The Other Boston Busing Story

Susan E. Eaton

The Other Boston Busing Story

What's Won and Lost Across
the Boundary Line

Yale University Press   New Haven and London

Printed in the United States of America

Library of Congress Cataloging-in-Publication Data
Eaton, Susan E.
The Other Boston Busing Story: What's Won and Lost
Across the Boundary Line / Susan E. Eaton.
     p.   cm.
Includes bibliographical references and index.
ISBN 0-300-08765-9
1. Busing for school integration—Massachusetts—Boston—
History.   2. Metropolitan Council for Educational
Opportunity (Boston, Mass.)   3. Boston (Mass.)—
Race relations.   I. Title.
LC214.523.B67 E38 2001
379.2'63—dc21   00-011667

A catalogue record for this book is available from the
British Library.

The paper in this book meets the guidelines for permanence
and durability of the Committee on Production Guidelines
for Book Longevity of the Council on Library Resources.

10 9 8 7 6 5 4 3 2 1

For my family of men
Mark
Will
Eli

Contents

Acknowledgments

This book would not have been possible without the generosity of dozens of former METCO participants who took time out of busy lives to share their memories, perspectives, and ideas with me. Without you, there would be no book. I am honored to share your stories so that others may learn from them. I have tried to be careful, respectful, and empathetic. Thank you.

My husband, Mark Kramer, is my best friend and best editor. He has been a brilliant but gentle critic, an endless source of amusement and joy. And thank you to Will and Eli, my two boys. This would not have been possible without the three of you—my family—keeping me grounded to earth.

Gary Orfield at the Harvard Ed School provided tremendous inspiration for this work and steadfast encouragement during the long-running project. He has helped and influenced me in incalculable ways over the years, not merely in matters academic. A generous mentor, a good friend, he is my model for how to use life well.

Susan Moore Johnson, also at the Ed School, worked closest with me on this book from the proposal stage to the editing of the final manuscript. She reviewed and edited this manuscript expertly and with great care to detail. Her wise critiques and comments shaped this work in significant ways. Her thoughtfulness, wisdom, and care run through this book.

Beverly Daniel Tatum also reviewed an earlier version of this manuscript and offered helpful suggestions and direction as I began shaping the book's organization in 1996. A. Michael Huberman was an invaluable, generous technical adviser and an even more important guide for my soul.

When I started graduate studies at Harvard, I was fortunate to be taught and advised by Jay Heubert. His passionate teaching about the intersection of schools, law, and society cemented my interest in the field and greatly improved my mind.

My editor at Yale, Susan Arellano, expressed tremendous enthusiasm for this book from the beginning. Knowing that she believed in this work was especially important during the usually isolating editing and revision process. Thank you also to my manuscript editor, Jeff Schier, at Yale. Deborah Kops edited an earlier version of this manuscript. Their talent and precision improved it immensely. Thanks also to Candice Nowlin, editorial assistant at Yale.

My parents, Nancy and Guerry Eaton, gave me the gifts of perseverance and self-discipline. Their pride in my accomplishments helped me push this book forward. Sidney B. Kramer, my father-in-law, who conveniently happens to also be a literary agent and lawyer, generously worked out contractual details for me. For this, and for the interest and pride that he and his wife, Esther Kramer, have in my work, I'm grateful.

Many METCO administrators were helpful to me during my research. Jean McGuire and John Shandorf at the central office in Roxbury talked with me several times and reviewed the manuscript. They were always open and never sought to influence my work. Jean, METCO's dedicated, long-standing director, is an inspiration. Thank you also to Adreene Law, Manuel Fernandez, Veronica Valentine, Thelma Burns, Dana Johnson, and other METCO administrators who helped me get the project off the ground.

A special thanks to my friend and former Boston news reporter Nick Mills, who gave this book its title. He has expertly named books now for both me and my husband.

Thank you also to friends and colleagues who listened and gave me advice, encouragement, inspiration, and criticism over the years: Jennifer Jellison; Ann Donlan; Ed Kirby; George Counter; Jacqui Deegan; Everly Macario; Elissa Kleinman; Adrian Nicole LeBlanc; Joan and Bob Weiss; Mitra Shavarini; Miguel Morales; Jane Ewing; Karen Armstrong; Judy Pace; Jim Sparrow; Bob Crain; and A. Michael Huberman.

Any errors or omissions, of course, are my own.

1

The Other Boston Busing Story

No horde of newspaper photographers showed up in the suburban town north of Boston to record Barbara Michaels'* small moment in history one summer day. In June 1975, Barbara was the town's first student to graduate through a voluntary program called METCO, which bused black students from Boston to public schools in white suburban communities. Barbara was asked to give a speech, and she had good things to say.

Looking back that day on her years as one of a handful of black METCO students in her school, Barbara was glad she had left her neighborhood school in Boston and come to this small, suburban town. She had grown accustomed to the hour-long highway commutes from and to her city neighborhood. Barbara had a nice suburban "host" family, who had helped her become more familiar with this town.

Barbara still chuckles when remembering the day that she and her mother visited the town before school started. They had never even heard of the place before Barbara won a coveted METCO spot at the start of her eighth-grade year.

*Barbara Michaels, like all the identifiers of past METCO participants, is a pseudonym. See Appendix I for details.

"I remember driving out there with my mother one day in the summer before school," Barbara recalls. "Just to see it, to check the town out, and at first looking at all the big houses and thinking, 'What's with all these big houses?' But it was so quiet. You see all these big houses [and] you think, 'Well, people must be living there, right?' But where were all the kids? You know, in the city, it's more active, kids are out, playing together. It feels more alive. So, that was strange to me. Just that small thing. It all seemed so strange."

Barbara remembers, though, that she eventually made good friends. And she overcame the academic struggles of junior high through hard work. By the time she was in high school Barbara earned good grades and by her senior year, she was looking forward to attending college the next fall. Barbara felt fortunate.

But Barbara recalls disappointments, too. She was a track star whose record runs had helped get her suburban track team to the state finals. But Barbara suspected she had failed to win votes for team captain because she was black. She had tried out for cheerleading, but the white parents doing the judging had said Barbara didn't "jump high enough" to make the squad. Even the white teachers looking on during tryouts had sided with Barbara when she complained to the vice-principal of "blatant racism." Barbara had said: "C'mon, if I'd have jumped any higher I'd have been in the rafters," and the teachers had nodded in agreement.

Then there were the classroom discussions about slavery and Jim Crow. All the white kids had turned and stared at Barbara, seeming to search her face for reactions, for answers. That had made her angry. "Turn around," Barbara remembers having told her white classmates. "Turn around. I'm trying to learn this, too. I wasn't there. I'm just trying to learn, here."

Today, Barbara thinks she never did learn enough black history. And her response was to "take every black history course I could in college. Because I was lost. I was totally lost. I did not know my history."

If Barbara didn't learn black history in her white high school, what she surely did learn was how to "survive intact" in a white-dominated society. For Barbara, METCO was a preview of what her life would be. She says, "It taught me how to work with all different types of people, how to find my way and just survive intact as a black person in a white world. So, I was collecting information out there, collecting my information for the world. And you learn it. You have to learn it. And you do need it. This is something you find out later."

Crossing the Lines for Three Decades

Decades after Barbara's journey, thousands of racial minority students from Boston still travel to suburbia for their educations. Thirty-four-year-old METCO is the longest, continuously running voluntary school desegregation program in the nation and one of just a few of its kind. An acronym for Metropolitan Council for Educational Opportunity, METCO was founded in 1966 by black parents and activists who originally saw the program as a partial and temporary remedy for the poor conditions in Boston's then-segregated, predominantly black schools. Urban activists and some suburban ones alike wanted desegregation through METCO and developed it peacefully, some eight years before Boston's now infamous struggle with a very different, mandatory form of busing, which began within the city in the mid-70s.

Though not a government-initiated program, METCO had a relatively warm political welcome in part because it helped the city of Boston comply with a new law. By busing black children from urban schools to predominantly suburban ones, METCO helped meet requirements of the state's 1965 Racial Imbalance Law. This law, designed to diminish racial segregation, gave certain monetary benefits to local school districts, which drew up desegregation plans whenever more than 50 percent of students in a school were racial minorities. (This law is being challenged in a 1999 lawsuit filed in U.S. District Court in Boston.

Plaintiffs argue that admission decisions in one community are encouraged by the law, and based on race, in violation of the students' equal protection rights.)

But despite the link between METCO and a law designed to encourage racial integration in education, parents who signed their children up for METCO were rarely searching for racial integration, or, to use the more modern term, "diversity," per se. According to surveys, these parents were searching for what they thought would be a "better education" for their children (Batson and Hayden, 1987; Orfield, 1997). It is important to draw a distinction here between the goal of "equal educational opportunity" and that of "diversity." While the two are surely compatible, from the perspective of parents, they are very different. Giving students equal educational opportunity implies that resources are being distributed to them that previously had not been made available. One might think of it as evening up the score. The goal of diversity, however, speaks to the need for all children—including the most privileged white students—to interact in learning environments with colleagues from varied racial, ethnic, economic, even geographic backgrounds. Diversity, then, is a pedagogical interest, in which varied perspectives, and ways of thinking, informed by family backgrounds and culture, are viewed as necessary elements of a full education.

The two concepts—equal educational opportunity and diversity—are usually treated separately in the courts, but often are muddled together in discourse about educational policy. From its founding, METCO clearly has encompassed both goals. For urban blacks, it has provided equal educational opportunities; for suburban schools, it has provided some racial diversity.

At the time of METCO's founding in the mid-1960s, even the program's initiators expected METCO's life span would be short—about three years, until Boston "straighten[ed] out" (Batson and Hayden, 1987). In METCO's inaugural 1966 year, 220 black children, from the first through the eleventh grades, traveled to seven suburban communities. More than three decades later, in 2000, about 3,100 Boston students traveled to 32 participating METCO communities. About 4,300 men and women have graduated from the program in the last three decades.*

Though some suburban communities pick up a share of the costs themselves, METCO is paid for primarily by the state. In 1998, the program received an increase of $400,000 from the state, its first funding increase in 12 years, bringing the state's total contribution to $12.4 million. Before this increase, METCO had operated for a decade on $12 million in state funds annually, even as education budgets rose elsewhere in the state.† The program has two levels of administration. Administrators in the central office, located in the predominantly black Roxbury section of Boston, make policy decisions, oversee placements and transportation, coordinate special programs such as college tours, work directly with state officials, and counsel and advise parents and students considering the program. Out in the suburbs, METCO directors, assistant directors, counselors, and tutors work with METCO students, their parents, and the personnel in the school district. They often act as advocates and coordinators for the students, set up special programs for them, and maintain files to keep track of students' progress. Most often, these directors have offices within METCO schools; others, stationed at district central offices, make frequent visits to students and teachers at the schools. Students are assigned "host families" at the start of their schooling. The host family usually will include a child in the METCO student's classroom. The suburban family is supposed to act as an informal guide to the community and also provide transportation when needed, help the child if he or she

---

*Technically, there are no admission standards for the program, though some districts employ informal standards for students to remain in their district and will "counsel" students out because of discipline or other problems.
†METCO Central Office, Boston, Mass.

becomes ill, and be a friendly, reliable, close-by contact for the METCO student and his or her family.

The central goal of METCO parents—to get a better education for their children—has remained unchanged over the years. In a 1996 survey, 73 percent cited a school's "academic program(s)" as the "most important" reason for sending their children to METCO (Orfield, 1997). The program enjoys an enduring popularity among black families. In fact, METCO cannot accommodate all the families that apply. In 2000, there were nearly 13,000 children on METCO's waiting list, and getting in requires thinking far ahead. A quarter of METCO parents surveyed in 1996 had signed up for the program before their sons and daughters were a year old (Orfield, 1997). Technically, METCO is open to all Boston schoolchildren, including white students. But in practice, it remains a program for racial minorities. There are several reasons for this. The waiting list is long, with racial minority families likely ahead of white students who might have applied in recent years. The program's administrative offices are in a predominantly African-American neighborhood, and METCO has a decades-long reputation as an equal education program for racial minorities. It is thus responsive—through its tutoring programs, college counseling, student support groups, and diversity training workshops—to that population.

Despite the unquestionable demand for METCO, the program has not escaped criticism. Even though METCO administrators have repeatedly requested public funds to pay for a systematic study of student performance, the legislature has never allocated the money. Even program supporters admit that educators, suburban administrators, counselors, and METCO administrators need to pay more attention to improving the academic performance of some students in the program. While the program boasts a 92 percent college-going rate, administrators in local school districts commonly complain about poor performance of a sizable share of METCO students.

These problems were underscored in 1999 when the school superintendent in the nearly all-white, middle-class suburb of Lynnfield complained of the poor academic achievement of some METCO students and threatened to end the program in that community. The reaction to the threat was swift and angry and illustrated METCO's political power and popularity. Hundreds showed up to protest the superintendent's statements, including many white Lynnfield residents. The superintendent backed off from his original threat, and town school committee members tried to refocus the contentious debate on how to improve METCO students' academic performance. During the controversy, a racially diverse collection of educational leaders from other suburban METCO communities spoke publicly, in television and radio broadcasts, about the program's benefits. These educators, while acknowledging some of the METCO students' academic difficulties, focused on the program's contributions, not just to the lives of black students, but to the otherwise isolated white students living in an increasingly diverse nation (Eaton, 1999).

Feeling the Weight of Separation

Though one can't tell from watching their routine, daily disembarkations off the school buses, the black METCO students' lasting presence in Boston's suburban towns is anything but ordinary. The small degree of racial integration that METCO creates in its participating schools is an anomaly among the more standard, long-standing patterns of racial and economic segregation in metropolitan Boston.

In 1990, about 24 percent of all Boston residents were black while about 11 percent were Hispanic. But in the combined population of all suburban communities that participate in the METCO program, just about 1 percent of the total population were black. In 1990, just 2 percent of this suburban population were Hispanic. The state's total population of black residents was about 5 percent. Likewise, about 5 percent of the state's population were Hispanic* (U.S. Census Bureau).

The public schools reflect the pattern of segregation in the Boston metropolitan area. Public school districts in the north are usually divided along municipal boundaries, and children go to school in the community in which they live.† Most of the white suburban student population attends schools that are largely white, and most of the black population in Boston attends schools that are predominantly composed of racial minorities.‡ In 2000, 50 percent of the students enrolled in Boston's public schools were black and 27 percent were Hispanic.§ Without METCO students, the public school enrollment in many of the participating suburban communities would be less than 1 percent black or Hispanic.

The general pattern of racial segregation in greater Boston means that white suburban students usually need not confront racial issues. Likewise, Boston's black students, while they probably interact with whites more than suburban whites do with blacks, still can form social groups, go to class, and live in neighborhoods made up entirely of other blacks. They need not adapt to a foreign, all white suburban school nor feel isolated in any nearly all white classroom. There is little racial conflict precisely because there is little racial contact.

---

*Statistics calculated by the author from U.S. Census Data. Race & Hispanic Origin in 1990: Massachusetts Cities, Towns, and Counties Ranked by Per Cent Minority. 1990 Census of Population and Housing, Summary Tape File 1A, Table 10.
†In contrast, public school districts in the south often follow county lines, which encompass cities and suburbs. And in many areas of the south, rates of black suburbanization are generally higher, as blacks there have traditionally lived outside of cities
‡Boston public schools
§Of course, there are exceptions. Some schools, including Boston's prestigious exam high school, Boston Latin, enroll a racial mix of students. And many traditionally white suburban communities near Boston have become more racially and ethnically diverse in the 1990s.

Bouncing between two worlds, METCO's black students not so much cross but blur these racial boundary lines. One world is predominantly black and urban. The other is predominantly white and suburban. Thus, perhaps more intensely and personally than anyone else, these young students of METCO experience the possibilities and challenges associated with any effort to reduce the separation between city and suburb.

The Troubles of Racial Integration

This examination of the perceived impact METCO has had on the lives of its past participants touches on important issues of our time. A better understanding of METCO, enhanced by the recollections and perspectives of the men and women who lived through the program, informs and expands public debate over the appropriateness of this and other racial integration programs in our race-conscious society. It may also broaden the knowledge of policy makers and advocates who see METCO-like programs as potential routes to achieving racial integration and providing racial minority children with access to high-prestige schools where advanced curriculum is available as a matter of course and large majorities of students go on to four-year colleges.

Public school programs such as METCO are also significant because they can potentially provide legal remedies for segregation and unequal educational opportunities. Since the 1970s, forms of mandatory desegregation, typically confined to one school district or municipality, have become increasingly difficult to achieve. In 1974, the Supreme Court cut off routes to integration in its 5–4 *Milliken v. Bradley* decision by ruling that surrounding suburbs cannot be compelled to participate in their city's desegregation plan. This ruling effectively closed off predominantly white suburbs outside the south from the requirements of desegregation. Thus, by the 1970s, for urban school districts, whose pool of white students was small and shrinking, racial integration became nearly impossible. As whites increasingly moved to the suburbs, *Milliken* cemented in place the now-familiar pattern of predominantly minority, poor central city schools surrounded by white suburbs.

The north's persistent segregation and the state of the law under *Milliken* have led some civil rights lawyers and advocates in search of new approaches to educational equality. A handful of lawyers and advocates, hoping to get around *Milliken*, have sought remedies to racial segregation and inequality under state rather than federal constitutions (Eaton & Orfield, 1994; O'Connor, 1997). They argue that urban systems, because of their racial isolation (and accompanying concentrations of poverty), offer neither adequate education nor education of quality equal to that enjoyed by suburban children.

The argument was successful, in the landmark 1996 Connecticut case, *Sheff v. O'Neill*. In July of that year, the Connecticut Supreme Court ruled that the severe levels of racial segregation in the Hartford metropolitan area violated the state constitution's guarantee that "No person shall be denied the equal protection of the law nor be subjected to segregation or discrimination in the exercise or enjoyment of his or her civil or political rights." In her opinion, Connecticut Supreme Court Justice Ellen Peters wrote: "The public elementary and high school students in Hartford suffer daily from the devastating effects that racial and ethnic isolation, as well as poverty, have had on their education. . . . The issue is as controversial as the stakes are high. We hold today that the needy schoolchildren of Hartford have waited long enough." (Though a victory, the decision did not address the effects of concentrated poverty, which had concerned plaintiffs.)

The court ordered state legislators to correct the problem. But a state panel appointed to make recommendations to the legislature never resolved the circular question of whether the state should provide integrated schools or instead improve urban schools within the current structure. A legislative package, which disappoints plaintiffs in its modesty, mixes both strategies. Regional magnet schools that draw a racial mix of students began there in the 1990s.

Efforts of the type under way in Connecticut are still rare and hardly signal a new trend toward metropolitan solutions. Even so, advocates are looking to these legal avenues and educational paradigms as models for racial integration and equal access (Duchesne & Hotakainen, 1996; Judson, 1996). But hopeful as they may appear, METCO-type programs, funded with state money, surely may be vulnerable to the now ubiquitous legal challenges to affirmative action and other race-based equal opportunity policies. Under such challenges, often backed by prosperous conservative groups, plaintiffs argue that race-conscious programs are discriminatory. Supporters, however, might argue that diversity, as it is achieved through programs such as METCO, fulfills a compelling interest by meeting specific educational goals.*

The state of the law in the area of K–12 education is still

---

*When challenged in court, any government program that provides preferences to a certain racial group must be reviewed under the "strict scrutiny" standard, requiring that it meet a "compelling state interest" and be narrowly tailored to meet that interest. This applies even to programs that are intended to aid a group, such as African Americans, who have been victims of government discrimination.

Several circuit court decisions are relevant. For example, in *Wessman v. Gittens,* the United States Court of Appeals for the First Circuit struck down Boston Latin School's admission policy, which had given preference to some racial minority groups. But the court left open the possibility that achieving racial "diversity" may very well be a compelling state interest in specific circumstances. However, the court ruled, the "abstract" justifications offered by the Boston School Committee were not sufficient justification.

Similarly, in *Eisenberg v. Montgomery County Public Schools,* the United States Court of Appeals for the Fourth Circuit struck down a race-sensitive transfer policy at Montgomery County, Maryland's elementary and secondary schools. But that court also chose not to decide whether racial and ethnic diversity is or might be a compelling state interest. But the 2nd Circuit in *Brewer v. The West Irondequoit Central School District* reversed a lower court finding that had granted a unclear, for as of 2000, the Supreme Court had not ruled on questions related to race-conscious policies in K–12 public education. But whatever its legal standing now or in the future, understanding the experience under METCO allows all of us in our increasingly diverse nation to better comprehend the challenges and possibilities that come with crossing over racial and ethnic boundary lines. In fact, it is those sitting outside the world of legal scholarship and equal rights advocacy who view racial integration not solely as a remedy to inequality but as a way to prepare young people of all races and ethnicities for life in a racially and ethnically changing United States (Smith, 1997; Bok & Bowen, 1998). And many educators and policy makers in the northern states, who are constrained by fragmented, racially isolated school districts, recognize that the only way they can provide diverse environments for learning is by fashioning cross-district or metropolitan solutions.

Voluntary, metropolitanwide programs, such as METCO, are significant too, because they may simply be more popular among racial minority parents than traditional, mandatory forms of busing. Surveys suggest that a majority of black Americans still

---

preliminary injunction to a white student who had wanted to participate in a suburban transfer program designated for racial minority students. The court remedying segregation could be a compelling government interest.

Thus, the question as to whether the achievement of racial and ethnic diversity in education can be a compelling government interest appears to be open. In fact, as of July 2000, the 5th Circuit, in *Hopwood v. Texas,* is the only circuit court to hold that using race in admissions or attendance zoning for reasons other than remedying specific acts of past discrimination can *never* be compelling.

Consequently, the U.S. Supreme Court's decision in *Regents of the Univ. of California v. Bakke,* which held that race may be one factor in a college's admission policy, appears to remain good law. In his opinion in *Bakke,* Justice Powell reasoned that a university derives benefits from enrolling a diverse student body, which contributes to a vigorous exchange of ideas in the educational environment.

strongly support integrated schools for their children. But surveys also suggest that parents desire more educational choices (Orfield, 1994). Ironically, as the popular press reports increasingly on African Americans' disenchantment with busing in Boston and elsewhere (i.e., Yemma, 1997; Fineman, 1996), the waiting list for METCO continues to grow, even though it buses students much farther than typical desegregation plans.

What METCO Is All About

Perhaps the program's enduring popularity stems from the rare, dual solution it offers. This and similar programs are true efforts to combine desegregation and quality education. This is significant because public discourse about school desegregation reflects a frequent dichotomy between the goals of "quality" education and of desegregation (Orfield & Eaton, 1996). Desegregation critics and local school officials commonly argue that desegregation requirements must be eliminated or greatly reduced so educators may focus on teaching rather than social policy. Under this popular argument, so-called quality education and desegregation are in opposition. Even the most well-respected public opinion polls ask respondents to choose between the two concepts (Orfield, 1994). Putting oppositional rhetoric into action, lawyers trying to dismantle desegregation and affirmative action policies have used the dramatic quality versus integration dichotomy to great success. More than a dozen desegregation orders have been lifted since the 1980s as "quality" became a new buzzword and the Supreme Court loosened standards to free school districts from their duty to desegregate—a move that commonly prompts a return to segregated schools (Orfield & Eaton, 1996).

Yet, METCO has always been viewed by activists and parents as an educational program *and* a racial integration program, thereby avoiding these popular debates. People may attach to METCO whichever priority they wish. While scholars and social critics disagree about whether choice-based programs undermine racial integration and about whether racial integration even matters, METCO circumvents these controversies by being at once a racial integration and a school-choice program. And for now, METCO has managed to sidestep traditional objections to affirmative action and so-called quotas because, while it does not cater to whites, it does not displace them either. Indeed, METCO is a racial integration program for the mere fact that it does create some racial integration where otherwise there would be little to none. But perhaps more importantly, METCO is a public school–choice program that gets black students into high-performing schools, which greatly appeals to parents who believe these suburban schools are better than those in the city (Batson & Hayden, 1987; Orfield et al., 1997b). The politicized debates over the worth of school desegregation and the appropriateness of school choice and affirmative action surely will continue. But for parents, enrolling in METCO is not a political act. It is a practical one.

Even so, there is still much nationwide disagreement over METCO-like programs that bus racial minority children to predominantly white schools, a debate I discuss fully in chapter 7. Briefly, the most common complaint is related to human and monetary resources. Race-conscious choice programs like METCO are certainly responsible for the departure of some good students with involved parents from urban school systems. A related complaint is that money spent on such programs would be better used improving predominantly black city schools so that black children and their families will no longer feel compelled to leave their neighborhoods.

Second, critics often complain that educational choices such as METCO denigrate black communities and contribute to their erosion. According to this theory, black children, exposed to

suburban lifestyles and white settings, will abandon their neighborhoods and their culture. Though one argument is about
money and the other primarily about culture, identity, and belonging, the two complaints often are linked. (See, for example,
Yemma, 1997; Schlinkmann, 1997; Shaper Walters, 1996; Fineman, 1996.)

Despite years of criticisms, supporters of racial integration
programs such as METCO for the most part have not directly
addressed these crucial questions about culture, identity, and
community. Equally true is that critics of racial integration, in
their speeches and position papers, usually fail to address the
fact that METCO, if a student can get in, does not keep families
waiting for the ever-elusive promise of urban school reform.
Through METCO, parents simply see well-functioning, well-
connected, prestigious suburban schools that offer their children
opportunities that already exist.

Looking more deeply at METCO won't silence such public
debates, which are often rooted in emotion and ideology rather
than research and fact. But this book explores, through the
words of the former METCO students themselves, the experiences
and lasting impressions of people who actually went through an
unusual and extreme form of racial integration. What they say
forces us to think about contemporary questions and narrowly
constructed controversies in new, more sophisticated ways.

What This Study Can Teach Us

In this study, adult former METCO students speak about what they
think they gained from their experiences in METCO and what they
think they lost. They also discuss whether they think METCO was
worth the displacement and inconvenience it required. By allowing past program participants to talk about their educational
experiences in their own words, I do two things that previous

research on racial integration in schools has not: I consider myriad aspects of the educational experience simultaneously, and I consider an integration program's perceived impact over the long term rather than just the short term.

Desegregation-related programs and policies have typically been studied by scholars from various disciplines, each asking questions related exclusively to his or her field. Sociologists and policy analysts, for example, generally look for external indicators of success. They might compare the college graduation rates for desegregated and segregated blacks. Social psychologists, meanwhile, would scrutinize individual internal processes associated with an integration experience and focus most often on self-esteem, development of racial identity, and relationships with family. Thus, research on public school integration usually increases our understanding of one aspect of the experience, or the perceived effect of integration on one element of a person's whole life. But social scientists have rarely considered the entire experience of public school integration from the perspective of black students who then went on to live their lives after the experience.

Certainly, there has been considerable research and even more speculation about the effects of racial integration on black students. Most of the research considers desegregation's effects on student test scores and self-esteem while the students are still in school. But as other researchers have noted, this focus on the shorter-term impact of racial integration as measured by test scores does not speak directly to the earliest goals of the school desegregation movement. The argument underpinning the pre–*Brown v. Board of Education* cases, which sought access to higher education, was this: Ensuring blacks entry into predominantly white, middle-class schools would improve their changes for social mobility by linking blacks to social networks and prestige associated with these white-dominated institutions (Kluger, 1975; Wells & Crain, 1994; Orfield & Eaton, 1996).

Thus, to assess a program's longer-term impact on human lives, it is necessary to talk with program participants not when they are children and teenagers immersed in the process of integration, but later, when they are adults with life experiences well beyond high school. Such adults can discuss not only their recollected school experiences, but, more important, their mature perceptions of the ways these experiences affected choices, behaviors, attitudes, relationships, and career paths.

A few studies do examine the longer-term effects of school desegregation. Generally, this research—including some on Hartford, Connecticut's Project Concern program, which is similar to METCO—finds that blacks who participated in desegregation programs are more likely than their segregated counterparts to have high aspirations, consistent career planning, and career patterns that would prepare them for their desired occupations (Gable, Thompson & Iwanicki, 1983). A follow-up study of the Connecticut program found that blacks who had attended desegregated schools were more likely than blacks from segregated schools to have a racially mixed social network of friends and acquaintances and to live in racially mixed neighborhoods (Crain, 1984). Yet another study, published in 1985 and comparing the graduates of Project Concern with those of city schools, found that the desegregated black students were more likely to enroll in college and work in occupations traditionally dominated by whites (Crain & Strauss, 1985). Other studies have shown that higher college graduation rates and particular types of job opportunities were also associated with prior school desegregation for blacks (Wells & Crain, 1994).

My study gains focus and many of its principal questions from this previous body of work. But this study differs markedly from previous research. These longer-term investigations were almost all statistical and thus, by their nature, were not designed to probe either the human processes benefiting from integration programs or the meanings people attach to their own experiences under such programs. Asking open-ended questions that give people the opportunity to reflect, qualify, and fully explain themselves, their opinions, and their perceptions surely will add to our understanding of the gains, the losses, and the complexities found in the kind of experience that METCO offers.

This study was guided by three groups of questions. The first group focuses on respondents' memories and the meanings they attach to them. What salient recollections do black adults have of their experiences of attending suburban schools while living in the city, and what recollections do they say best characterize such experiences? As they look back on some of the events, what have those memories come to mean and symbolize? For example, if a student remembers fondly a cross-race friendship, does that memory help sustain hope for racial harmony?

The second group of questions focuses on the adults' perceptions of the long-term effects of their early integration experiences. In answering this question, the past METCO participants speak about the ways their educational experiences helped shape their attitudes and the choices they made over the courses of their lives. Many of the themes that emerge in discussions about memories of METCO—cultural isolation, the bridging of two worlds, increasing comfort—reemerge when respondents discuss their current lives. Necessarily, the former students also place in perspective METCO's role among their many other life influences, such as family, church, friends, and other educational experiences.

The third group of questions focuses on students' current assessments of their experience. Balancing all aspects of the experience, how do post-METCO adults characterize and explain the worth of their experiences? In answering this third type of question, I ask adults to consider whether they would repeat the program if they could go back in time and why they would or would not want their own children to enter METCO.

The Summary Story of METCO

As past participants tell it, the story of METCO is one mostly of clear gains put to practical use after high school ended. This seems to be the case even when the road traveled to get those benefits was rocky. The adults I spoke with often trace their current feelings of comfort, diminishing self-consciousness, and growing self-confidence in white settings to their earlier METCO experiences. And it is these acquired attitudes that, from the participants' perspectives, increased their willingness, even eagerness, to enter predominantly white settings when they perceived opportunity there.

Once in white settings, many of these adults speak of playing a role best described as a "bridge" between white and black communities, cultures, and individuals. Their ability to straddle and blend two worlds is, to many of them, a payoff for their childhood and teenage experiences in METCO. Some of the adults have professional jobs requiring them to act as bridges between cultures and communities. Others apply the same straddling skills in less conspicuous ways. They may feel adept at getting others to see and question their prejudices, or they may use casual conversation to make cultural and racial differences non-threatening and enriching rather than intimidating and awkward.

Scattered among the stories of gain and increased personal power, however, are tales of real loss. Many of the adults still struggle today with questions about where they "fit" in society. Specifically, these black men and women don't always feel at ease in all-black settings and report that they are sometimes criticized there for "acting white." Many are acutely sensitive to what might seem like lighthearted ribbing or mock insults about cultural integrity. But to them, the joking is a painful, even maddening, a continuation of taunting they received from neighborhood friends and family members who didn't go to suburbia.

Some former students remember that as black children

bused out to white suburban schools, they did develop negative attitudes about their own neighborhoods or about blacks in general. But those opinions, born from simplistic analysis, proved transient and, as the adults recall, rarely lasted even through high school. Many of the reactions articulated by these adults seem to follow the course of normal racial identity development as described by other scholars (Tatum, 1997; Cross, 1995; Cross, 1991). Nevertheless, these men and women do perceive that their reactions at least were heightened by their stark, daily crossings over to the white world and back to the black world. The adults speculate that this straddling forced them to deal with issues and conflicts that they would not have had to confront had they stayed in Boston for their schooling. And past participants often express ambivalence, wondering whether they missed out on something important by not attending predominantly black schools.

But the oft-repeated charge that urban/suburban choice programs will rip black children away from black communities and black culture and make them aspire to suburban lifestyles does not match the experiences and sentiments of these adults. In fact, after high school, past participants of METCO reconnected to their neighborhoods and to black culture and history by deliberately seeking out predominantly black social groups and organizations. This pattern of reconnection is well described in the literature on racial identity development (Cross, 1991, 1995). But many past METCO participants do trace their reconnection impetus directly to their suburban educational experiences. Some assert that these reconnections were more deliberate and pronounced than they would have been had they never been displaced from their communities. These former students often see the reconnection as a remedy for the disconnection that METCO had imposed. But for others, community involvement and connections with black culture and the black church expressed values learned in their childhood homes. Going to suburbia for school had neither negated nor diminished those values.

Remarkably, nearly all the adults represented here said they would indeed repeat their METCO experience could they go back in time. (Just four of the sixty-five said otherwise.) There surely is a range of enthusiasm and a score of conditions that come with such decisions but, interestingly, even those adults with primarily negative memories of suburbia say they would indeed return to METCO. In considering whether they would repeat their experiences or send their children to white suburbia, the adults weigh more than the negative and positive aspects of their experiences in the program. Their decisions, they say, are influenced more by their discoveries that the exposure they had in suburbia comprised fair approximations and decent preparation for life as blacks in white-dominated America.

The chapters that follow explore these themes and findings more deeply. In chapter 2, post-METCO adults discuss their current understanding of their families' decisions to send them from their urban neighborhoods to suburban schools. The former students speak about what those understandings were when they were children and what their own mature reflections add to that picture. In chapter 3, the men and women recall their experiences as young people straddling urban and suburban communities. They look back on their experiences and explore what the memories have come to mean to them. In chapter 4, adults describe the gains they perceive from the METCO experience. The emphasis of this chapter is on how, concretely, the men and women used those benefits in later life. Conversely, in chapter 5, adults describe the negative aspects or losses they perceive were associated with METCO and how they resolved or failed to resolve those problems. In chapter 6, the post-METCO adults weigh both the positive and the negative aspects they associate with their suburban desegregation experience as they consider whether they would repeat METCO and whether they would en-roll their children in the program. Chapter 7, the final chapter, considers the implications of these findings. It details how this study might best inform debates over school desegregation and race-conscious choice programs such as METCO. It also reviews in detail the study's relationship to previous research and its contributions to current scholarship, and it suggests avenues for further study.

Who's Talking?

This study is based on in-depth interviews with 65 of METCO's past participants who have been out of the program for at least five years. The sample includes 30 men and 35 women. Forty-two of these adults could be classified as middle class and college educated; 17 could be classified as working class, either with a college education, some college credits, an associates degree, or high school diploma; the remaining 6 could be classified either as working poor or poor with no college education.

Forty-nine of the 65 adults I talked with had graduated from a four-year college or, at the time I met with them, were finishing work toward their degrees. Twenty of the 65 had completed some graduate work (either a law degree or a master's degree) or were working toward graduate degrees. Several more were planning to pursue graduate studies.

Of the 65 adults in this sample, 58 graduated from a METCO high school. Seven had dropped out of the program in high school and graduated from another school, earned a graduation equivalency diploma (GED), or never graduated from high school. Thirty-nine of these adults live in the city of Boston. Fourteen of the 65 live in Boston suburbs. Some of these subur-ban communities are affluent with relatively few black residents, but others are more diverse, both culturally and socioeconomi-cally. Eight live outside Massachusetts, and all of these adults characterize their neighborhoods as racially and socioeconomically diverse and primarily urban. Four others live in Massachusetts, but well outside metropolitan Boston. Two of these reside in diverse, primarily urban neighborhoods, while two others live in suburban communities that are predominantly white.

The past participants are of various ages. Eighteen graduated high school or were of graduation age (18) between the years 1971 and 1977; 24 graduated high school or were of graduation age between the years 1978 and 1983; and 23 graduated high school or were of graduation age between the years 1984 and 1991.

METCO *in the Shadow of Busing*

Despite its relevance to so many important issues, METCO's story has never been told. This small program has long been overshadowed by the drama, racial violence, and political tumult spurred by Boston's school busing order that went into effect in 1975.

At its most controversial, the desegregation order led to students being bused from predominantly black, poor, and working class Roxbury to predominantly white, poor, and working class South Boston and vice versa. The ensuing violence and racial tension were so intense that the busing order still ignites controversy. In 1997, more than two and a half decades after busing began, community leaders in South Boston even speculated publicly that the disintegration caused by busing was in part responsible for a rash of teen suicides in the neighborhood (MacQuarrie, 1997).

For many observers, both in and outside the city, busing in Boston did display desegregation at its most destructive and human beings at their worst. It wasn't long before busing in Boston became a popular symbol of the "failure" of liberal social engineering and the futility of trying to legislate racial equality and racial harmony. Meanwhile, though, few onlookers noticed an irony not too many miles away. As the rocks flew, the tempers flared, and the fears escalated in Boston, black city kids were strolling with little incident into lily-white suburban schools. It was not always easy. But so close to the municipal boundary line, just out of sight of the gathered reporters, television cameras, and busing's now infamous race- and class-based rage, there were, and still are, other stories. These are stories about racial integration in what might seem the most unlikely of places.

2

Why They Went

Mae Rogers kept a map of metropolitan Boston in a kitchen drawer of her city apartment. A few years after her daughter Shirley was born in the 1960s, Mae took the map and began circling in red ink some of the rich towns ringing the city. Mae had learned about some of these towns when a few neighborhood children started going out to them for school every day through a new busing program. Mae didn't need to know much more about this program except that it got black city kids into some of the "best" public schools in Massachusetts.

Mrs. Rogers had never been to any of these towns herself. The subway line out of her Boston neighborhood didn't go directly to them. And she didn't own a car. "You have to understand this," says her daughter Shirley, now in her thirties. "A lot of people in some parts of Boston, they don't have knowledge of where things are outside their little neighborhoods."

According to Shirley, her mother did cling to a flowery image of the suburban towns and small cities that lay beyond metropolitan Boston's racial boundary line. In her mother's mind— and so in Shirley's mind too—there would be a lot of green grass out that way. "Greener! The grass was going to be greener," says

Shirley, giggling at the cliché embedded in her and her mother's imaginations. But Mae Rogers, though prone to "sugar coating" life, would also, Shirley remembers, "get right in there and dig, dig, dig for her family. Always looking out for her kids, looking for the best."

But Mrs. Rogers' image of the suburbs included more than manicured lawns. Shirley's mother had heard of well-stocked libraries with new books, and, of course, high-school graduates who went on to the best colleges, which in turn gave students access to economic power and professional accomplishments. Sure, she'd heard about some of the problems—racism, name-calling—but Shirley remembers her mother telling her, "You are going to get that nonsense wherever you go."

Mrs. Rogers had seen only the outside of the nearby Boston schools, she had never been in one. But she'd heard stories. And she had images. Disorder. Fights. Chaos. And their own brand of what Shirley said her mother termed "prejudice." But what Shirley remembers her mother emphasizing most of all—to relatives and friends—was that she just could not imagine the local schools getting her children farther than the city limits. "They [the city schools] were in this world, the world my mother already knew, you see?" Shirley says. "And those suburban schools were in another world and this was the one she thought we better get our feet in."

And so Shirley (and her siblings after her) rose at 5 a.m. to wait at bus stops. After a trip of an hour or so, the bus's accordion doors sprang open, and out came Shirley, onto a suburban school campus that at first glance exactly matched the image she and her mother had carried in their minds. To Shirley, this bus ride, and the displacement it symbolized, was just the way life was. She didn't think very much about why.

" 'A better education' is what we always said," Shirley recalls now in the living room of the house she and her husband own in Boston. It is a solidly middle-class home, not far, in miles anyway, from the more working-class neighborhood where Shirley, her siblings, and mother lived. "A better education. A better education." Shirley repeats this old mantra learned by a dutiful daughter from a mother empowered by hopefulness and resolve. "I just said it over and over again and it got me through, I think, just saying those words: 'a better education.'"

The justifications for enrolling in METCO that Shirley remembers her mother passing on to her kids are typical in several ways. To Mrs. Rogers and Shirley, METCO wasn't so much an escape hatch as it was a bet on the future. To go out to those towns circled on the map was to pursue a share of the American dream. Education was viewed unquestioningly as a sure route to options and success in life. Also typical is that Mrs. Rogers' decision rested at least in part on unconfirmed images about the "best" suburban schools and the "chaotic" urban schools, neither of which she had seen. Mrs. Rogers' decision to put her children in METCO rested on her understanding of the things that suburban schools could offer children, not just in the day-to-day experiences but for the future. Putting her children on METCO's buses represented the execution of Mrs. Rogers' plan to give her children access to a world beyond the city boundaries, beyond the confines of the neighborhood her family not only knew, but also loved.

Leaving Love and Security for What?

As it was for Shirley Rogers, a decision to attend a METCO school is a commitment to tolerate more than inconvenience. There are early risings and late homecomings, certainly. But for nearly all students, METCO also requires uprooting from community and comfort.

The choice to uproot for five days a week is especially curious since nearly all the past participants characterize their neighborhoods and their family homes as warm, nurturing places.

These are places often anchored by active black churches, abundant, close families, and a lot of strong mothers. Some of the neighborhoods and homes were poor, though most of the communities these men and women describe were, at least at the time of their growing up, of mixed incomes. The streets or apartment buildings usually included working class, working poor, and a sprinkling of others with higher incomes who owned homes and cars and traveled during vacations.

But today, those adults who attended METCO as children and teenagers living in or near the edge of poverty do not romanticize their neighborhoods. Though they rarely remember threats to their own physical safety, many families had been victims of lesser crimes, including burglaries and muggings. But the stereotypes that many suburban white children held—of urban shootings and violent death and guns—do not figure prominently in the portraits METCO's past participants paint of their childhood communities.

The former students, do, however, recall vivid symbols of neglect and collective lack of opportunity. These are some of the negative images: the drunks or the idle men who seemed to do nothing all day; cracked sidewalks; garbage piling up; slow response from police; leaky roofs and gutters; drug dealers. They remember other people's schemes for getting rich quick. In later years, old scratch-card lottery tickets littered sidewalks. The former METCO participants also remember friends who didn't go to METCO, friends who began losing hope. These were the old friends who began to use drugs, skip school, or drop out and devote energy to looking and acting tough.

But there are different images that are even more potent and more important to these adults. These are memories of Sundays at church and around family and food, of joyful parties and get-togethers, easy conversation on the sidewalks and apartment steps. These adults recall most commonly feelings of gladness in their homes, their churches, on friends' front stoops, in community centers, basketball courts, playing fields, and neighborhood streets. Even if they were dead certain that going to school in suburbia was a good choice, Boston was still clearly home to these young people, just as it was to their parents. Boston was the place nearly all the past METCO participants associated with love and security. Many still call it their "comfort zone."

Former METCO student Marquise Bell, who graduated in the mid-1980s, echoes the sentiments of many of his fellow METCO students for whom Boston was more than simply an address. A Boston neighborhood—be it Mattapan, Dorchester, South End, or Roxbury—remains a strong anchor and touchstone for nearly all the former METCO students. Marquise still lives in Boston. While he was in METCO he had many white friends in his suburban schools, did well academically, and played on varsity sports teams. Because of his demanding sports schedule, Marquise frequently slept over at his teammates' houses. Marquise remembers being sure throughout his school career that METCO was a good choice for him. But his positive experience in suburbia didn't erase the love and respect and longing he often felt for the security of his neighborhood. He recalls, "It was always clear that Boston was home. There was no doubt about this. You could sleep out there every night but still, you know where your family is, where your center is. It was always like coming home to your comfort zone where you'd you know, just, I'd just feel like letting out this big sigh. It was relief."

Marquise explains that beyond "feeling comfortable" in his Roxbury neighborhood, his neighborhood is an integral part of his identity, part of "who I am." He says, "I guess because it was where I always felt the most like me. I still go there—to Roxbury —to get my clarity, to get some peace back in my life. I still use it that way, it's part of who I am."

So, if METCO, in the eyes of its participants, was not a paternalistic, white suburban life rope to save black children drowning in urban despair, what was it? To former students and their families, METCO was an essential part of a plan for maximizing future options. METCO was the vehicle that connected children and teenagers to what they expected would at first seem alienating and unwelcoming places where many weren't sure they'd ever like to live. But it wasn't just the schools these families wanted. It wasn't only the day-to-day educational experience to be had inside the tony, white schools in towns like Concord, Wayland, and Newton. They wanted the world that lay beyond those schools. As Samuel Dean, an early 1990s graduate, explains simply: "Why was I doing it? I had my little bullets in a row. A better education. Better opportunities in my life."

What Does a Better Education Mean?

Nearly all the former METCO students learned the "better education" mantra early in their suburban educations. Like Shirley Rogers, they used it to shoo away the taunting of neighborhood friends who wanted to know why anyone would want to travel out so far to any school, let alone a white school. Adults today recall moments as children and teens when they, too, questioned the wisdom of their attending METCO, and a lot of them used the mantra to push away these doubts. As they look back at METCO today, it is extremely difficult for adults to explain why they once left the familiarity of their home neighborhoods for the new world of the suburban schools.

At first, the old words "for a better education" fall almost mechanically from past participants' lips. But it is more difficult for these men and women to explain what the phrase meant then and what it means now. Once they do find the words for it, we learn that a better education means different things depending on the individual. Generally, adults subscribe to two broad meanings of "a better education." These meanings are interrelated in their minds. One refers to the more immediate educational experience and the academic preparation a suburban education might provide for college. The second meaning refers to the potential future value of obtaining the type of education that American society's gatekeepers—college admission officers, employers, even potential colleagues and clients at work—perceive to be better.

Within this first category are several subcategories people associate with the nature of a good, or better, education. Most past participants, while holding meanings that combined two or three of these, recall one prominent characteristic of a "better education" that was most important to them and their families. For example, past participants remember that they believed the suburban schools would provide them with access to better educational resources, including books, supplies, libraries, lower student-to-teacher ratios, and nicer buildings and grounds. Past participants recall that this "better education" would include an environment that was more conducive to learning than urban schools and would be more likely to simulate college-level work. The participants remember their parents' hopes for orderly classrooms with fewer interruptions for discipline problems. Inherent in these images lay another essential ingredient: physical safety.

Past participants also associate a "better education" with the expectations that a community has for its children. For example, the former students recall that their parents expected the suburban students would have more serious attitudes toward learning: course work would be more rigorous and challenging than it was in the city schools, and teachers would expect and demand a lot from their students. Students and their families valued the fact that students in these suburban schools rarely dropped out and that high school graduation was taken for granted. But most important was the fact that in the suburban METCO towns, most students went on to college.

But How Do They Know?

Among the many families with little or no firsthand experience with Boston schools were strongly held beliefs about the superiority of suburban education that were based strongly on perception, hearsay, and first impressions. But about one-third of the adults in this sample had attended a city school for at least part of their education. And these adults base their comparisons of urban and suburban schools on three main factors. It is these recollected differences that provide for them today justification for having attended a METCO school.

First, while in the city schools, the students were often advanced academically or working at a high level in various subjects. Some former METCO students recall that after transferring to suburbia, they often were put in lower-level tracks. Or, students who thought their work was satisfactory were told that they needed to improve. Second, many former students recall that the As and Bs they earned in Boston often changed to Bs and Cs in suburbia. For some students, those grades eventually went up; for others, the grades remained average C or below-average D. Sean Thomas, for example, recalls, "I was a superstar academically in Boston. Well you had to kiss that status goodbye, and that hurt at first, but it confirmed to us, I believe, that we were in a better environment, a higher standard type of environment."

Likewise, Bethany Cross says, "I was used to getting As. I had to get used to Cs, then Bs. Then, finally, I was getting As again. This was a big challenge for me, for my self-esteem, but my mother thought it was a good thing—we were looking for a better education and this was an indication to us."

The third factor is related to the classroom environment and the comparative frequency that learning was interrupted as a teacher tended to discipline. The adults recall that in the city schools, it was much more difficult for a teacher to get through a lesson or a discussion without objects flying across the room, a student yelling out, a squabble erupting.

Also, some students, whose families wanted to escape the disruption to education and the racial violence spurred by Boston's busing order, found calm in suburbia compared to the tumult they had experienced under busing in Boston. As Beth Davidson recalls of her years during the 1970s in suburbia: "The whole racial thing? I never really had a problem with it at all. This was just not an issue. And I mean, this was the time that busing was started and people were having really bad fights. And there were really bad problems everywhere else and I was just going to school. That's all. I just got on the bus, went to school and wondered, you know, 'What's the problem?'"

Ironically, the families who saw METCO as a way around the problems caused by busing were not seeking escape from integration or busing per se, since they chose an even more extreme form of integration and longer bus rides. As these adults remember thinking about it, integration was acceptable, even desirable, but only if it were a vehicle to "better schools."

Though their parents and guardians usually made the decision for them to attend METCO, the past participants recall that, as children, they amassed their own evidence to justify their going to suburbia. Today, the adults remember having two, even three times the amount of homework as their neighborhood friends. The symbol of the book bag was ubiquitous and important to them: METCO students remember that they carried heavy loads while neighborhood friends carried nothing, save for occasional pieces of paper. Some adults recall that in high school, as they marked the dates of the SATs on their calendars and prepared for the test, neighborhood friends did not even know about the SAT.

But there is still another particularly powerful piece of evidence used by both adults who did and who did not attend the city schools. These adults look to the seemingly unchanged life of old neighborhood friends who did not attend METCO—friends who are hanging around the street or still struggling to find good jobs and financial security. Rightly or wrongly, it is quite common for the post-METCO adults to compare their own relatively successful lives with those of their less-successful old acquaintances and use these examples as justification for attending METCO.

For example, when George Gardner goes to visit his mother in his old neighborhood he sees "the same guys hanging. Smart black men, just hanging. I was always mad that I couldn't just hang, when I had all this homework. I'd be mad about it. Now I walk by and I'm thinking, 'I'm glad they gave me all that homework. I'm glad my mother made me do it.'"

At times in her suburban educational career, Shirley Rogers wondered whether she might be able to get just as good an education in the city. She sometimes found the long bus rides difficult to justify. But today, Shirley visits relatives in her former neighborhood and runs into old acquaintances who seem to her to be unchanged since "old days." She explains:

> It's not that everything was good for me in [town] and I did used to think that with my mother, and I always was a pretty good student, sort of self-motivated depending on the subject. I probably would've been alright, probably gone right on to college, anyway. . . .
>
> There is still the question of influence, of who's influencing you and examples and what have you. And the same ones who were hanging til' 2 a.m. on, you know, Tuesday nights! They were the ones harassing me, calling me "white girl" for doing homework? They're still there, talking the same shit, like it's a time warp. . . .
>
> I'm not saying if I went to Boston, I'd be out there with them. My mother would not have stood for that, okay? But she made me go [to METCO] for a reason, you start to see that, and it was to get me moving on another road.

There are likely many factors contributing to what the former students perceive as others' relative failures compared with their own relative successes. Similarly, there are probably many graduates from the city schools whose financial or other external measures of success surpass those of many METCO graduates. And there are surely complex and varied reasons black urban children were placed in low-level courses and received poor grades upon entry to suburban schools. It's plausible that the placements and lower grades were neither true reflections of a better-quality education in suburbia nor accurate reflections of the students' abilities or efforts. But these recollections are, nevertheless, lenses into the reasoning and thinking of the former METCO students.

Besides the more immediate perceived day-to-day benefits of attending a METCO school, participants remember that their families understood something else. Mothers and fathers or grandmothers believed that going to a well-regarded suburban school carried prestige in American society. The suburban diploma, parents told their children, might one day open doors previously shut. Adults today recall parents impressing upon them that college admission offices, or even job interviewers, would think better of them for their diploma from a suburban school. A suburban education, Michelle Parker understood as a young child, would place her in a world that was "close to power." And Bruce Paynter's mother told him to " 'get your foot in there.' She said if I got my foot in there, I'd see, I'd see people would treat me different. 'Right or wrong,' my mother said, 'people will treat you better.' "

Similarly, Marquise Bell recalls, "My mother was like, 'Get out there, take in that world, learn that world. Be a part of it. Open up your life.' And somehow she knew, I don't know how, but she knew it'd give you that edge. My mother, she never left Roxbury really, but she had it figured out somehow. That's what amazes me to this day, that she knew all this."

Logic of Parents, Logic of Legal Activists

The logic of these parents—who chose METCO on the basis of perception, reputation, and access—mirrors the logic of the Supreme Court in two cases that were crucial legal stepping stones to the more widely known *Brown v. Board of Education* in 1954. This common sense social theory, of mothers, fathers, and grandmothers in some of Boston's poorest sections, is echoed by scholarly research as well as by the rulings of the High Court.

In the 1950 Supreme Court case *Sweatt v. Painter* (1950), lawyers for the NAACP asked that Heman Sweatt, a black man, be admitted to the all-white University of Texas Law School. The civil rights lawyers argued that Sweatt be admitted despite the fact that a black law school had been established with "faculty of five full-time professors, twenty-three students, a library of 16,000 books serviced by a full-time staff, a practice court and a legal aid society" (Kluger, 1975, p. 282). The Supreme Court ruled in the NAACP's favor, reasoning that the newer law school for blacks was not in keeping with the "equal" part of the then-operative *Plessy v. Ferguson* (1896) "separate but equal" mandate. The black law school was not equal, the Supreme Court ruled, because the larger white university had in more abundance other important qualities that defied objective measurement. These characteristics included reputation of the faculty, the position of alumni, standing in the community, and prestige (Kluger, 1975).

Then–Chief Justice Fred Vinson wrote in the Court's decision: "What is more important, the University of Texas Law School possesses to a far greater degree those qualities which are incapable of objective measurement but which make for greatness in a law school. . . . It is difficult to believe that one who had a free choice between these law schools would consider the question close" (Kluger, 1975, p. 282).

Simultaneously, in *McLaurin v. Oklahoma State Regents for Higher Education* (1950), the High Court applied this principle to other graduate programs. In this case, George McLaurin, a black doctoral student in education at the University of Oklahoma, had been forced to sit outside regular classrooms for instruction, assigned a segregated desk in the library mezzanine, and forced to eat alone in the cafeteria (Kluger, 1975, p. 280). The Court ruled that the restrictions were not consistent with Plessy's "equal" mandate because the segregation restricted McLaurin from exchanging views and engaging in discussions and making contacts with other students, namely the white students who would be potential future colleagues. In the *Sweatt* and *McLaurin* cases, desegregation was viewed as a policy intended to alter an unequal structure of opportunity imposed on the basis of race. Under this theory, the opportunity in these cases is unequal at least in part because segregated blacks were denied the prestige and connections associated with the white schools.

These cases were important because they established that objective measures, such as facilities and staff, were not the only appropriate measures of equality. Rather, these cases said, schooling must be understood within the context of the larger society. Equally important measures of equality and "quality" are the social milieu and powerful networks within a school, and the reputation that school carries in the community and broader society. And this is exactly what many past METCO participants and their families believed too.

So, like the law and graduate schools of *Sweatt* and *McLaurin*, METCO's suburban schools were, in the eyes of past participants and their families, clearly connected to wider opportunities in American society. Therefore, the fairest measure of the utility of METCO-like programs would be their longer-term effects on students after high school. A handful of scholars has taken this view. Most recently, Derek Bok and William Bowen (1998), who took a long view of affirmative action in elite colleges, conclude that it has benefited blacks over the course of their lives. Similarly, in their research review on the longer-term effects of desegregation, Amy Stuart Wells and Robert Crain find evidence that the early legal activists, in the researchers' words, "knew what they were talking about" (1994). The researchers note that black students who attended predominantly white schools were more likely to be integrated in, and obtain success in, other realms of life than were their counterparts from predominantly black schools.

Of course the METCO families based their decisions on neither scholarly research nor the logic of legal decisions of the 1950s. But as we have seen, many of these families did have an acute sense of the unwritten requirements for success in American society.

Something Else Besides the School

In addition to the "better education" mantra, there was, for more than two-thirds of these men and women, a second mantra. The program's past participants recall that METCO was not only a way to get to a better school but also a journey that would "broaden their horizons." It is particularly difficult for the adults to recall what, as children, they thought that phrase meant. But the phrase does mean something to the adults now: feeling entitled and accustomed to participating in a white-dominated society. As 1970s graduate Laurel Yale describes it, broadening her horizons meant "seeing that world as mine, too . . . as belonging to me as much as it did to them." Similarly, Mike Carter explains: "It was to get used to this idea that this was where I was going to be operating, this was part of my life." And Dwight Stephens offers simply: "It's about practice, really, for me, I guess. It was practice for thinking of yourself as belonging there . . . having a right to be there. You start to just assume that that's the way your life is going to be."

This idea differs substantially from gaining power from association with a powerful, prestigious social institution of a suburban school. Power of association relates more to what opportunities people in the larger society might provide you because of your status as a graduate from a prestigious school. But broadened horizons speaks to the effects the METCO experience had personally on its participants. More specifically, if METCO did successfully broaden a participant's horizons, that person would become more confident, more at ease, and more familiar with learning, work, and social interaction in a white-dominated setting.

Renee Samuel understands this mantra too, after years as a child "not totally understanding the purpose" of "broadened horizons." Renee explains, "You go through your days out there and pretty soon, you just sort of forget about it, that it's different there. Then, you realize, 'Hey, I'm not worrying about this anymore.' The fact that people are different out here, that this is different from where I'm from. You start to feel like this is just the way it is. Then, it's just how you function. And you continue thinking like that, like, you can go anywhere, really. It's all part of your world."

That is not to say that everyone achieved a sense of belonging during the years they were in their suburban schools. For most, it took years after METCO to see what they had gotten from the experience and to understand what relevance the simple, overused words "broadened horizons" had in their lives.

Watchful Mothers and Fathers

Despite repeating METCO's mantras in their minds as young students, most of the adults I talked with remember having doubts about METCO's worth. And just more than half even remember wanting to drop out (five in this sample did drop out). There was also a range of intensity here, with some former students remembering having "hated it, every minute"; "begging, just begging not to go"; "despising it most of the time." But others simply "went through stages of liking it and not liking it," and "hating it one day, hating all white people one day and then thinking the next (day) that it was okay, liking the white kids and not minding it so much." The reasons for wanting to leave ranged from cultural isolation and loneliness to sheer physical exhaustion from early morning bus rides and long days.

Sandra Robertson, for example, complains of "getting sick of being the only black in my college prep classes" and "being just really tired all the time and tired of getting on the bus." Still, Sandra stayed, despite her longing to go to school in her neighborhood on the Roxbury/Dorchester line. "I kept going because I had to. My parents made me," Sandra says.

By junior high, Rita Wood was growing tired of the ignorant questions from white students in her wealthy suburban METCO school, such as, "Are there bars on your windows?" and, "Have you ever been shot at?" Partly for this reason, Rita wanted so much to return to Boston and go to public school with her neighborhood friends. Shirley Rogers longed to just "roll out of bed, walk to (school) and not have any homework." But Sandra, Rita, and Shirley, like other METCO students who at some point wanted to leave but did not, usually had just one reason for sticking it out.

"My mother would not let me leave," Rita says. The only way Rita would be allowed to leave, her mother insisted, was if she took the entrance exam and was accepted to Latin Academy, an exclusive, well-regarded public high school in Boston. "Then, she made sure that I missed the test there," Rita says. "I remember I wasn't so happy about that. I did want to get out." Today, Rita appreciates her mother's forcing her to stay. But left to make up her own mind 15 years ago, Rita, like Sandra and many other graduates, probably would have returned to Boston. As Shirley Rogers explains, "On the one hand, I was glad for METCO even as a small child. But there were days, you know, I just didn't want to deal with it and I'd be questioning my mother on it, you know, 'Why do I have to do this? Can't I drop out for a couple of years? Can't I just drop out to graduate with my (neighborhood) friends?' And I'm nagging on her while we are eating breakfast at 5 a.m. so I can be on time for the bus. And she'd say, 'You're going. Eat your cereal.' And she was right."

So, in addition to the better education mantra, many METCO students had another reason for getting up at dawn, waiting at those bus stops, riding those highways, accepting those home-work assignments, and toughing it out even when they would rather not. It was because of a mother or father, grandmother or grandfather, older brother or older sister, because at least one of these important, watchful adults said, "You have to go." It makes sense then that those participants who feel they benefited from METCO or who have successful lives would give much of the credit to their families. If not for their mothers or fathers, these past participants say, they might have either left METCO altogether or foundered for the rest of their lives.

The Meaning of Participation

Looking back on it today, the adults generally see METCO as a direct step into a world of privilege and opportunity that they or-dinarily and wrongly would have been denied. Leaving the se-curity of their own communities wasn't always what they wanted to do and it was not taken lightly. And their choice of school was often made for them by parents who had their own maps for their children's futures. When they were young children and teen-agers crossing the color line few others tread past, they usually found ways to justify their attendance at white suburban schools. But it wasn't until they were grown up, in college, working, raising families, and living on their own that they really began to understand the reasons their parents signed them up for METCO in the first place.

The post-METCO adults' understanding of why they went to

white suburbia for school is based not on rejection but on the desire for full participation. Michelle Parker, in terms similar to those of fellow past METCO participants, expresses this sentiment:

> When you leave your family to go to college, the way that I did and my mother did not, my father did not, either. Does that mean you are rejecting them? Who would dare say something that stupid, hmm? And when you become, when you have a kind of a middle-class lifestyle when your father drove a bus when you were a child? Is that rejection of him? No. No. METCO is not rejection of anything, really. It is the choice of participation in something that maybe wasn't all set up right just for you, maybe they've been trying to keep it from us, even—not like a kind of conspiracy, but just the way things got handed out, you know, people in positions of power forgot about certain communities. It's not something made for you. But you want a stab at it anyway.

Like Michelle, the post-METCO adults today don't see themselves as having left a black world in favor of a white one. Most now understand that their parents wanted them to have the choice and skills to meld those worlds. And in the following chapter, adults speak about their days in suburbia and the challenges, disappointments, and triumphs that came with the requirement to learn, to live, and to survive simultaneously in black and white communities.

3

What Remains in Memory

Ask past METCO students what they remember about their years in white suburbia, and their first responses usually have little to do with the weighty subjects of race, culture, and class. It's the logistical aspects—5 a.m. wake ups and bus rides that went on for as long as two hours one way—that begin their conversations.

Michelle Parker, a 1980s graduate, relives what she calls "the boring, tired, physical exhaustion part of METCO" every time she sees or hears a yellow school bus rumbling around the streets. Her nephew goes to a METCO school, about an hour outside the city, and from him Michelle hears echoes of complaints she made two decades ago.

"I tell him, 'Listen, I know it can be bad. But having quality morning time to sit with your feet up?' I tell him, 'This not what METCO's for.' The bus ride . . . it was like torture, okay? But there was this feeling like everyone on the bus was in it together, doing this. It was just the way it was for us. And slowly you got kind of used to it. I say 'kind of' because it could wear you down. It was long—long, long, long."

The rides and long days—often from 5 a.m. to 6 or 7 p.m.— were constant features of school life. Past participants remember

that the bus rides often seemed interminable at the start of their
METCO careers, but eventually, many say, the rides became routine. Former students rarely focus on such topics for more than a
few minutes. It is with more serious tones that the adults move on
to other salient memories of their days as black city children and
teenagers in white suburbia's schools.

These adults' recollections are important not because they
accurately describe the experiences of METCO students. Surely,
current students would be better sources for that information.
They are most interesting and informative as mature adult perspectives on childhood and teenage experiences. An important
first question is: What did these experiences feel like to the
adults when they were children or teens? But more relevant
questions are: What sense do the former students, now adults,
make of these experiences? What remains in their memories after
all these years? I asked past METCO participants to talk about the
events or images that stand out in their minds and the memories
that best characterize their experiences in suburbia. The memories are generally of three distinct types.

First, the adults tell stories or recount anecdotes that seem to
reveal or spotlight difference—difference not only from white
children in suburbia but difference, too, from black children
back home. Differences between the communities where they
lived and the communities where they were schooled meant
that as children and teens, these adults lived in what they often
termed "two worlds." These were worlds marked most obviously
by distinct speech patterns, tastes, habits, and social behavior
with friends.

This chapter is divided into three sections. The first, "Dis-
covering Difference," explores these memories and tries to make
sense of them through the eyes of the black adults who attended
suburban schools. There are both negative and positive sides to
this discussion. On the one hand, white suburban students and
teachers often appear in these stories almost comically unable to

socialize, learn, and teach gracefully amid racial and cultural difference. But there are also examples that spotlight circumstances under which racial and cultural difference is not only nonthreatening, but enriching too and that underscore the potential of cross-district school desegregation.

In the second section, "Crossing the Line," former METCO students recall events or images that symbolize to them a crossing of a constructed color line. Often, this crossing was accompanied by an increasing understanding that difference, in whatever form, was merely one part of their experience as blacks attending white schools. Important in this process were friendships with white students or families and a gradually diminishing self-consciousness and intimidation that had expressed itself in racial terms. Some students also remember what were usually failed attempts to bring up race as a general topic. Students look back on these crossings of the color line in a variety of ways and with some mixed feelings. Some gained empowerment and faith in humankind. Others were and remain disappointed in what they see as whites' general inability to address issues related to race.

In section three, "Peering into Privilege," the adults speak about their first realization of class differences between the suburban communities and their home communities. As children, they had a range of reactions to these differences. Today they often say that their early observations of class differences between communities helped contribute to their understanding of the social significance that such class differences have in American society. Some students continue to resent two class-related attitudes they felt white students had. White students did not seem to have a sense of, or perspective on, their own privilege and seemed unable to get past stereotypes about black poverty.

With mature eyes and the salve of time, the adults looking back on their days as black city children in white suburban schools usually fit into one of three general categories. Just more than 20 percent recount days in suburbia as nearly all positive. They fit in well, had black and white friends, were rarely personally affected by blatant racism, and were spared all but the most typical adolescent identity crises. By far the most common description—about 70 percent of post-METCO adults fall into this category—is of years mixed with good and bad. Acceptance and rejection. Confusion and clarity. Fear and strength. A far smaller number—about 10 percent of the 65 people in this group— characterize their experiences as entirely negative. These men and women focus on stories of incessant racial name-calling and exclusion by blacks at home and whites at school.

The black adults now learning, working, and child rearing in the years and decades since high school commonly view their experiences in school as a microcosm of their subsequent experience. For most of the post-METCO adults, their atypical educational experiences constituted a fair approximation of post–high school life in white America. Being a black child in white suburbia was a head-on run into America's racial quandaries and preoccupations—all its persistent misunderstandings, consistent clumsiness, occasional ugliness, and hopeful transcendence.

Section I—Discovering Difference

The recollections of difference, of "feeling [as if] from another world," as METCO graduate Samuel Dean describes it, take many forms. They include: the first-day shock of so many white faces; the silent, penetrating stares; the palpable awkwardness during dispassionate classroom discussions of slavery and Jim Crow; being the only black child in an advanced class or clumped together with the other METCO students in a low-level learning group. Few can forget the questions from white students that revealed stereotyped images of blacks and of urban life. These were the images of drugs, violence, deprivation, and parental neglect—images that didn't include the love, faith, work, and ordinariness of the black students' actual lives in Boston.

Most of the black students from the city felt that when they were in suburbia, they needed to learn to talk like the white kids. Speech was and is the most powerful symbol of their need to straddle "two worlds." School years were commonly marked by feelings of being fundamentally "different," "out of sync," and "not quite a part of" white suburbia. But as the long days in suburbia and their cross-racial friendships began to influence their values, their speech, their dress, tastes, and personal goals, METCO kids also began to feel different from friends back home, too.

The power of difference intensified around adolescence. In these years, taste in music and clothing seemed to split clearly down racial lines. These differences today seem small and funny to adults, but years ago seemed to have the power to mysteriously place great distance between black and white children who had been friends in elementary school.

Years and decades after high school, the post-METCO adults explain that the differences they confronted and learned to live with in METCO are similar to ones they encountered in predominantly white colleges, workplaces, and social situations. And as they talk about their past experiences as black children in white suburban schools, the adults' stories reveal that it wasn't the differences per se that were innately troublesome. For them, it was white *reactions* to difference. That is, the way teachers, students, and administrators reacted to the black METCO students shaped the black students' suburban experiences. And now, those reactions from whites leave impressions and affect the way the former students look back upon the suburban communities.

The post-METCO adults hold dear the times when difference opened the door to cross-racial communication and new understandings. And they use the narratives from these experiences as evidence for the potential of cross-racial understanding, even friendship and equality. This is the case even when such experiences were rare, compared with the far more common memories of disconcerting confrontations with difference.

Reflecting today on past experiences with cultural difference, childhood anger has mostly faded, though the adults haven't stopped thinking about their years in suburbia and the significance of past events. Most likely, these black adults attribute past difficulties to suburban whites' own isolation from African Americans and urban life. In their eyes, the problems stem from big, unseen forces that METCO doesn't touch—a mix of history, economics, and politics—that drew the isolating boundaries between whites and blacks in the first place.

The irony isn't lost on METCO graduate Mike Carter, who comments:

> That's why we had METCO, or one of the reasons—to get rid of some of the isolation out there. So, we get there and there are some problems with blacks and whites, there is just a huge, huge distance between all of us. And that's no one person's fault, it's the isolation that's the problem. So we end the isolation by coming out there. Fine, but before that, the isolation has already set up misunderstandings, and that's what you get. You solve the problem of isolation by ending isolation. And then you say, "Hmm. Isolation has bred out all these other problems, all this junk has kinda' spawned off of it." Now, someone's gotta deal with it all. It's how you deal with it that's gonna mean (METCO's) a good thing or a bad. I don't mean the METCO kids, I mean how everyone deals with it.

THE QUESTIONS, BOTH ASKED AND UNASKED

In fourth grade, Patricia Baxter, a new METCO student, was paired with a white girl. Their teacher asked the two to make a presentation at the blackboard. Patricia, now in her early 30s, can't recall the content of the assignment. But she remembers what happened as she and her partner, standing together at the front of the class, neared the end of their talk.

> I do remember that my partner was so fascinated with the fact that I was black, this fourth-grade white student. I think the fact that they hadn't experienced a black student in the classroom, that she, you know, picked up the eraser off the board, and she started to put the chalk all over my face. The teacher immediately ran up to control her. At the time, I didn't really understand what was going on. Then, after I got out and started to grow, that story always kind of came back to me, because I started to realize what was going on with them. They were so isolated, we were strange to them. I didn't understand at the time how really isolated they all were.

Like Patricia, most of the post-METCO adults today now see even the most audacious acts—such as the spattering of a black child with white chalk dust—to be helpless manifestations of white curiosity and ignorance bred from isolation. But when these black adults were children, the white students' behavior, be it compelled by ignorance or curiosity, often felt humiliating and invasive. In addition, many adults recount examples of what several respondents call "unasked questions." These came in the form of stares and whispers that were often overheard.

Like many of the adults I talked to, Barbara Michaels, who in the mid-1970s was a member of the first METCO graduating class from her northern suburban high school, was once frustrated by white children who turned to stare at her during classroom discussions of slavery and black history. "And it happened in just about all of my classes when it came to social studies and these discussions," she says. "And it was really strange: whenever it came to any kind of black history, it was like they thought I was there on the plantation, picking cotton. They seem[ed] to be looking at me for some kind of answer about what was it like. I'm full of questions, too. I'm just like them in that way."

Sometimes the questions were asked. White girls routinely asked black METCO girls about how they did their hair and what kind of makeup black girls bought. The respondents reacted to these questions with a range of emotions, from anger and annoyance to amusement and playful scorn for the white girls.

But the questions were far less threatening when they came from white students who were already friends or acquaintances, than from white classmates the black girls did not know well. Such questions could be preludes to more substantial discussions about race and difference, *if* the white girls asked them in private settings, rather than in public places, such as hallways or the girls' bathrooms, where the black girls often felt as if they were on display.

Carla Lyon, who graduated in the 1980s, explains that "questions themselves weren't bad in and of themselves"; what mattered was the person who asked them.

> You could get the exact same question—the exact same words—but it just felt different. A stranger in the bathroom would say, "Oh, my God, look at those braids." And at that point, of course, all the white girls stare and you're like: "What? Get out of my face."
>
> But then, [with my] white friends, I'd braid my hair real tight, close to my head. And my friend Marisa would say, "Oh, my God, look at those braids." But we'd move onto a different subject, something with a bit more content, something about us, the people inside, and with her it was different even though the words were really the same. And I also knew she was curious, and we'd ask each other stuff about black girls or white girls or whatever but there was more to it, I guess was why it

didn't bother me with her. And it was never like I was on parade. So it can be different, depending.

There were other kinds of questions, too. These were the questions that, as the adults remember, revealed to them as black children, white students' steadfastly negative stereotypes of blacks and of Boston's predominantly black neighborhoods. Like many of the past METCO participants, Thomas Mitchell, who graduated from a wealthy suburban high school in the early 1980s, recounts frequent public humiliations during discussions about drugs.

We were doing a unit on drugs, a science unit, I think it was. And it was a technical kind of discussion, like what was a stimulant, what's a depressant, things like that. We didn't have a lot to do with the white kids really; the METCO kids kind of all stuck together in this class, maybe because there were not that many of us to begin with. But when we started on the drug unit, they started asking us questions, like: "Do you know a lot of people who OD'd' [overdosed]" or, "Do people try to sell drugs to you?" And we thought it was ridiculous, I did especially, because we were heavy churchgoers and my family was just so straight. But that was when I felt like we were really seen as the "other," something from another world to them, like something to peer in and then pull away from. And when we answered those questions, it didn't matter because they just fired more and more and more at us. Even though, right from the start of the discussion, they should have known that we couldn't give any great stories about black people and wild drug parties.

As was generally true among black girls who were asked incessantly about their hair or makeup regimen, the post-METCO adults say that questioning from white students was not, as

Thomas Mitchell says, "the thing itself to be feared." As Thomas and other former METCO students typically noted, "it was the attitude that came with the question" that "really got to me in a bad way." Or, as Paul Hammond puts it: "Ignorance is okay. It can't really be helped. What's bad is when there's no real effort to stop that ignorance. They [the white students] just hung on tight to it."

More specifically, two factors commonly turned questions asked of black students by whites into negative forces. First, and most important, is that the white suburban students seemed unreceptive to explanations that ran counter to white stereotypes about black people or city life. Second, as these adults remember it, teachers often unwittingly built the barriers even higher by failing to guide students toward more empathetic and less stereotypical questions. The first complaint is more common than the second. Most of the adults recall feeling frustrated by the white students' unyielding, false images of blacks and of the neighborhoods where many of the black students lived. It wasn't usually until years after high school—often as their own children begin school—that the post-METCO adults began to reflect upon the potentially positive role teachers could have played but usually did not.

The ways that past participants remember acting on those feelings of humiliation vary considerably, ranging from a seeming lack of concern to physical fighting. Generally, men were more likely to recall their mocking the white students. But black women, interestingly, were more likely to recall their angry protests and public, verbal challenges to the stereotypes implied by white students' questions or comments. For example, Mike Carter, who, in his words, was "socially popular among all kids, black, white, whatever," just "made jokes about it," when a white student asked such questions as: "Can you go out after dark?" and "Have you ever shot a gun?" Mike recalls that he would then put the white student "on the spot," replying sarcastically, for example, " 'Oh, yes. I'm terrified there in Fort Hill (economically mixed, largely professional section of Roxbury). Yeah man, you gotta look out for them killers, man, they are everywhere up there.' Back home, when you're hanging out in Roxbury [and] you live way up there on the Hill, they think you must be a snob. [To the second question] I'd say, 'I shoot every night, man. Go home? I'm on the street, shootin'. All night, shootin'.' So, they don't know what to think. To this day, I have never held a gun in my hand."

Women, on the other hand, are far more likely to recall sincere efforts to discuss and confront the misperceptions and stereotypes that the questions revealed. Similar to many other women, Margaret Redford remembers a constant refrain from her METCO years. It was: "Wait a minute. Stop right there."

> I'd always be trying to get everyone to look at the question, to examine it in some way—"Why is this question being asked?" and "Where did you get this question?" —trying to turn it around so it might sink into their head. And so, when someone said: "Can you hear gun shots in your room at night?" And we lived not like they (the white students) did, in a fancy place, but it was comfortable and it was safe. As long as you knew your way around, it was fine. Today, now, I don't know, maybe not so safe. But I'd just try to get all the METCO kids to not answer the question, to just refuse. To say: "Wait a minute. Let's think about that question and why you would ask that question, where you get your ideas about life outside this little town?"

About one-fourth of the respondents were unconcerned and even amused by the white students' questions. They saw evidence of white stereotypes almost daily but either laughed them off or ignored them entirely. These students didn't try to change the white students' views, and, as METCO graduate Michelle

Parker explains, "didn't let ourselves get all worked up about these things." Unlike the other former students who remember with clarity past feelings of anger or disgust, this relatively smaller group does not remember being affected by persistent stereotypes.

In fact, no matter what their reactions were as children and teens, few of the adults who experienced such questions or comments report feeling angry about them today. Most say the inquiries are not something they think about very often, and that the comments and questions that displayed ignorance or stereotypes didn't end with METCO. Today, these adults hear similar questions and comments while they are out socializing, in their workplaces and their colleges. That's not to say they blindly accept the comments and questioning. Rather, the questions and comments were as Thomas Mitchell sees it, evidence of racial isolation, which is, "part of the American landscape."

However, the more than two dozen past participants who have contact with METCO today, through a relative or friend who is a parent in the program or through their jobs or volunteer work, report that they hear very familiar stories from current students and METCO administrators, who complain about negative stereotypes manifesting themselves in questions, stares, and comments. When past participants witness such events in METCO schools or hear of these stories, especially from their own children, an old frustration gets re-ignited. "You get impatient sometimes," says Laura Gates, a 1980s graduate whose daughter attends elementary school at a METCO suburb north of Boston and comes home with "all-too-familiar" stories. "It can make you mad."

Likewise, Mary Carson, whose goddaughter attends a METCO school, says, "You think it couldn't still be like that. Then you hear these stories, like the white kids still ask the same stupid stuff. And you know—I know—this child is happy with her school and this is a good thing for this child. But you still feel for that child, and then you remember, it's you in that place, all over again, and it can really get you mad again."

Few today locate the source of the problem in the children and white teenagers themselves, even though these classmates were once the exclusive focus of the black students' frustration and anger. There are two standard responses. About half of the post-METCO adults assign blame at least partly to the adults associated with the suburban schools, including teachers and, occasionally, parents of the white students. This is especially true among the black adults whose contact with METCO continues today in some form. Most commonly, the adults say that white teachers and administrators should have encouraged better, more substantive questions and been sensitive to black students' frustrations over the form and tone of certain questions. Also, the adults believe that the children's parents should have guided their own children to more sensitive questions, though few think that the adults themselves had such skills or practice in interracial settings.

The post-METCO adults located the source of their childhood problems most often with suburban isolation itself. About three-quarters of the adults, while they might feel that the whites had some individual responsibility, lament the powerful race and class boundaries in the metropolitan area separating blacks and whites. This structural reality, then, is responsible in the minds of most of these black adults for their having been subjected to moments of humiliation, invasions of privacy, or, as 1980s graduate Cara Ross describes them, "these questions that just didn't let you be."

WHEN QUESTIONS LED TO LEARNING

Good occasionally came of questions that white students asked. Usually, two characteristics made the questioning positive or, at least, neutral experiences for the former black students. One, the white students demonstrated that they were listening carefully

and seemed to be gaining something from the black students'
explanations. Two, like the hair and makeup questions, these
positive questions were asked not in classrooms as eyes turned to
gaze, but in smaller groups or in private, between friends.

Kim Peters, a 1970s graduate, holds dear a brief exchange
she had with a white acquaintance as they worked on a school
project at the white girl's house:

> Everyone was going around pretending like we [METCO
> students] were white and we were just like everyone else,
> and teachers would say these things, happy little stupid
> things like, "We may all look different, but really, we are
> all the same." And I'd be sitting there, thinking, "Huh?
> No. We're not all the same and you know it, honey." And
> that was what I wanted to say.
>
> And so, this girl, she was all right, and she asked
> me: "It must be hard sometimes, is it, being the only
> black kid in the class, huh?" And I remember wanting to
> cry, you know? And I was a tough kid, but I was so
> relieved. And then we kind of talked more and more, not
> always about big race issues. You can really tell when a
> person's listening, and she asked me, "Oh, tell me about
> your house and your mother," things like that. And she
> was just learning about a different life, you know. You
> could tell she was curious and that was fine.

Douglas Baker, who graduated in the 1970s from a large
suburb west of Boston, recalls surreptitious phone calls with a
white girl who was in the midst of challenging her parents' racist
views.

> She asked, "What's Boston like?" And I said, "Nothing
> like you read about." And she said, "Would there be a
> problem if I were to go in there with you? I mean, is it
> dangerous?" And I tried to explain, "Nancy, if some-

thing were to happen there, to you, the whole community would be held hostage until they found out who did it." And she understood the repercussions of something happening to a white suburban girl in Dorchester or Roxbury [and] that she probably wouldn't be in danger. She'd be in less danger than a girl who lived there. And she indicated that she didn't think that was right, that it wasn't fair. Then I said, "You know, Nancy, if anyone should fear, I should fear, since I am very easily identifiable in [Nancy's suburb]. And I don't feel afraid coming here. I don't feel the town is hostile toward me." So, she really thought about that, about seeing the situation I was in. And we talked about a lot of things and she appreciated our relationship.

To the past participants, memories such as these are the personal treasures from their suburban experiences. Such events stand out in their minds, even for men and women for whom such positive encounters were uncommon. Most often, the adults portray their suburban experiences with a nearly even mix of hopeful stories, such as these, and stories about questions and attitudes that made the blacks feel excluded and somehow foreign. Nearly everyone has stories about the incessant questions. And nearly everyone has stories about events, no matter how brief or unsensational, that inspired in them hopefulness that blacks and whites might learn to understand and accept each other.

THE UGLY SIDE OF FEAR

Just as there are small treasures from METCO days, so too are there stories that reveal an uglier side of the experience. Several of the students heard the word "nigger" directed at them or at other METCO students. The word "nigger," many past participants recalled, often was uttered during an argument or dispute when a white kid, unable to think of a better retort, aimed where he knew it would hurt. A few past participants had racial epithets etched into their notebooks or lockers. And there was often racist graffiti here and there, aimed at no specific person.

Then there was exclusion based on race. Tara Beck, a self-described shy METCO student, sat at the opposite end of a table from white girls during a study hall one day in the late 1970s. The white girls moved away to another crowded table, leaving Tara alone with her homework. The next day it happened again. Then it happened a third time. This time, Tara heard a girl whisper "nigger" under her breath while walking away. As Tara remembers it, each day, the white, male teacher supervising the study hall looked up, saw the movement, and went back to his paper-grading or newspaper.

When it happened the fourth time, Tara walked out of the room, looked around the corridors for her black friends from METCO, found none, went to the bathroom and cried quietly in a stall. The following year, she returned to the Boston public schools, dropped out, and later earned her GED. Today she's a teacher's aide in a racially mixed educational facility. "It doesn't have to be that way, the way it worked out bad for me," Tara says. "Those were unhealthy children out there—scared, sick children."

Such stories of blatant racism, dramatic and disturbing as they might be, are far less common than are the stories of more subtle and unwitting prejudice on the part of whites. About one-third of the adults either referred to the outwardly racist events briefly or discussed and characterized them at some length. Former METCO participants generally focus less on blatantly racist incidents, even when I ask for elaboration. And such events are mentioned with much less frequency than are other aspects of the METCO experience.

Indeed, even those men and women who ran head-on into unsubtle racism more than just occasionally—about one quarter say this happened—today tend to view the events as merely one aspect of a larger and multifaceted educational experience. For example, Laura Gates, mother and 1980s graduate who attended a suburban school south of Boston, reports her confrontations with obvious racism in this typical way: "I enjoyed METCO mostly. I mean, of course, though, there are certain people, they call you niggers and stuff like that. Stupid stuff. I either just ignored that or I insulted them back. And then, I did get into fights."

Like many fellow post-METCO students, Derrick Talbot also speaks dispassionately about the blatant racism he confronted as a child. In Derrick's case, the racism was so bad, he said, that he left a wealthy METCO town to transfer to a more diverse METCO community.

"Sure, you know, there was the occasional kid who would say the N-word. So, yeah, it was pretty blatant," Derrick recalls. "But that was then."

And Alicia Holmes, who said she was often verbally harassed by "tough, white girls—tougher than me," today laughs lightly, with an apparent sense of absurdity. "Oh, it was so stupid, they'd scream, 'Nigger,' or they'd say, 'Go back to the jungle.' And the teacher would tell them to hush. It's just amazing thinking about it now. You realize how stupid people are to make such asses out of themselves like that."

The dispassion in most of the adult voices doesn't mean that they weren't hurt by events like these as children. In fact many of them, including Kim and Derrick, got into fist fights with white students who taunted them with racial slurs. Neither does the general dispassion mean the adults are passive when they see racism in their current lives. To the contrary, as we will see in the following chapter, these adults today tend to speak out and take action against racism in its subtle and blatant forms with frequency and passion. And they quite often attribute some of the motivation for this activism to their METCO experiences.

Generally, when describing their confrontations with blatant racism in METCO, participants fall into one of two categories. The first group dismisses the racism as having been practiced, for example, by a few "jerks." This group is far less likely to even bother with locating the cause or the reasons a person might have made racist remarks to them. A second group attributes the racism to whites' own fears of difference and their threatened sense of identity. Thus, to these students, the name-calling or exclusion was principally fear *expressing* itself in racial terms. Today most past participants say they are affected by current-day blatant, unsubtle racism the same way they remember experiencing it in METCO—it is stark, blinding, and hurtful but not representative of their general experiences in life or even in predominantly white settings.

There is another, smaller group whose members said that they have experienced far more blatant and more frequent racism since high school. This group—just fewer than ten—is composed entirely of men, each basing his perspective on extensive experience in predominantly white, working-poor or working-class environments around Boston. For example, like several other METCO participants, Jackson Xavier, an early 1980s graduate of a diverse METCO community west of Boston, was shocked to confront blatant racism on his first job out of high school before entering college. "I was real disillusioned while I was working there because it was my first experience working with, or really dealing with, white people from the city," he explains. "It was a totally different experience. People wouldn't even talk to me, they'd make racial slurs, comments. It was really, really bad. And for me, it was kind of hard. I had grown up with white people. I had been around white people in school; it was not perfect but I was really feeling very comfortable and then, because of this, I'm not thinking anything about going into a white place to work."

NOT MY MUSIC, NOT MY CLOTHES, NOT MY FOOD

Anyone who has been a teenager in America knows there are unwritten rules and powerful symbols of teenage culture. Following certain rules and adopting certain symbols will affiliate a teenager with certain groups. These symbols exist for both urban blacks and suburban whites. Former METCO students recall that it was around adolescence that they began to notice differences in musical tastes between themselves and suburban resident students. During adolescence, music was a powerful vehicle for the expression of identity, racial and otherwise.

As former students consider their past experiences, these differences symbolized two things. First, they were constant reminders that the students were living simultaneously in two worlds. This arrangement carried the implicit requirement at least to experience and learn about a world outside their neighborhood. Second, these divergent tastes were to the former students clear and simple examples of the differences between black and white. The students' attachment to the symbols occurred at the same time that the students became conscious of the social significance of their race. This, in turn, enhanced the power of music, clothes, and even food.

But as with some of the questions, these apparent differences didn't always separate and divide. In rare circumstances, the differences could provide powerful material for sharing culture and building friendship. Peter Quint, for example, an early 1990s graduate of a suburb west of Boston, adapted well to his schools, having started in kindergarten. He formed friendships and excelled academically. Music was for Peter, as for many other students, the first clear mark of difference between black and white adolescents. "That's the only time I think I really felt the differences between us in a really clear way. There was always something different, a little different. But when you are little, you can't totally describe it and you didn't think about it. But with the music, I remember going to a friend's house, a white kid, and he put on a tape, I don't remember what it was, but I heard it and I looked at his [other tapes] and I said: 'Hey, we don't listen to the same music.' Then I realized that the other METCO kids liked the music I liked and that the white kids all listened to the music that my friend liked.

For Peter, who had a leadership position in student government and had many close black friends and white friends all through his METCO career, this new consciousness of race-related difference was to him, "not a big deal, just something interesting that I noticed." Most significant, Peter recalls, "it could be a way to start to talk about things, to open people up to really talking."

But for others, divergent musical tastes happened simultaneously with a growing distance between black and white friendships that had formed in elementary school. Some of the adults recall that it appeared at the time as though music was the very *thing* that separated them from their white friends.

Some of the past participants remember that music played at school events—in some cases disk jockeys were hired—was nearly always songs that were popular among white students. Funk, house music, hip-hop, blues, and jazz were not commonly played. But when an occasional rap or hip-hop song was played, the past participants said, it seemed that those genres, favored by some of the METCO students, were openly scorned and ridiculed by white students. At these times, the apparently negative sanctioning of certain brands of music seemed to some of the METCO students to be evidence of white suburbia's rejection of black modes of cultural expression.

Just as there were differences in musical taste, so too were there differences in style of dress. Many former METCO students recall that, like their friends in Boston, they dressed up to go to school by wearing trousers, shirts, and leather shoes—formal clothing compared with the jeans, sweatshirts, and sneakers suburban students wore. Or, as the former students recall, they might have adopted a casual but distinctly urban style—jeans worn low or baggy, baseball hats or wool caps, unlaced sneakers, sport team jackets.

Teachers rarely seemed adept at discussing racial difference and culture as it manifested itself in music and teenage fashion trends. (Just about 20 percent had such stories.) Those teachers who led constructive discussions about difference stand out in the minds of the former METCO students, who see in these events the potential for openness and acceptance between blacks and whites. For example, Lana Wymon, a late 1970s graduate, recalls two teachers, a married couple, who tried to help students talk about racial difference openly.

> I will never forget the time that we were all walking into class and everybody was joking around and kind of ranking on each other, and then we started talking about music and [the male teacher] asked the white kids, "What music do you listen to?" And they'd answer and he'd look at me and say, "[Lana,] you ever hear of this?" I'd say, "No." And then, he'd say, "Okay, what do you like?" And I'd say, "Oh, Funkadelicks, you know." And they would all say, 'Huh?' And laugh. And this was how kids really identified at that age. When you have different music, it's a major, major big deal. But he made it easy to talk about sort of freely. He and his wife were really trying to bring out the differences, make people aware of them and really see how exciting and interesting and fun it could be. It was just always a natural kind of safe discussion about difference. Instead of the more common idea, which was that you are different and that's bad, so we just won't bring it up. We'll just pretend we don't notice that you're black.

Similarly, when black and white students had previously formed friendships, usually through athletics or extracurricular activities, the apparent differences in music, clothes, and food did open doors to important cultural exchanges. For example, Mike Carter recalled the breakfasts at suburban students' homes, where he occasionally slept after weekend basketball games. After many nights and mornings in suburbia, Mike and his white friends began alternating visits to Boston and to the suburbs for meal exchanges. Mike considers those exchanges to be the most important and formative experiences of his school years.

> I was used to real food with a lot of flavor, a lot of life to it, and I used to say, "Man, I can't eat your food." And it was a joke between all of us. And so, we started this thing where they'd come to my house and eat my mother's and my aunts' breakfasts that would go right into lunch.
>
> And I still do remember that moment when they said, "Sure, let's go to your place." Their parents thought it was a good idea and so, it kind of started, this sharing around food. Our house, it was so alive, full of people and kids in and out, little feasts all the time that kept on running. And their meals, they were quieter kind of weekends, but they really came over to my world and they had to learn to fit in, mix with my crowd. It was a good thing, and that memory sort of lasts.

Nathan King, who graduated in the early 1990s from a small suburb west of Boston, sees the discovery of teenage differences in style and taste to be one of the most enriching parts of his METCO experience. Like Mike, Nathan also had white friends who were on a basketball team with him.

"It allowed me to interact with people who didn't quite understand the things that I like and I didn't quite understand the things that they like," Nathan recalls. "I was fortunate enough to be paired up with people or to be part of an athletic team. I had a host family and when I had late games I would stay at their home. And there were many evenings that we would just talk about things I didn't quite understand, differences in styles or in dress and such and we would just talk openly about them."

In such environments, there were usually two characteristics that made emerging or apparent differences between METCO and resident students enriching rather than negative experiences. First, differences were discussed among children or teenagers who were already friends or acquaintances. And second, the white students did not scorn or reject out of hand the black students' preferences in music, clothing, or food, but instead expressed a desire to learn about and experience those new things.

The black students sometimes used cultural artifacts such as music and food as tools with which to flaunt their rejection of the white world. For example, former students recall accentuating the tastes or styles that they or white suburbia associated with being black. Many former students said they did this in part as pure expression, but also as a form of rebellion against the dominant white culture's accepted musical tastes or norms of dress. For Mary Carson, the hip-hop music she listened to on a portable cassette player, along with the heavy, faux gold jewelry she wore, were defensive symbols of blackness that set her apart and protected her from the dominant white culture at her school. Mary, like many METCO participants, recalls that by high school, in the late 1980s and early 1990s, she felt compelled to "not seem white at all." She shed that need slowly, eventually making assessments about her true taste and desires more independent of what she refers to as "the racial rules about what you did."

Now, Mary says, "the music, that's still there, still what I choose when I'm at the store. But there's other white stuff that I like, some of the folk music that I got into in college. I do like it when I hear it, and this is funny because this is the music that I wouldn't have gone near in high school."

Why? Mary explains: "I wouldn't want people seeing me liking this. That would have been too white of me. But now, it doesn't matter so much. I like what I like. I don't need to make a statement with everything I do, with what kind of music I listen to."

Conversely, when wanting acceptance in their suburban schools, some students, usually temporarily, adopted the dress styles of the white students in their schools. As Lauren Baldwin recalls with derision, "I did the whole white girl preppy thing. That was me." Similarly, Cara Ross recalls, rolling her eyes: "You should have seen me. Little Miss Prep."

However important the differences were then, former METCO participants now view differences in music and clothing as things that were powerful only because they came to be symbols that expressed identity, belonging, and culture. The adults now generally see that the differences in music and clothing that emerged in their school years were potentially enlightening and instructional. This sentiment is most common among nearly half of the past participants who offer stories in which the differences between black and white students served, if only rarely, as entry into substantive discussions about culture, tradition, and race. But even the students who didn't have such positive experiences still see the potential these differences might have in opening up discussions among young people. However, the men and women stressed, because neither they nor the white students had the skills to talk about those differences gracefully, the negative power of their divergent tastes grew exponentially.

THE TALK OF TWO WORLDS

The METCO bus ride, that burdensome journey about which nearly everyone complains, was often the scene of some relief. With the accordion doors closed and the bus rolling toward home, the young black children and teenagers could finally talk with the pace and inflection that felt just right.

At school, the children had, in varying degrees, learned and employed white suburbia's styles, rhythms, and manners of speech, including whatever adolescent suburban vocabulary was in fashion that year. During one period, for example, the suburban word for thrilling new music, clothes, or phenomena was "pisser" or, spoken with a Boston accent, "pissah." There also was "wicked," as in "wicked cool" and "wicked nice." Later, it was "awesome." In the city, the word was "bad."

Some METCO students made changes in their ordinary vocabularies too. A few former students even swapped "my mama," for "my mom." Rita Wood, who graduated in the early 1980s, recalls, "I think I learned those rules from trial and error. If you hear the METCO kids in school all day long, you hear them talk one way. But it's not the way we would talk once we got on the bus. It was completely different—we were back to city talk. We learned how to switch back and forth. The way that you heard [METCO students] talking on the bus would not be the way that you heard them talking in the classroom."

Former students also recall making deliberate changes in grammar. In METCO, the adults remember learning the codes and rules of what they now commonly refer to as "proper English." There was, of course, tremendous variation in how much "slang" (the participants' most common word of choice) or "Black English," which is how some linguists refer to urban black dialect was used. It is important to point out, too, that not all black students spoke such dialect in their homes. Several students said they were always expected to use conventional forms of grammar and pronunciation in their homes and that parents admonished them for slang or language commonly heard in the neighborhood. The degree to which the former students recall altering their speech varies. Nevertheless, nearly all former METCO students recall altering their speech to match suburban habits in some manner.

These changes might have included, Bruce Paynter recalls, not using an "f" or a hard "t" for words ending in "th," or "d" for "th" beginnings. If they customarily used "no" in place of "any," as in "I don't have any/no homework," as Sean Thomas did, that usually stopped, too. Bruce Paynter, for example, soon learned to "talk plain, quiet like, with no ups and downs." And

Sean Thomas learned to "not be so expressive when you talk, to just say it straight out, without punctuating a word, or moving your head or face around to get a point across." In her wealthy suburban schools, Kim Peters adopted "smooth and steady and flat sentences" without inflections and changes in tone that had been her habit in her Boston neighborhood. Kim remembers the reasons her speech changed.

Kim explains, "Basically, you learn that what you think is just you being happy, or having a good time talking to a friend, or just being a strong minded individual—saying what's on your mind in your own comfortable way, [the white students would] look at you and then at each other like, 'Whoa, is she an angry black chick, or what?' "

Kim gives a pithy description of the process of acquiring suburbia-speak when she recalls the forms of speech "just sinking in, and before you knew it, it was all coming out your mouth." In other words, these children and teenagers understood suburbia-speak as something they needed to acquire. And then they, quite simply, acquired it.

The participants' speech and the ways that it changed, however, are not evidence of mere adaptation or assimilation in suburbia. And changes in speech to match the suburban setting were not a function of their ambition to succeed or get ahead in school. The students did it merely to avoid creating awkwardness in social situations. As Bruce Paynter says, "It's not like you're 15 years old and you go in and you say, 'Gee, what do I need to do in order to get ahead here?' It's just a thing you get into to avoid feeling on the spot all the time."

And it was not a situation in which the black students came to suburbia, learned the language codes, used them, called them their own, and thought themselves the better for it. More accurately, they acquired the language of suburbia while retaining the language of the city. The children and teenagers, then, didn't elect to change their speech forms entirely. They simply chose a speaking style to fit the setting and audience. This maintenance of *two* sets of language codes—one for the city, one for the suburbs—symbolizes better than anything the degree to which METCO students lived in what so many respondents called "two worlds." Speech marked and revealed them. If they weren't careful, they could give themselves away as being "different" both in their suburban schools and, maybe even more catastrophically, in their urban neighborhoods. So as Rita Wood says, they "switched back and forth." As Marlene Gibson describes it, she "walked a line" between city and suburb. Cara Ross, too, "turned the speech switch on and off in my head." Or at least she tried to.

Donald Isaac, an early 1980s graduate, began his schooling in a small suburb west of Boston when he was in kindergarten. He recalls expending enormous energy adjusting his vocabulary and speech to match the setting he was in. But as with other METCO participants, code words and inflections invariably "slipped out" of Donald's mouth. "Whether I realized it or not, I was accused of speaking a little differently," he explains. "And because of that, I really did deal with a lot of the internal stuff of not really knowing who I was—not really knowing if I was black enough, really. I was always being called 'Oreo' and 'white boy.' I remember being really careful about how I worded things. If I let any of that [suburban town] talk slip out, I'd get beat up. That would be it; it's over."

In their neighborhoods, a lot of the METCO students' friends, acquaintances, and cousins seemed to sense there was something besides speech that was different in the kids who went to suburbia. A lot of the METCO students were accused of not just talking white, but "acting white," too, just by doing homework or going to bed early. The post-METCO adults recall that when they were so often accused of "having attitude" or "acting better than," they'd simply deny it. Or, they would do as Dwight Stephens did—walk away, using a loud "fuck you" as a cover for inner "confusion about what world was really mine now, about where I belonged."

But they could not walk away from speech. Speech, with embedded, audible signals, just rang true. In words, tone, and inflection, other black children and teenagers could actually hear difference with their own ears. They could name it. Then, they might very well say the sentences so many METCO students learned to expect and fear: "You talk like a white girl." "You talk like a white boy." These familiar sentences so clearly told the METCO students that they should camouflage characteristically white outward behaviors to avoid rejection. Usually in less direct but equally oppressive ways, the dominant culture in suburbia communicated that, to avoid embarrassment and discomfort, METCO students should camouflage behaviors whites associated with urban blacks. Speech was how the young students could comply with demands from both worlds.

Like clothes and music, speech was used by some students with heightened racial consciousness as a tool to express their identities as African Americans in opposition to the white world of school. Speech wasn't used universally in this way, as less than a quarter of them remember using speech so deliberately. It was most common among students who also recall an intense desire —usually around adolescence—to identify themselves racially. For example, in her suburban junior high, then-METCO student Marie Lawlor proudly adopted the inflections and vocabulary she heard, not in her parents' middle-class home, but in the neighborhood where she was growing up.

Marie recalls, "My father was a professional man, around white people his whole life, and I know how to speak properly, or should I say I know how to speak in a way that makes white people comfortable? Listen to the way I talk now, for example. Do I sound white or what? Around eighth grade I start[ed] up with the slang—you know, the street talk. And it wasn't to fit in at home. My father's like, 'What are you doing talking like this, girl?' This was so I could say to these white kids, 'I am black.' I don't remember when I just stopped [talking like] that."

GROUPED TOGETHER, GROUPED APART

There is quite a bit of variation in the ways post-METCO adults recall their academic experiences in suburbia. But two types of events and experiences remain potent in their minds today and profoundly affect their lasting impressions of the educators in their suburban schools.

Adults vividly retell stories about their placement in the academic sorting systems that separated students by school performance or perceived ability. When placed in higher-level academic courses, usually by middle or high school, METCO students felt uncomfortable because they often were the only black in the class, or, at most, there might be one or two others. When placed in lower-level courses, the post-METCO adults associate that experience with shame and embarrassment. Either track left the students feeling "different," "looked at," "burdened by expectation," "forgotten." When in advanced classes, the former students recall feeling culturally "isolated from people like myself," "alone," "abandoned," "made to feel I didn't deserve that," "watched," "spied on all the time," "totally left to drown," "like I had to work harder than everyone to prove black people were smart," "like the smallest slip would land me in trouble." These students commonly recall that they felt somehow different from the other METCO students at the school, who, they remember, were in other academic tracks. Even students who took on the informal role of tutoring fellow METCO students still felt guilty. April Patterson elaborates.

"Even when I was helping, I worried about making them feel bad and them hating me because I was nerdy, a little bit different," April says. "I was always feeling guilty."

Placed in lower-level classes, the men and women recall

feeling "like maybe black people weren't as smart," "stupid," "worthless," "embarrassed," "like I had something to prove in there," "abused," "like the school was against you," "like they didn't see my promise," "totally misunderstood, just different from everyone," "angry." For Paul Hammond, who later attended college and went on to a successful career in government, his low placement was "evidence of their bias, and it pissed me off. That's the deep-down reason I was getting into fights all the time."

There seem to be three general stories here. One is about METCO students who had great success in the Boston schools, ranked near the top of their class, identified with academic success, and then, upon arrival in suburbia, found higher standards and were placed in low-level courses or got relatively low grades in middle-level courses for most of their time there. The second story is of the METCO students who began their education in suburbia, usually by first grade, but who still found their skills lacking in comparison to the suburbanites. They struggled, eventually meeting standards of suburbia satisfactorily at least in some subject areas. (Sometimes this didn't happen until high school.) The third story is of METCO students who excelled academically and were thus removed, to some extent, from their fellow METCO students. No one story is strikingly more prevalent than the others, though the third story—of extreme academic success—is somewhat less common than the other two.

But some of the adults—fewer than half—view their course placements as stemming not from impartial, objective evaluations of their academic potential but rather from whites' preconceived notions of the capabilities of METCO students. Even some students assigned to high-level courses commonly said that they felt that other METCO students in lower tracks had been underestimated. Bruce Paynter says, "I knew those kids. Those kids were smart. It was a waste. They weren't thought of as smart because they weren't behaving, some of them. They needed basic study skills, some time to get into it. They could have done it."

This theme of having been underestimated is even more prevalent in stories about meetings with guidance counselors assigned to help students choose colleges. Post-METCO adults remember clearly their meetings—even the briefest and most routine exchanges—with white guidance counselors and teachers who gave advice about college and post–high school life. The comments educators made during such meetings, usually held in students' junior years, became for the students powerful evidence of two things. First, black students viewed the comments as evidence of the school's general judgment of their worth and potential. Second, students heard in the comments and character of the exchanges evidence of an important school representative's general attitudes about black students' potential in general. Most often, such meetings were disappointing, even for many students who excelled academically. Just more than three quarters of the adults recall with intense emotion their meetings with guidance counselors. Wanda Carter, for example, was told that, although she might "make the team" that was going to college, as a member of that team she'd likely be one who mostly "sat on the bench." The sports analogy enraged Wanda, who, directly after high school, attended a well-regarded, competitive, predominantly white women's college and began a successful career in higher education administration. Recently, she began graduate studies at an Ivy League school.

"To always be thought of as the one that would have to sit on the bench!" Wanda exclaims. "My record didn't reflect that. It didn't call for that attitude. Not in the least."

After receiving good grades at her four-year college, Barbara Michaels began a varied, full career as an educator, including work as a financial aid specialist in higher education and, more recently, as a high school administrator whose job requires her to counsel students. But even after years of professional success, she "won't ever forget" being told by her guidance counselor that she wasn't qualified to attend college. She tells this story: "I had to go back to my high school for something when I was in financial aid. I told him I remembered what he said, that he said I wasn't college material. And I told him, 'Hey, look at me now. You still feel that way?' And he said, 'I never said that.' And I said, 'Oh, yes you did and I've remembered it my whole life. And you were wrong.'"

Few have Barbara's opportunity to confront and correct past insults. But a remarkable number of the post-METCO adults carry with them fantasies of revenge in which they show off their current successes to the guidance counselors who suggested the students lower their expectations about college and modify their ambitious career goals. Marlene Gibson, who was told she ought not "even think about a four year college," finished a community college program with "never, nothing, anything, less than A's." The work, Marlene recalls, "was just way, way too easy for me. I was so bored. I was so ahead." After two years of working and saving money, Marlene went to a well-regarded business school and "was on the Dean's List every term. Professors loved me. I was the prize student, ahead in every course." Marlene was urged to go on for her MBA degree, which she's earning part-time. Still, Marlene can't let old insults rest:

> That was the only thing, really, one of the only things that just gets me going. I was a plugger there, working so hard, oh my God, I worked hard. And my teachers, I thought they knew that. I wasn't all A's. But I was B's, and in English, I didn't have as much interest, it came slower, so I'd work and work and study and my teachers knew that. I wasn't a slacker. My SATs weren't great by any stretch, but my math was strong enough to get me by, no question. I had a shot and I knew it. But they look

at you and, "Wrong." I'd love to shove it in his face, in public, in front of the METCO kids there now. I imagine being on a stage, and I'd point right at him and talk to them, to the METCO kids and say, "See him? This guy's gonna tell you that you can't make it, and I'm here to tell you he's wrong." Sometimes I think about writing a letter. But I don't know what good it would do.

The METCO students who got good grades in high-level courses and did well on their SATs were certainly encouraged to attend college. Even so, these students also occasionally complain of meetings in which guidance counselors suggested that high-achieving black students were an extraordinary aberration from the general pattern of intellectually slow and undisciplined METCO students. Such comments, the former students said, made them feel "different" and "alien" from the other METCO students. April Patterson recalls such a discussion with her counselor:

> I was supposed to be thankful for being a credit to my race or something? I just said, "You should really get to know some black students, and you'd find out that they're just as smart and that they need some help maybe 'cause they don't have every advantage in the world just there for them." I was not his favorite after that. And my teachers were [wondering], "What are you so upset about?" They're saying, "All that matters is that you go to college, that you do well." It was not how I felt. I wanted to make a statement for all the others, that people shouldn't make judgments about things they don't know anything about.

Few students remember the particulars of classroom discussions or the specific assignments and subjects at which they excelled or failed. They can, of course, recall their general academic strengths, weaknesses, and interests. But the stories of situations in which they felt their potential—and the potential of blacks in general—was being formally assessed by whites are more significant to them. The results of tracking and grouping, like so many experiences in suburbia, often made these young students feel uncomfortable and anxious. And brief exchanges in guidance counselors' offices could deliver devastating blows. To-day those memories can still resurrect strong indignation.

YOU ARE READING ME WRONG

Like his father and grandfather before him, Sean Thomas is a big man and has a hearty, loud laugh. It begins with a shriek and his head flies back and then forward. He stomps his feet, as if run-ning in place and then raises a hand high to slap hands with whoever else is sharing in the moment. His laugh is "not under my control," Sean explains. He still laughs this way, even though people—white people—stop and stare in the store he manages. He'll always laugh with "vigor," he says, even though some twenty years ago, adults in his suburban high school tried to make him stop.

"I was laughing," Sean recalls. "Laughing! You'd think I was waving a gun around the hallway, ready to shoot anything that moved. The way they looked at me, I will never forget that. They call me into an office, I don't remember if it was the assistant principal or the principal. But they ask me what's going on and I say, 'What's going on? What's going on is you are reading me wrong. What's going on is me laughing with my friends.' And they say, 'Well, cut it out.' I leave and I'm thinking, 'What the hell was that?' "

Sean's story of rebuke and bewilderment is typical of his fellow METCO participants. It was common for METCO students—mostly men—to recall events in which they were, as Sean Thomas describes it, "just being myself," and getting punished or lec-tured for loud or rowdy behavior. Often they were told, as Sean and other men remember, to "pipe down." Even men who don't recall being personally admonished for social behavior do recall students—most often young men—who were. They remember being angered by whites' dismay at what seemed to the black children and teenagers to be ordinary behavior. Former students commonly recall that when this scolding occurred, fellow METCO students and METCO staff provided important support. The white adults' admonishments to black students brought many METCO students closer to each other, they said. And a sizable share of those scolded did seek explanations from and, as Thomas Mitchell puts it, "vent anger on" black METCO administrators. To complicate matters, what early 1980s graduate Lauren Baldwin calls "sticking together" seemed to perpetuate white stereotypes about threatening behavior on the part of black students. "In elementary school me and four of my friends sat together all the time at lunch," she says. We always wanted to be together, play together, laugh a lot. I remember my mother talking to one of the other parents and she was saying, "they think these kids are in a gang. Literally, in a gang. Like a street gang." I mean, please! So, they had expressed some concern to my mother about this, about our being in a gang. We were confused. We just liked to be together . . . I remember a lot of things like that."

Nathan King, who was a popular athlete and an elected leader in student government, speaks quite positively about his METCO experience. Nevertheless, he also speaks eloquently about whites' frequent "misreading" of black students' behaviors that were "taken out of context."

> We had issues where the METCO students were being perceived as loud, rowdy, just out of control. But if you look at where we come from, we come from a culture that emphasizes music, laughter. If you go to our churches, there is music, there is dance. We shout. It's being vibrant and alive. All of those things were things that my community emphasized and things that my community

valued, and this carries on into your day-to-day behavior. So, here we are, we're leaving our community and we're going out to a community that doesn't exactly emphasize these kinds of things. You are then taken out of context. It's misreading. They tell you, "Hey, you're loud, you're this, you're that. You're boisterous. You are always singing." Well, that's not a small thing. That's where we come from. And I think, to this day, it's still not understood in [his school's suburban town]. And so now, I think, it's our job to go back and educate this community. To say, "Hey, okay, look, when a child is singing, they are not out of line. When a young adult is talking to one of their peers from the community and is using slang, or almost a slang, they are not being disrespectful. They are just being them. They are communicating. This is where they come from."

To mitigate the misreading, most former students remember that they modified, to varying degrees, their behavior in hallways, lunchrooms, and gym class, and during breaks in the day. As with their speech, the former students recall switching between the generally more reserved, staid atmosphere of suburbia and what several former students characterized as the more "vigorous" life in the city. Even though they tried to adopt suburbia's unwritten behavior rules, though, most past participants remember it being impossible to repress all mannerisms, styles of discourse, and expression all the time. Even when the students thought they had succeeded in adapting to suburbia's codes, they commonly found that, in the eyes of white adults at their schools, they had not done so completely. This caused some students simply to stick even more closely with other METCO students. Others withdrew and remained as anonymous as possible. And still others worked even harder to comply with suburbia's rules. Likewise, at home, when they thought they had fully reverted to their more comfortable ways of being, the black students were told that they were "acting white."

Jeremy Shepard characterizes his METCO experience as "very, very negative," mostly because of what he said were white adults' persistent misinterpretations of his behavior when he was with other black, male METCO students. Teachers and administrators, he said, commonly labeled his greeting of other METCO students in the halls or his laughing and clowning around as "loud" and "obnoxious."

"It was like, 'You need to come here and you all need to understand that we are going to fix you all up and make you appropriate,'" he says, or "'You need to learn how to act, to behave, to do things a certain way and aren't you lucky that you get to come out here and have this privilege and all.' Well, you're a kid so you are thinking, 'Yeah, okay, they are right. I am lucky. I'm saved.' But, these people out here might be sophisticated in some way, but they know nothing about a world five miles from them. Five miles! And couldn't I make their lives richer? Of course. But no one even considers that. It's all about us getting fixed up."

Like many fellow graduates, Jeremy feels that whites in the suburban towns had remedial, assimilationist goals for METCO students that did not match his reasons for coming to suburbia. From Jeremy's perspective, and that of some other past participants, it is this erroneously construed remedial goal of METCO that led whites to label black children's behaviors as inappropriate and in need of improvement.

WHAT CAN WE LEARN FROM DIFFERENCE?

These stories and recollections teach us that confrontations with difference were inescapable for black city children in white suburban schools. The experiences take various forms, of course—from stares to blatant racism to moving conversations that increased understanding between black and white students. But whether adults today look back fondly or with pity or with anger or with scorn depends largely on the way white suburbanites reacted to difference.

As Shirley Rogers explains, "Being different wasn't a problem for METCO kids. They were always different no matter where they went, and I for one was used to it really early in my life. Being different isn't bad in itself except for that normal adolescent time, but everyone gets that. The problem is what people do when they see difference coming their way. Do they hide? Do they run? Are they cool with it? Are they open or closed? That's the issue."

Eventually, the students came to discover that the difficulties inherent in being a METCO student exist in the world after school, too. In this way, METCO came to be seen by these adults as a fairly accurate reflection of both the remaining problems and the vast potential for race relations in American society. And these adults soon began to see METCO as a type of training ground for life as a black adult in white-dominated America. While difference is surely a basic part of this reality, it is certainly not the whole of the experience. Although difference often bred intimidation, children who spent years in white suburbia often felt that race-based fear fade as they slowly, often imperceptibly, blurred the racial lines that once seemed indelible. In the next section, the adults describe that line between white and black, and the steps they took to cross it.

Section II—Crossing the Line

Most of the former METCO students refer matter-of-factly to "a line" between blacks and whites. On their side of the line, black students experienced fears and misperceptions about white students and their families as well as feelings of self-consciousness that were sometimes brutally painful, but more commonly, just made the black students feel awkward, out of place, even invisible. These feelings tended to diminish over time.

With blacks and whites on separate sides of an invisible line, neither group talked to the other about race—the very thing that appeared to be separating them. As a result, race frequently felt to the black students like a family secret. To keep life going smoothly, everyone compliantly locked the race subject away. It was too potent to open, too delicate to touch.

Today, these black adults remember vividly the moments when they felt they had crossed over this socially constructed race boundary. What some of them found on the other side of the line were relationships with white students and families that were positive, even transforming experiences. The adults still view these relationships as evidence of the potential for cultural sharing and tolerance. Even more important, memories of these friendships and positive exchanges reassure post-METCO adults that they can succeed in interracial settings. Having confronted life after high school, however, some of the adults question whether, as METCO students, they grew too confident, thinking that race would not matter in American society.

Some of the adults recall crossing the race line simply by broaching the subject of race or by offering analyses 'from a distinctly black perspective. Speaking out in this way, however, usually bred palpable discomfort, most commonly in the form of silence or reproaches from teachers and administrators. Today, some adults see those events as evidence of whites' limited capacity to examine, much less correct, their attitudes and stereotypes about racial minorities. But whether or not speaking out was immediately successful, these adults still look back on their actions as moments of moral strength.

POWER OF PERSONAL CONNECTION

In her school years in the late 70s and early 80s, Mara Taggart carried three keys on a chain, each of them a symbol of safety and belonging. One key was to the home Mara shared with her mother and brothers in Boston—the place where she usually slept and said her prayers. Another opened the door to Mara's grandmother's lively three-room apartment where Mara, her brothers, and cousins came and went, cooked for each other, and did weekend errands for their grandma, who was at times shut in with health problems.

The third key opened the door to the kitchen of a big, "very fancy" suburban house with a "new-looking" stove and refrigerator. There were a few pieces of antique furniture that Mara remembers no one was allowed to touch, a family room with a big television and a stereo, shelves crammed with board games, and, most important to Mara, "a lot of warmth" and "good friends."

This was the home of Mara's host family in the suburban town where she went to school. Mara often "just hung out with my host sister" or did her homework there before her host mother drove Mara back to Boston in the early evening. Sometimes, especially if an after-school activity made her late, Mara slept over. To Mara, this spacious suburban house felt to her like "a third home," one where "I felt completely accepted and appreciated for who I was as a person. They cared about me for me, not as a poor little black girl from the projects."

Mara most fondly remembers graduation day when her host family searched her out in a sea of snapping cameras and small family celebrations. She recalls, "[My host mother's] screaming, '[Mara, Mara] there you are!' You know, and I'm waving, 'Hey, c'mon over' [because] I wanted them to meet my aunts. But it was funny, because my aunts are saying, 'Who is this white lady?' And my host mother just comes bouncing over and she's dragging the whole family along and [my host sister's] saying, 'Finally, there you are!' and [host mother] has her camera and she just gives me this big hug and tells me they're looking for me everywhere. And I'm thinking, 'What's the big deal?' And they tell me: They weren't going to take their family picture til' they found me."

Douglas Baker, who went to suburban schools west of Boston in the 1970s, also, like Mara, carried a key to his host family's suburban house. Similar to some of the other past participants, Douglas said the relationship with his host family taught him that racial difference need not inhibit true acceptance. But for Douglas and the others, the relationships were powerful then and are memorable now because they not only offered the daily personal comfort of acceptance, but provided to them lasting models of successful interracial relationships. In Douglas's case, the power of the experience has endured for more than 25 years.

> I had a black host family and a white host family. And I guess one would assume that that relationship would automatically exist with my black host family. But with the white host family, it was equal if not a little better in some respects. I don't know if it's possible to ever get to this point again, but I really didn't see race at all in that household. And I mean, I knew that I was black and they were white, but that's where it ended. For all intents and purposes, I was treated like one of their children. I really was. I mean, they went somewhere and I went with them. The whole makeup of the host family, the idea was that you had a child in your class. It got to the point where I didn't need my host brother to come home with. I would come home anyway. I mean, he (host brother) went to Switzerland for a little while and I would come home there anyway.

Certainly, not all the adults recall such intensely positive relationships with their host families. Just less than forty percent of the adults I talked with recall such intensely positive relationships, while the remaining adults describe the relationships as generally positive but not necessarily life changing or even particularly important. Somewhat more typical are the comments of George Gardner, whose host family served more practical than emotional purposes. George explains:

There was a feeling with this family that if I really needed help, I could probably turn to them. They were good people, no doubt about that. But there wasn't a connection there with them, really. They'd give me rides (home) if I missed the bus. A couple times I was sick and [the mother] came and fetched me and she was real responsible—taking my temperature and taking care of me until my own mother could come—that sort of thing.

By high school, I didn't have much to do with them. I'd bump into my host brother in the hall or something and he was cool, but it was like running into an *old* friend, not a friend that you had at that moment. He'd stop, we'd talk, he would ask me questions about how I was, how was school, my family, then his friends would call out to him and he'd say he had to go. I got the sense that they cared about me, but they just didn't connect. I should say *we* didn't connect, not in any deep sense.

Similarly, Marie Lawlor explains that she saw her host family as "guides in a new world," not as friends.

I know some people became really very close with their host families. I remember at the time knowing that that wouldn't happen to me. I kind of thought of these people as guides for me in this new world, nice people who would help me—who would answer my questions and be a good resource. And I do know that my host mother and my own mother did talk quite a bit and she was helpful in that way to us. And my host sister was very kind to me, showing me all around the school, introducing me to people, taking me around her neighborhood. But that was it for me. It kind of felt weird: these people are assigned to you [and] there's supposed to be this automatic connection and there's not? Not as friends, anyway, in the sense that I think of as a friend.

Despite the fact that the positive, yet not intense, relationship is more typical than the very intense, important relationship, the lasting power of the more intense relationships should not be overlooked. Indeed, for the past participants who had such impressionistic relationships, they use the human connection as *the* one example that best characterizes their METCO experience. Thus, these narratives are important not because everyone tells similar stories, but because so many do tell such stories and because the narratives reveal the power and long-term potential of such relationships that would not have been possible without METCO.

Friendships with white suburban students have also endured in the former students' minds as evidence of the potential for acceptance and understanding across racial lines. These are not stories of benevolent, paternalistic whites making nice gestures to disenfranchised black students. These are stories of friendship in which two young people came to know and trust one another. Some of these friendships lasted through the students' school careers, and several continue. For example, Wendy West was one of the first METCO students in her suburban elementary school south of Boston. Her most vivid and one of her most important memories of her suburban experience is a white student's first gesture toward friendship in what was at first a very isolating setting.

> I remember this distinctly. I sat alone on the swings at recess because no one wanted to talk to me because I was the [only] black kid in the class. We were the first [METCO] students in this particular school. It was hard for me because my host sister stayed as far away from me as possible. Her mother, her father were very nice and really tried their best. But their daughter, she wanted nothing to do with me. So, finally, one day, a girl came over to me and asked if she could push me on the swing.

I wondered, "Okay, is she going to push me right off? Or will she just push me, like you push someone on a swing when you are playing nicely together?" So I didn't know what was going to happen. And I was scared, really scared at that moment. And I don't know [why] but I said, "Sure." So, then she just pushed me like you push someone on a swing, and we ended up becoming really good friends. We even went off to college together, to the same college.

This effort by a white student that developed into friendship was to Wendy a sign that she could find comfort and belonging in an alien environment. Black-white friendships developed during METCO have tremendous symbolic power for many of the adults I talked with. For Reggie Carlton, who dropped out of his suburban high school, his middle-school friendship with a white boy was alone "worth the trip." The friendship, Reggie said, "is what I think of when you say METCO, even when there were more not-so-great things." And when Ray Newsom is "feeling pessimistic" about the state of race relations "at my job, in the country, everywhere," he thinks about his friendship with a white student named Kevin. "He was open to me," Ray says. "He got something out of me and I gave something back to him. And it opened the door for me to say, 'Okay, you can't judge people on skin color.'"

These compelling narratives aside, the degree to which students remember having friendships with white resident students of course varies. Among the former METCO students, there are three categories—of nearly equal size—related to cross-racial friendships. One group of students were socially very integrated into the suburban system, counting many friendships with whites. There were many more boys in this group than there were girls, a ratio that mirrors findings from previous research suggesting boys were more socially integrated than METCO girls, probably because of athletics (e.g., Raju, 1992; Ezeze, 1983). The boys in this group were frequently athletes or received school-wide recognition for their talents in such things as the dramatic or visual arts. Girls in this group were also likely to be athletic and to excel academically. Among the adults I spoke with, how-ever, there are no differences between men and women with regard to the content of the friendships or the general meaning those friendships have for them today.

Another group—this one includes mostly girls—usually had a lasting and close friendship with at least one white student. And there is a third group of students who did not have sus-tained friendships with white students. Sometimes such students did have white friends in elementary school, but those friend-ships usually faded by middle school or high school.

The sense that adults make of these relationships today is complicated. The process is not a simple chain reaction in which black students have prejudices and fears, form relationships with some whites, and see all distrust and apprehension evaporate. The long-term utility of these past relationships, from the stu-dents' perspectives, was not that the friendships cured blacks' own racial prejudice and fears of whites. Nor did these relation-ships lead black students to the simplistic conclusion that racism does not exist or that black people are not at times victimized by whites. Rather, with hindsight from these relationships, the for-mer students say that because of METCO, they felt more confident than they might have otherwise of their abilities to form healthy cross-racial relationships in white-dominated settings and social situations. Their relationships with host families and friendships with white students did cause many students to question old assumptions that blacks would always be victimized within white settings. These kinds of self-limiting "blanket statements," as Mara Taggart calls them, would no longer "hold us back" from seeking opportunity.

"After this experience of really loving people who were from a very different world than you, it would be impossible to make blanket statements like 'All white people are this way' [or] 'All white people are that way,' " Mara says. "It's not going to hold you back, (your) thinking that all white people are out to get you."

But there is also a group of adults, including several who had strong and lasting friendships with whites, who insist that building one-on-one friendships, while enough to make a day-to-day experience better, is not enough to erase what are more systemic problems for METCO students and for blacks in American society.

WHEN COUNTING WAS NO LONGER NECESSARY

In his suburban junior high and high school, when Samuel Dean walked into classrooms, up to hallway social gatherings, into lunchrooms, he began to count. Samuel needed to answer two essential questions: How many white people are here? How many black people are here? More than once, Samuel was the only black person around and this, he recalls, was often "intimidating." This kind of racial head-counting that Samuel mentally performed is a common memory among past METCO participants. But even more meaningful to the nearly three-quarters of adults in this sample who recall stories similar to Samuel's is the moment that they realized they were no longer counting. To Samuel and other past participants, this realization meant that they were no longer controlled by a fear of being black in a white place. Samuel explains his process.

"You start off like I did when I was a teenager just starting in [town], believe me, you go around and you count: how many white people? Any black people? You make these counts, constantly, all day. Then you do it a little less each day, and maybe by junior year or something, you kind of stop the counting. Because it starts to be reality, your reality. And it's no big deal. You are surviving."

Like many other past program participants, Samuel can trace a change in himself. He started his suburban schooling as a teenager, painfully self-conscious about his race, and then he became less and less so over the course of at least a few years. Even students who began their suburban schooling early often engaged in some kind of mental assessment of their cultural isolation. Samuel is very typical of other METCO past participants who cannot recall or describe exactly the process of changing but who do hold dear a single moment in time when they realized they were no longer obsessed with counting and what it symbolized: the fear and discomfort of being the only black person in a classroom or a crowd. Marie Lawlor, for example, vividly remembers the simple act of walking late into gym class, where she was the only black face in a cavernous room.

> It was a surreal experience. I was late, I don't remember why, and I walk in, in my little shorts, and I'm sort of looking at the scene from outside and I just walked into it, so natural-like. Then I'm in it, starting up on a volleyball team, just joining in without thinking about it. I'm playing along and then, it's like I'm in my own little world all of a sudden cuz' I'm realizing that I just did that so easily. I wasn't thinking, "Oh no, I'm standing out, sticking out," that kind of thing. I just walked in and I realized just at that moment for some reason that I had been doing that for some time, just walking in without that yuck feeling, just a bad feeling that used to be there. And it was this moment of happiness for me, like, "Yes! I beat this. I can do anything."

Though the respondents remember these changes as mere moments in time, the diminishing self-consciousness surely did not occur with the flip of a switch, and neither did their feelings change immediately from pain to obliviousness. More accurately, the interviews show great variation in degrees of race-related self-consciousness. For the adults, the symbolic moment meant that they were no longer being limited and held back by their personal fear of inevitable victimization. This fear is one that respondents believe they built up in their own minds because of two factors. One factor is simply their inexperience with inter-action in a white-dominated place. The second factor was fear or distrust of whites that had been expressed by black adults, such as friends, neighbors, and relatives, whom the METCO students knew and trusted.

There is, of course, a difference between the fear of the unknown built up in one's own mind versus distrust or wariness based on actual experiences with racism; in these cases the adults are speaking only of the former. The manifestations of this di-minished fear varied. Some adults recall feeling more confident speaking in class. Others said they expressed opinions more frequently. As one adult said, she no longer "hid" herself, but instead "walked proud." Another said that "it was just a feeling of empowerment on the inside." Indeed, many remember taking no outward action on their diminishing self-consciousness, at least during their school days.

That said, just getting over their own fear, the adults dis-covered, was not enough to guarantee great opportunity and success. There were other factors—including racism—work-ing against them in their schools, colleges, and the job market. Adults needed to balance their own acquired feelings of em-powerment with their continuing confrontations with discrimi-nation and differential treatment on the basis of race. There is then, quite frequently, an ambivalence about their learned confi-dence. It is common for the adults to wonder whether they might be too naive, too hopeful, even wrong to feel powerful as black people in a race-conscious America. As Margaret Redford ex-plains simply, "Just because you are out there after METCO, feel-ing strong, feeling good about yourself, walking into any place feeling like you can own it, and [thinking that] white people are cool, that doesn't make you not black. People still see the black."

Jeremy Shepard explains the dangers of feeling overly con-fident or comfortable:

You're going along with that strength in you, not full of this obsession that a lot of blacks have, like they can't cope in a white place they feel so on stage all the time. I don't have that. I did. But you are out there every-day. It turns into being just your life. And so you go along but then, bang: something reminds you it's not just about being strong. You can't change other people's racial attitudes, so you have to deal with that, too. You might be okay with the white-black issue, but they are not, and that is going to affect your life most definitely. And so sometimes [I wonder,] "Am I being too optimis-tic here?"

Samuel Dean, who graduated from high school in the early 1990s and later from a predominantly white college, now is in his third professional job where he is the only black in an otherwise all-white work setting. Samuel does notice that he is less race-conscious and more willing to enter predominantly white situa-tions than many of his black friends who never had sustained experiences in such settings. He generally sees this lack of fear as a positive attribute that has helped him gain educational and professional opportunities. Still, Samuel wonders whether he is conscious enough of how his race might affect the way whites treat him. Like many of the adults, Samuel and Jeremy are trying to find a balance between their own earned confidence and the reality of life in a belligerently race-conscious society. As Samuel explains:

You get to the point where you aren't doing it anymore, you don't do that counting, [and] you do have to start to wonder, "Hey, do I have some false sense of reality that it doesn't matter that I'm the only black person here?" I don't want to lose sight of the fact that it really could matter. I'm not naive [by] thinking there are no racists out there. It's something that I'm in the middle of, still trying to balance a bit, [but] because of [the town where

I attended school], I feel comfortable anywhere. I walk in [to my job] everyday, and I am the only black face. And you get used to that and you forget a little bit, you're focused in on your work and it's going well. But then, it's sad,[because] you always have to defend, like if something political happens, like discussions about [racial] quotas—all of a sudden, you are the spokesperson.

WHEN THE CROSSING IS ACADEMIC

Former METCO student Jane Staunton remembers the terror and pressure she used to feel just before she spoke out in suburban classrooms. Jane almost "always knew the answers" and "almost always came up with an intelligent thing to add."

"I was always well prepared," Jane recalls. But still, she remembers, "I was so afraid of slipping. I was thinking, 'If I miss it, that's it; they'll think all black people are dumb.' "

Similarly, Cherisse Clarkson, who earned "average and below average" grades for most of her METCO career, says, "Okay, you make a mistake—and how do you learn without making mistakes—and you think everyone's saying to themselves, 'Oh, black people don't get that stuff as quickly. They're slow.' "

But for these adults, and for many other former METCO students, the basic requirements of learning were fraught with self-consciousness caused, they believe, by being one of so relatively few blacks in such a heavily white setting. While most remember similar discomforts, they also recall that this academically related tension also diminished as time went on. Ann Edgar, whose stories are typical of other students', remembers raising her hand in class to "ask a simple question" about a math problem. "I'm thinking, 'Okay, cool, I have my hand up. I don't get it and I'm asking for help,' not worrying that people are [thinking], 'Oh, there's that dumb METCO kid who is so retarded.' I was just me not getting it," Anne says. "And it was just realizing that fact—that was intense for me—that I had changed just into a person who didn't get something in class and dealt with it without worrying [about being] a black person not getting it. It sounds like not a big deal, I know. But it is. It was."

Regardless of their past academic performances, former METCO students typically reinforce this view as demonstrated by these representative comments: "It felt like you had to represent all black people in an intellectual sense"; "like people were watching you to see what black kids could do, not what you could do"; "like any fucking up on grades was going to be confirmation to them that blacks couldn't cut it"; "it felt like they're seeing blacks doing bad on science, not me doing bad on science"; "that you had to watch it in class, what you said, how you said it, 'cause if you don't, it's going to get attributed to your race." But as Ann Edgar did, they also recall that the feelings Bruce Paynter calls "intrusions in your mind that stopped you short" diminished as time went on.

"It's just time doing it, I think. First it's a big deal when you start to become self-conscious of yourself anyway and you are always wondering what people are thinking," Bruce recalls. "And then it's just easier in time. You can do what you need to do without constant fear about what they're thinking. You just do it."

There are, of course, striking similarities here to the stories of intimidation or anxieties that surrounded everyday social situations in school, which were described in the previous section. There also are differences. In social situations, the adults recall their discomfort having diminished dramatically—so dramatically that they found other blacks' relatively higher levels of discomfort around whites to be extraordinary.

But intimidation related to intellectual ability is much more likely to have lasted longer during the METCO years than did other forms of intimidation and awkwardness. While such anxieties or fears usually are significantly diminished over time, they tend to crop up again later in life, in relation to job performance, especially where one is required to display competence publicly, as in a presentation or speech. These are situations that are characteristically different from everyday situations such as making a phone call to a client (white or black), chatting in the employee cafeteria, or speaking up in a routine staff meeting. In these arenas one's intellectual or professional capacities are on display and up for judgment. Certainly, these types of situations may create increased anxiety for any employee or professional. But with these adults, the anxiety and pressure does clearly express itself racially, with adults fearing that one slip will bring out whites' racial prejudices.

Several adults suggested that the greater intensity surrounding academic intimidation is the result of pervasive white stereotypes about blacks' lack of intellectuality. Many of the former METCO students recall being warned by their parents that such stereotypes exist and that it was important for their sons and daughters to counteract such misconceptions. And after high school, in the workforce, the post-METCO adults remained aware of such stereotypes.

In their research in predominantly black high schools, anthropologists John Ogbu and Signithia Fordham (1986, 1988) found that the history of white stereotypes about blacks' lack of intellectual skill led black students to resist learning. As is discussed in greater detail in chapter 7, researchers found that students rejected academic pursuits precisely because learning and academic success had come to be seen by black students as the domain of whites only. To protect themselves against the racist attitudes of whites, then, the black students consciously disassociated themselves with any behavior deemed "too white" by peers. The students' fear of "acting white" was, Ogbu and Fordham suggest, a major reason why the black students performed poorly in school.

Interestingly, however, the former METCO students simply do not recall resisting academic success during their METCO years. Certainly, some of the higher-achieving students recall feelings of guilt that other black students were "left behind," "not doing as well," "having personal troubles that made school harder." And, as we know, the students were often criticized by friends for acting "too white," or for being a "white boy" or a "white girl." But according to the adults, they don't recall that their response to this negative sanctioning was poor academic performance.

Even when the students did perform below standard in school, the adults simply do not look back on their lackluster performance as a manifestation of their fear of being "too white." It is more likely that the adults attribute their poor performance to such factors as, "a lack of discipline," "not enough preparation before I got there," "no time management skills," "too much thinking about sports," "a lack of confidence, maybe." Certainly, the reasons for low academic performance are complicated and varied, but the conflicts that research indicates are so common for other students were not present in the METCO adults' accounts of their past schooling experiences.

NAMING IT

In characterizing the treatment of the race subject in their suburban schools, METCO students sound as if they are describing a family secret. They remember that race was a subject more or less untouched by constructive, open dialog. Many past participants remember feeling that white students and teachers seemed afraid of taking on the topic. That's not to say that all the past participants wanted to engage in substantial dialog about race. Some of the former METCO students—about a quarter, in fact— said they never wanted to hash out racial issues when they were at school because their principal mission was to receive a better education. Nonetheless, even these students who were not compelled to talk about race quite frequently sensed that race was unapproachable as an official topic. Surely there were private chats among friends and acquaintances, but as a topic worthy of debate and discussion, Mara Taggart recalls, race "was just about as taboo in the classroom as sex."

This common recollection of silence and awkwardness

around race issues usually drew one of three responses from METCO students. One group of former students remembers being angry that the teachers and administrators failed to acknowledge that the METCO students were, in fact, black and that it wasn't taboo to talk about it. Another group of students said the silence didn't make them feel so angry, as much as it made them feel "invisible," "not there," "a nothing," "unrecognized." A third group, as mentioned, felt the awkwardness but reported that they didn't pay it much mind, focusing instead on other matters. Many of the students who struggled with what one past participant termed "the forced silence on race" found strong, reliable supports from fellow METCO students and METCO administrators and from the institutionalized METCO office at school and the central METCO office in Roxbury. These were places where the students could talk informally about their experiences and feel listened to.

Prominent in the memories of just less than half the former students are moments when they tried to break the silence on race. Such efforts rarely spurred constructive dialog. And soon after the silence was broken, the black students recall feeling uncomfortable, even humiliated after whites failed to respond to invitations to examine the issue. But years after the fact, the adults most commonly recall those awkward moments as ones of personal strength and moral courage, though some just remember them as comically embarrassing. Even when the adults look back on these moments with pride, they also tend to view the white reaction as evidence of how difficult it is for whites and blacks to have a rational discussion on issues related to race.

Nick Marshall, who graduated in the early 1990s, remembers sitting in a history class, learning about the Civil War, "feeling frustrated about what I knew," and speaking his mind. As he recounts it, in the middle of his teacher's lecture he blurted out something like: "Blacks weren't treated fairly in that war. Even when they saved lives, they weren't treated fairly and they didn't get credit." His comment was met by silence, save for another

METCO student in the class who applauded in steady rhythm. Nick recalls that usually this particular teacher would scold anyone who interrupted him. After Nick spoke out, the teacher cleared his throat and continued his lecture. As Nick remembers, "the other kids in the class didn't really look at me, they just looked at each other, you know, with these really wide eyes, like: 'Oh shit, what's going to happen now?' or, 'Can you believe he said that?' That was the end of it."

Similarly, Cara Ross, an early 1980s graduate, recalls a classroom discussion about a presidential election and her suggestion that her teacher take a critical look at voting trends in America.

> Basically this woman was saying, "If people don't vote, then well, they have no right to complain. Everyone should vote in this wonderful democratic country. There's no excuse not to and it's irresponsible if you don't." How one-sided. I said, "For a long time this country didn't even allow blacks to vote and then when they did, they just tried to make it impossible for them to do it, and now a lot of blacks I know don't see anyone out there worth voting for and there are a lot of reasons why that actually makes a lot of sense." Something like that, only probably angrier. Then, I know I said: "Maybe we all should talk about that?" I think [the teacher] said something like: "Are you finished with your speech young lady?" And the other METCO kids just smiled at me, but everyone else, all the white kids sorta just shifted around in their chairs a little. And that was my big activism. Hey, it didn't change the world, but I'm glad I did it for myself.

No matter how they reacted as children and teenagers, adults looking back today almost universally view the lack of dialog as a result of isolation and inadequate preparation on the part of suburban educators. In a typical assessment, Patricia Baxter, an early 1980s graduate, said of the educators in her first suburban elementary school, from which she later transferred for this and other reasons, "They just didn't know what to do with us. Here it is, we arrive in on buses and they have no idea how to act, what to say. So they play it safe. They don't say anything."

A LINE NEVER SEEN OR NEVER CROSSED

There is a small group of students—fewer than ten—who never mentally constructed a line between black and white. In this category were students of two types. First were students who were involved in the school through more than athletics. These students, for example, might have been elected to student government or achieved success in other extracurricular activities such as debate teams. None had serious academic troubles and all began their suburban schooling early, either in kindergarten or by first grade. There is a second, small group of students—four adults in this study—who did not see a color line in their suburban schools. These are students who either attended or transferred to one of the few suburban districts that are culturally and racially diverse. The two systems, one of which borders Boston and is accessible by subway, are characteristically more urban and economically mixed.

Patricia Baxter describes the difference between her initial placement in an affluent, nearly all-white district and the more urban district to which she transferred. She recalls, "It was night and day. There was more of a natural integration there of the METCO kids [into] the rest of the school. There were a lot of different cultures and no one really stuck out as different. Another important thing was that I could keep all my friendships from the city, which were important to me. I could meet my friends on [the subway], do things with them, stay later at school, choose whatever I wanted to do. It was completely different."

Just as there are those for whom this line did not exist, so too are there other former students who remember a line but don't remember ever even trying to cross this racial divide. In fact, several students recalled calculating the ratio of blacks to whites into graduation. And there are others who more or less stuck with their friends from METCO or the neighborhood and did their school work as best they could but interacted only minimally with the white culture. Sandra Robertson, for example, is typical of this group. She says, "I knew I was different. For me, METCO was about going out there, doing your work, and getting out. I had my head buried there, just doing what I needed to do so I could do well and get out."

CROSSING THE DIVIDE

Despite some important exceptions, constructing and then crossing a line between black and white is a frequent, repeated phenomenon that endures in many past participants' memories. Crossing the line is a metaphor for several actions and triumphs, including forming friendships, diminishing self-consciousness, verbal acknowledgment of racial difference, and display of critical thinking that emerges from the black experience. For the past participants who did cross the racial line, doing so was clearly a very powerful part of their experiences in white suburban schools.

As young people in these schools, many of the METCO students quickly realized that lines existed not only between white and black. They began to understand implications of the socioeconomic class differences between the communities where they lived and the communities where they went to school. In the next section, "Peering into Privilege," post-METCO adults speak about the ways they untangled the often perplexing relationships between race, class, stereotype, and image.

Section III—Peering into Privilege

A black child arriving at a white suburban school found not just more white faces but more wealthy people. The former METCO students remember that class differences between their urban neighborhoods and their suburban schools affected their educational experiences in a variety of ways. Many former students remember being impressed, on their first few bus rides into their suburban towns, with large homes on expansive lots. And many still recall, in great detail, their first visit to a home of a well-off classmate. They remember their "mouths dropping open," a palpable "fear of doing something wrong," of "spilling something," of not knowing dining rituals.

Before drying his hands in a new friend's house, Nick Marshall studied the position of plush bathroom towels to make sure he folded them back just as they were. At his first supper at a white friend's house, Bruce Paynter, usually talkative at dinner at home in Boston, sat silently with his friend's wealthy family. He wiped his mouth "like a compulsive," and was "awed" by the furniture, the "fancy" plates, the chandelier above the long dining room table, and the "waste of food." "I'll never forget," Bruce says. "They gave an entire steak to the dog."

While these memories are common, it is crucial to clarify that less than one-third of the respondents characterize their own families as "poor" or even "low-income." In fact, many of the respondents come from families who owned their own homes and traveled occasionally. None in the sample had parents with high-paying professional jobs that put them in the upper-middle or upper classes. But most had at least one parent who either worked steadily at her own business or had a steady, reliable job that carried health insurance.

Only a few of the post-METCO adults had parents who had graduated from college at the time of their children's schooling, though a good share of parents had either two-year degrees or training in the health professions, or were skilled in another type of labor, with a few owning construction, paper hanging, or plumbing businesses. (Some, however, did earn bachelor's degrees after their children were grown or while their children were attending college.) Despite the fact that most students' backgrounds were far from "poor," METCO was usually a respondent's first exposure to either concentrated middle-class or wealthy lifestyles.

A middle-class child growing up in the Roxbury or Dorchester neighborhood, for example, was far more likely than a suburban child to be exposed to and associate with families from a mix of economic backgrounds, including poor families. To many of the METCO students, the more affluent towns of suburbia felt more homogeneously wealthy. Many commented that in their home neighborhoods their families were always considered among the wealthiest. Thus the students had often considered themselves wealthy until they went to school in white suburbia and realized that, compared with others, they weren't wealthy.

Predictably, the significance and intensity of experiences related to wealth depended in large part on just how wealthy a respondent's METCO district was. In the wealthiest towns, students' realization of privilege was immediate, often intimidating, and the impression it had on them seems to have been more intense. The memories of feeling somehow "different" because of community disparities in wealth are certainly more prominent for students who attended school in the wealthiest districts. But students in the other types of towns—this includes towns whose median home value falls in the middle and lower ranges—the students generally realized class differences more slowly, though the differences in class were as unmistakable. The memories are of similar content, but what differs is the degree to which the adults recall being affected by the realities. Generally, the adults who were in the less-affluent or more mixed-income suburbs recall that the class differences between their school and their neighborhoods were not nearly as important to them as other aspects of their schooling experience.

Not all past participants were affected by the concentrated

wealth in their school communities. Just about a third said the class differences were of little consequence to them. Students who were at least somewhat socially integrated into the community—and thus regularly exposed to the home lives of a significant share of their classmates—were more likely to be affected by the class differences and to feel those effects more intensely. They include students who were members of athletic teams and who regularly stayed overnight at teammates' homes and others who formed friendships in the suburban towns. Some students were far less socially integrated into their schools but did have casual conversations with white students that forced them to confront the economic differences between their schools and their neighborhoods.

The black students had three common types of experiences related to the class differences between their neighborhoods and their school communities, and these are covered in the following sections. Such experiences have both positive and negative long- and short-term aspects. In many instances, what was temporarily painful and uncomfortable for a child turned out to be instructive in adult life. While the differences could surely make some students feel angry and resentful, the experiences also contributed to the way these adults see the world—or at least American society—today.

ASSUMING POVERTY, ASSUMING WEALTH

Many of the adults recall that white suburban students and teachers had two contradictory attitudes regarding economic class and the METCO students. On the one hand, in their comments and casual conversations it seemed that the white students and teachers assumed everyone had lives of privilege. But, at the same time, other comments and conversations—these were usually directed at the METCO students—made it seem that the white students and teachers thought that all METCO students were poor.

For example, classroom discussions and offhand comments

about vacations and leisure activities indicated to some of the METCO students that the white students did not realize that not everyone could afford lifestyles like theirs. Related to this, some former METCO students were continually frustrated with white students who did not seem to appreciate the fact that they, as white, wealthy teenagers had advantages in their lives that others did not enjoy. Most of the former METCO students said it wasn't until well after graduation that they were able to articulate the reasons for the frustration and anger they felt.

John Johns, a 1980s graduate, describes the type of brief exchange that was common among METCO students and white students and that symbolized for the METCO students, as he puts it, "the white kids' inability to see what they had." Split into groups for a high school classroom assignment, students were instead discussing their plans for the summer. One white teenager, interested in biology, said his father had gotten him an unpaid internship working in a science lab at a nearby college. Another white student, interested in government, had landed an unpaid position in state government, thanks to a well-connected uncle. At the time, John, a good student who also was interested in politics, was in the middle of a summer job search. He had hoped that a job loading materials at a warehouse was going to come through, since it paid more than the restaurant jobs for which he had applied.

> When I told them this, that I was trying for this summer job, they kind of looked at me like: "A warehouse? You're gonna work in a warehouse?" And one of em' says, "But this has nothing to do with your interests." And I said, "Right, but the money's good, it's really good." And they tell me that you aren't supposed to think about money in your summers right before college, you're supposed to do things that look good on your applications and that relate to your interests. And

I'm thinking, "Relate to my interests?" I'm trying to get enough money together so I can maybe go to college someday. I will not be using that money for anything else, my mother was going to be sure of that. And they didn't get it. They just kept giving me this advice. This one kid, he was a nice kid, he's saying [that] maybe his uncle could do something for me, hook me up with a position over there [at the State House], and he asks me: "Do you have a suit?" And I tell him, "I can't take a job for no money!" What are these kids thinking? I try to imagine going home, saying, "Hey Mom, I got this great job, but it doesn't pay anything," and the look I'd get for that one. So, I just kept my mouth shut. It was a totally different world.

For the adults who recall similar conversations that revealed assumptions about uniform privilege, it is not the existence of wealth or inequality per se that angered or perplexed them but the fact that the white students seemed to have, as John put it, "zero perspective" about their own privilege. Today, as adults, the former students most commonly attribute this attitude among whites as a result of whites' isolation. A smaller group, though, some of whom say they still resent such experiences, blame the white students' attitudes on parents who failed to impress upon their children the relative advantages they have in life. As Bruce Paynter, who is from a "working-class" background, began his fall classes at a new junior high school in an affluent suburb, his new school jitters were compounded by the assumptions of a teacher who asked students to talk to the class about a new town, city, state, or country visited over the summer. Bruce's vacation did not include extensive travel. As the teacher issued the instructions to the class, Bruce decided he would talk about the fun he had visiting younger cousins in New Jersey, where he played simple games of tag and basketball. But, as other classmates gave their talks, he realized that his contribution "was not in sync":

Not everyone had exotic stories. But then, there's this girl, I remember, who went to China. And I'm thinking, "China! She must be making this up." China? Who goes to China? And this other kid, he went to Israel. And I'm thinking, "Israel, like in the Bible, Israel?" And my eyes were just wide open and then I'm thinking this is crazy, crazy, and all of a sudden it's my turn. And what am I supposed to say? I didn't go anywhere, really. It wasn't because I was poor. I wasn't. But my parents, they were working all summer. My dad took a week [off], I remember, and he took me and my sister, to Jersey to see my three little cousins. And I couldn't remember the name of the city, even. I did remember that we went to this beach, this really crowded beach, and it started to rain about twenty minutes after we got there so we went home and hung out and had a great time running around my cousin's building, playing all these games in the rain. It was great and my Dad, he was in a good mood, playing with us out in the rain. And it was this great memory, but how am I supposed to explain it, here? I can't. It wasn't in sync with the discussion. So I said, "I went to the beach, in New Jersey, with my father. It was okay." That's it. I still remember. And everyone laughed. And the other two METCO kids, they didn't laugh at all. And then, I don't know, the teacher stopped the whole conversation and it was really uncomfortable and everyone was looking at me. And I think that one thing, that experience, kind of carried through and made me realize that I don't have what these kids have. I have a totally different kind of life. They can have this conversation about travel here and there and never even think that this isn't a totally natural conversation to have for everyone. They didn't see that they were privileged. They're just going on talking about China and Israel like everybody does it. Well, I knew everyone doesn't do it.

When Bruce was an adolescent, his discomfort with white assumptions about affluence was particularly painful and was part of what led, he believes, to his "long-lasting" resentment of wealthy people, which he acknowledges, "isn't personally healthy for me" or "really very fair." Today, these attitudes are complicated by the fact that Bruce, earning more than $50,000 a year and married to a woman who earns about the same, is clearly financially comfortable. As he considers buying a home in a predominantly white, affluent, suburban town, he says his adolescent and teenage confrontations with suburban attitudes about wealth cause him to impress upon his own children the extent of their advantage.

It seemed to the METCO students that while whites appeared to think their own brand of privilege was universal, they also appeared to think that poverty was universal among blacks. It seemed to some of the black students that no matter how many times they tried to correct the misunderstandings about social class, the stereotypes about poverty would not die.

Many of the black adults who came from middle- and working-class families today recall being particularly frustrated by whites' apparent failure to understand that there is diversity among blacks with regard to social class. And after high school, the adults said they still find that white people are surprised when black adults talk about travel or cultural experiences they had as children. These adults also say they are still particularly sensitive to such stereotypes and are quick to correct whites' erroneous views about race and poverty. These sensitivities, the black adults say, come at least in part from being treated like what Marie Lawlor calls "a poor little black girl."

Marie, who attended a wealthy suburban district west of Boston, did not grow up poor. Her father was a successful sales-man for a large corporation, and her mother was an executive assistant. The Lawlors owned their own home in Boston, reg-ularly went to the theater, and spent school vacations with relatives around the country. During Marie's school years, her sister attended a private college, an aunt was pursuing graduate study, and an uncle had opened a medical practice in another state. Yet Marie recalls comments and questions that revealed to her that students and teachers just assumed she was poor. In elementary school, a teacher took Marie aside and asked if she had enough paper and pencils at home. The teacher was willing to give Marie some extras, in case she needed them. One day, in junior high, Marie forgot her lunch money and asked a friend to loan her some. A teacher who overheard the conversation between the friends pulled Marie aside to tell her that whenever Marie needed extra money, the teacher would sneak her some, without anyone seeing. As Marie remembers, the teacher said, " '[Marie], this is nothing to be ashamed of.' And I'm thinking, 'Right, this is nothing to be ashamed of because I'm sure my mother makes more money than you do.' But I didn't [say anything]. I just thought, 'Yeah, okay, lady.' "

Similarly, when Ray Newsom, an early 1990s graduate, had trouble in math and asked for help, the well-meaning teacher asked if Ray had enough space at home to do homework and if his family could afford a calculator. What this teacher didn't know was that Ray and his brothers, sisters, and cousins had a full floor to themselves with a study area at his family's three-floor brownstone in Boston. They not only had plenty of calcula-tors, but they also shared a computer and a small copy machine. Ray's father owned his own business. The family "wasn't rich," but "wasn't poor either. We had everything we needed." After recalling the discussion with his teacher and other similar discus-sions, Ray says, "you hate to knock someone trying to be well-meaning and charitable, but there was not the slightest indication that I was poor. A lot of white kids were struggling with the math, too. It was the skin color they were looking at, saying to themselves, 'Black? Okay, then, poor.' "

Such experiences led Ray, Marie, and many other former

METCO students to be particularly sensitive to people's assumptions about their social class and childhood socioeconomic status. Ray, for example, said that the first thing he does when meeting with new clients or in social situations with whites is to make it clear that he comes from a financially secure family. He does this by talking about vacations he took or his father's business. Sometimes, he says, including these facts in a conversation can be "clumsy."

Ray says, "I don't know why I do it really. Maybe it's protecting them from saying something stupid. But then, why bother? Because they always do it anyway: 'Oh, that's interesting. Your father is a business owner? Your mother just started her own business?' Like it's the most amazing thing in the world, right? Or you get this: 'I thought you said you grew up in Roxbury.' That's the best line. I'm always making cracks about it, but really after awhile it pisses you off."

And years later, Marie is careful "to wear the right clothes, to show I've been exposed to the finer things, that I value the arts and things of that nature." Marie explains that "it comes from this feeling like you are assumed to be poor and deprived and low-class and so sort of backward. And that is far from what I was. I'm not a snob and it's not like I don't want to be associated with people who are poor, it's just [that] I don't want people assuming that because I'm black, they know all these things about me."

SEEING THE LINKS

Exposure to concentrated wealth and differences in class helped METCO students make sense of the world. They learned to think critically about the role that race and class play in perceptions of a community, how its residents are treated, and the opportunities available to people who live there. Just as they learned the social significance of race, they grew to understand the social significance of class as well. And they noticed that the two were entwined and affected many facets of life. In this way, many of these students became lay sociologists. Certainly the students did not come to the same or even similar analyses, but the emergence of critical ideas about class was strikingly common, with nearly three-fourths recollecting a new enlightenment.

For example, Ann Edgar, who dropped out of METCO in high school in the early 1980s, describes the role that exposure to class differences played in her developing understanding of class, power, and neglect in America. Her comments are typical of so many former students who recall the development of new critical perspectives. Ann says: "You look around you every day, at [the suburban town] and things are neat, things look good. And then you look around your [own] neighborhood. You start to say, 'Hey, that's why my garbage doesn't get picked up. That's why it takes a cop two hours to get [to respond to an emergency call]. That's why the schools are so bad. I get it. It's because people are poor. That's why the streets are so clean here [in the suburban METCO town], why they have the good schools, why their garbage gets picked up on time. Oh, I see. I understand.' And it gets you real angry."

Elaine Yardley also remembers realizing in high school the role of class and race in communities:

> You start seeing the differences pretty early on. And you might start by thinking rather ugly thoughts, like, "Hmm, this is a black neighborhood. Why don't blacks pick things up more?" Or, you think, "Everyone is white out here. They're so neat! It's so nice!" Those ideas don't sit right [because] you start to see there's more to it, like money and power, and then [you get] this sense that people in a white community [believe they] have a right to these services. And people listen to them, because of money, skin color, all those things. And you

realize it's not so simple anymore. You see that these differences just feed off of each other, lead to other things like some communities looking nice, some looking like crap, and then you build images off of that and then reputations begin and people will move in or they'll move out. When you are a young person, you are idealistic. You want to say, "Why should money matter? Money doesn't matter." Spend a few years out in [her school's suburban town]. You see it matters.

Each person reacted differently to these realizations. For some students the realizations were accompanied by anger. Elaine felt a tinge of "frustration" and that "I was so small under these huge forces." Rhonda Johnson felt "smarter for it, definitely, but also sad, like a little of my idealism was gone about everyone being equal regardless." Others, such as Reggie Carlton, who dropped out of a wealthy suburban district in the early 1980s to return to Boston, felt "ashamed for awhile" about being from Boston.

The adults recall that as they reached high school age, a lot of them started thinking, as many did, about the concept of "reputation." That is, they began to think about the ways that people perceived cities or towns in which they did not live. Cara Ross, for example, always knew her city neighborhood had a bad reputation or "image," as she put it. Race and class, she figured, had "something to do with it." Cara thought this "wasn't fair," but she also felt that if a town is wealthy, there might be something to gain from being there. This realization was part of what caused Cara to remain in METCO even though, by tenth or eleventh grade, she wanted to transfer:

You see this, and you start figuring shit out: where there's money, there's going to be power, right? These people are used to getting their own way, so of course the schools are going to be good. And that sort of feeds on itself and then there are opportunities in these places so it is a "good place." And then the reputation that certain parts of the city get, part of that reputation is because people are black and poor in certain areas so it's a racist thing. I think some of it is just pure racism. But it's true about unequal opportunity. It's just true. And a lot of it's just money that they have and we don't. This is the reality of the situation.

Similarly, Rhonda Johnson began to question the concept of a "good" school and a "bad" school. She explains:

You hear people [say], "Oh, that's a good school." Well, how do they know? It's a school where rich kids go so there's this assumption, immediately, that it's gotta be good because rich people are going to make sure that it's good. This assurance of quality thing, right? So, then people say, "Oh, that's a crappy school, that's a bad school." Does that mean it's a black school? Is it a school with a lot of poor people going to it, a lot of immigrants? If you've never been in the school, how do you know? It's a class/race thing. Rich school? Good school. Poor school? Bad school. This is real. This idea is real out there. Then isn't that part of why things are bad, because people think they are and people who can be involved, help the school, won't go there because of the class thing? It's a vicious cycle based on money. And in METCO, you see, "Oh, I'm part of this. I'm here because of this idea of this being a better school because it's full of rich kids." There's truth in that, isn't there?

While these realizations initially caused anger, indignation, and sadness, the adults don't view their exposures to wealth in suburbia as producing negative results over the long term. The adult respondents seem to feel that coming to their own understandings of the structure of society was informative and important. Most believe that they eventually would have been exposed to the class differences and their implications once they entered college or the workforce.

Ann Edgar, who years after METCO went to a two-year college, puts it this way: "What's the alternative? Keep me locked up in a room in Dorchester, pull the shades to stop me from knowing I didn't have what they have? I knew. We all knew. But it's better, don't you think, to have a child in a position that lets him think about why things are the way they are?"

FROM WIDE-EYED TO ACCUSTOMED TO ENTITLED

Just as the black adults who attended white schools remember their wide-eyed reactions to suburban wealth, some students also remember that this affluence started to feel familiar over time. And to still another group of the students, the wealth began to feel not just familiar, but within reach for the future. The descriptions of increasing familiarity with affluence are similar to the adults' descriptions of increasing comfort in predominantly white settings. None of the past participants was able to recall the specific process of increasing comfort and diminishing self-consciousness. But the vast majority of those who were at first shocked or made uncomfortable by the wealth that surrounded them also recall a later period when the differences seemed unremarkable. Nearly all those who reported initial feelings of discomfort said that this discomfort eventually faded. And within this group are some students who recall that the increasing comfort led them to feel more deserving of economic security and material wealth. A few students describe this as beginning to feel more "entitled" to the lifestyles the white families had. As adults looking back on those feelings, they experienced two divergent reactions.

One larger group of students is thankful for these acquired feelings of entitlement. A former student describes this attitude as "feeling deserving, it's like: I can have that, too." Another says, "it's part of your realm, now, that you can have what other people have." A third says: "I remember making a pact with myself: okay, I'm deserving of this too. I can have it if I want it." Some past participants said that such attitudes made them feel more powerful, confident, and ambitious in their own lives after high school. These individuals tend to think of themselves as successful in their own careers and express contentment with their level of economic success. Often they are confident that they will continue to get promotions and increased recognition or have ample job and economic opportunities in the future.

Trevor Baron, for example, said that contact and familiarity with wealthy families in his suburban high school were, in part, what motivated him to understand how those families became successful. Today Trevor, who grew up in a working-class household, has a high-level position in state government. Trevor explains, "It wasn't really until high school that I noticed the income disparities. I went over to a friend's house, and their house was the biggest one on the street. It was amazing. And I remember going to these kids' houses [and] talking to their mothers and fathers about how they achieved their success. And this was a very positive experience, starting to feel that this could be something in my life."

Another group of respondents, however, who developed similar feelings of entitlement as teens reported feeling disappointed following high school. Most of these former students, none of whom attended college, found that they did not benefit by just feeling deserving in the manner that suburban students apparently did. Clark Raymon, who graduated from a METCO school in the 1970s, said his immersion in the wealthy, privileged suburban lifestyle did not prepare him for the challenges of life ahead. What Clark said he failed to understand at the time was that it "was going to be easier to get success if your family already had money." Clark says he now believes that "it's a mistake to think that this is your world, because it is not your world. And you come out and you're thinking, 'Hey, I understand the good life, I can play in that game.' Wrong. If you are black and your daddy isn't rich, you have to earn your way, and that took me some time to learn. No one tells you that."

For example, former students like Clark remember thinking that if the suburban white students were confident about their own futures, then the black students, too, should be confident. But for some of these students, financial problems often prevented them from attending college, at least immediately after high school. In addition, these students say, they did not have the professional and personal contacts the white students had for jobs and other opportunities. Thomas Crayton, who left METCO in the 1980s, spent time in jail and struggles to find and keep jobs. He said going to school in suburbia fooled him into thinking that he would one day become a member of what he jokingly calls "the leisure class."

Thomas says, "I like that. The leisure class. Can't say it did much for me, thinking I'd be out making deals, riding around on planes. I used to tell my mother, 'Hey Ma, I'm going to be an accountant.' I couldn't even do my math homework straight, you know what I'm saying? But Ben's [friend in suburbs] father, he was an accountant, they had three houses, all right?"

WHAT ABOUT MONEY?

Going from a poor, working-class, or mixed-income city neighborhood to an affluent town spurred new realizations for these young people. It often meant lasting dismay with the attitudes and assumptions displayed by affluent white suburbanites. Today, the adults see some of their actions and resentments as lingering symptoms of school-day confrontations with whites, who simultaneously seemed to take their own privilege for granted and to equate being black with being poor. Being near all that wealth, though, also caused these young people to make connections and form theories about the forces that create and limit opportunity in a community. Getting used to the affluence around them contributed to an attitude that many students described as entitlement to economic success or simply an expectation that economic success was within reach. This view, of course, could lead to fulfillment or disappointment, depending on the successes or failures that the METCO students experienced after high school.

Understanding class differences and the implications of those differences in society was for most of the adults like finding a missing piece of the inequality puzzle. In the long run, their exposure to concentrated wealth didn't necessarily make them want more material things, or even feel as if where they came from was inadequate. Their day-to-day interaction with wealth enhanced their understanding of the structure of society.

Memories of METCO
WHAT DO THEY TELL US ABOUT TODAY?

As black children and teenagers living in Boston and going to school in white, usually affluent suburban towns, METCO students blur the lines of a racial divide that has been a long time in the making. On the suburban terrain, the black students discover differences that set them apart from suburban families and from the black families they know at home. How suburban whites chose to react to real or perceived cultural or socioeconomic differences ranged from mockery and exclusion to careful curiosity and celebration. The response had a profound impact upon the black adults' enduring memories of METCO. Thus, for these children and teenagers, going to suburbia could be humiliating, fascinating, scary, exciting, anger provoking, and eye-opening. Because METCO was often all of these things at once, its lessons were often difficult to sort out at the time. But for adults today, METCO fits coherently into their larger life picture. What the adults experienced, treasured, disliked, and learned in METCO they went on to see, feel, use, and revisit in their lives after high school. Beyond the personal, the METCO experience represents to these adults the problems and the potential inherent not only in racially integrated schools but in the society at large.

In the next two chapters, adults speak about the years after METCO and the myriad ways the questions, challenges, and lessons evoked during their school days play out in grown-up lives.

4

The Gains

What Black Adults Say They Gained
from Attending White Suburban Schools and
How They Used What They Got

"A foot in each world."

"Straddling a fence between communities."

"Following two sets of rules."

"Switching."

"Moving back and forth."

"Having a double life."

"Bridging."

These are some of the most common phrases black adults use to sum up their experiences as young African Americans in white suburbia. Years after high school, the adults use the same or similar phrases to describe their current lives. This bridging of two worlds and leading of double lives bring forth stories of lasting gains and losses. In this chapter, post-METCO adults focus on the benefits of their movements between the black communities where they lived and the white communities where they went to school.

The men and women generally speak about two different types of long-term gains emerging from their school experience. The first involves the ways the suburban experience influenced their personal attitudes, opinions, and actions. Most commonly, the men and women say they are more "comfortable" in predominantly white settings and more likely to enter and succeed in such settings than they suspect they would have been if they had not gone to suburbia. In story after story, adults characterize an acquired personal quality that might best be described as a gracefulness with racial difference. It is this grace that enabled them to transcend that race-based awkwardness they so often experienced as children, a grace that today affords them fluid movement between black and white worlds.

The second important gain involved getting over structural barriers. As the METCO students prepared to enter the world after high school, they quickly discerned that survival in white America required not just increased self-confidence and earned feelings of comfort. Success, they found, required special connections—one post-METCO adult termed them "inside tracks"—to education and economic opportunities. Many of the students did make such connections. This is partly because the students profited from some suburban school characteristics that had historically benefited whites, including social prestige and a constant flow of information about educational and professional opportunities. The new social networks created through the METCO program itself, meanwhile, hooked students to opportunities that seemed to multiply.

Getting Comfortable

Similar to the way they repeat the "better education" mantra, many former METCO students say almost as a matter of course that their days in white suburbia helped them later on to feel more "comfortable" around white people and predominantly white settings. Many former METCO students speculate that had they not been to METCO, they would be more likely to avoid white-dominated settings so as to evade race-related awkwardness so common in new situations. The adults speculate that without prior experience, they might have entered a new situation and incorrectly assumed that the initial discomfort they experienced learning, living, and working around whites would be permanent. And without that prior METCO experience, the adults speculate, they would have probably fled such settings.

For example, Kim Peters, currently a business professional in a large New England firm, is making a career switch to college-level teaching. Now in her early 40s, Kim has worked full-time in three predominantly white companies—first as a secretary at two different firms and most recently as an associate in her current firm. Even after all these years, and despite earning a graduate degree, Kim is still apprehensive at the start of new jobs and assignments with new clients. But her fears can't be characterized merely as new job anxiety. Rather, Kim is filled with worry over how the color of her skin might affect the way others perceive and treat her. Her initial apprehensions are fairly typical among her fellow METCO graduates, but so are her experiences of diminishing fear and tension:

> Even when I was support staff [secretarial] I was dealing with white people, white people, white people. That's it, really, once you're dealing with the CEO level. It's not the most diverse crowd. I had been through METCO and all, but this kind of threw me. I'd be assigned to executives who didn't hire me and there was always this [question], "What if he's a racist?" going through me at the start.
>
> You never really get to feeling comfortable anywhere, though, unless you give it a chance, give it time to get past the fact that, okay, you're black. But if you have

no other experience to go on? I don't know. Some of the
places I've worked, yes, I would have quit. I probably
would have quit if I didn't know from METCO that there's
going to be this at the beginning, this little transition and
then it gets normal. Some days [at workplaces], at the
beginning, it's like: "Hello, yes, I'm black." There were
days I just wanted to scream out: "Yes, people, okay, I'm
black. Can we please get on with it?" Everyone was
either incredibly nice to the point that it came to being
ridiculous, or they'd just run away because they're afraid
they're gonna say something racist and not even know it.

Despite these difficulties, though, Kim knew from METCO and
from her sustained experience in the workplace that the tension
"eases up, it always just eases up."

When adults such as Kim recall their METCO years, it is quite
common for them to remember initial impressions of white suburban schools as "new worlds," "another world," even as places
"out of this world." But the adults hardly ever describe predominantly white settings in such terms today. Of course, predominantly white workplaces, colleges, or neighborhoods may
not always feel "like home," and adults often question periodi-
cally whether they are accepted in such settings. But the offices
and classrooms are no longer frightening and no longer feel
so foreign.

Those who recall being bewildered and confused as children by the cultural differences and unwritten rules of suburban
behavior and speech today say that METCO prepared them well
for the expectations of the academic and working world. Their
knowledge of what to expect—this subtle ability to recognize as
familiar the behavior, lifestyles, and unwritten rules—was, for
many METCO participants, a powerful prerequisite for life on predominantly white campuses and in workplaces.

Thus, two things, *knowledge that time would probably di-*

minish self-consciousness and *familiarity from prior exposure to similar surroundings*, contributed to the adults' willingness to enter and remain in predominantly white settings over the course of their lives. Post-METCO adults typically suspect they had, what 1970s graduate Barbara Michaels calls, "a running start" for developing navigation strategies required for later periods of adjustment in their lives. For example, Wendy West, who graduated from a small, predominantly white liberal arts college in New England, is among many of the adults who say that the "biggest thing METCO prepared me for was going to a predominantly white campus." Wendy recalls comments from the handful of other black students, all of whom wondered how she could tolerate being the only black person in her dorm.

> I was the only student of color in that dorm. The only black person in that dorm. And for a lot of people that might be a little isolating, but I looked at it as an opportunity. I said: "Wow, I get to meet all these different people." And there were all kinds of people there. There were upperclassmen, younger students, there were gay[s], lesbian[s]. Football player jock types and guys in the basement who had reefer plants growing on the ledge. There was every type of person in that dorm. The black students would say, "Oh God, how can you stand being there? Those people are so weird." But I didn't see it as weird. Not at all. It opened up a lot for me. A lot of the kids who ended up leaving [that college] were from Harlem, South Bronx. Their world ended at the end of their driveway or their boulevard and they couldn't see past that. Anything outside their world wasn't new and exciting, it was strange and they didn't know how to deal with it.

On college campuses particularly METCO students frequently would become informal counselors to other black students from predominantly black high schools. The former METCO students recall empathizing quite easily with these fellow black students whose college experiences mirrored some of the difficulties METCO students had already faced in suburbia. For example, Nathan King, who began METCO in his freshman year of high school, found that just four years of exposure to a different culture and lifestyle in high school prepared him for college socially as well as academically. Nathan recalls his efforts to help racial minority students who had difficulty adjusting to a predominantly white, though culturally diverse, New England campus.

"I met a lot of people in college. When they got there, they had to struggle with the adjustment," Nathan says. "I found out [in college] that by the time I got into my senior year, I was helping younger students make the transition and help them deal with the fact that 'Hey, you are not in Brooklyn, you are not in Roxbury.' These were African-American kids, kids from other countries. It didn't matter, they were still having to make that tough transition from coming from a place where they were in the majority to a place where they are in the minority. I had, however, been fortunate enough to make that trip, that transition."

What's Comfort?

It is important to understand not just the process of acquiring comfort, but what, exactly, "feeling comfortable" means to these adults. They fall primarily into two groups. The first group associates comfort with familiarity, with becoming accustomed to the atmosphere, culture, habits, and ways of being in a setting. Former students who characterize their acquired comfort this way describe movements from white suburbia to a white college or workplace as transitions to new, yet generally familiar, settings. The mere passage of time more or less eased race-related anxieties.

As time passes, many members of this first group draw maps in their minds based upon what they perceive others' racial attitudes to be. They gather evidence about people or groups and then deem them to be hostile, friendly, or unproved. These adults have keen senses of acceptable behavior and styles of discourse and have the ability to adjust to the setting they are in, *if* they choose to. Some members of this first group strictly follow these rules, not in an effort to be financially or professionally successful, but to put others at ease, thereby avoiding personal discomfort and awkwardness. But a nearly equal number of members of this group reject the rules knowingly. Whether they follow these rules or consciously reject them most of the time, being familiar with the rules alone brings comfort to this group.

If one accepts the rules, he or she still consciously engages in what Carl Pierce, a 1970s graduate, calls "switching." For example, one might use what is perceived to be "white" speech patterns in predominantly white settings and what is perceived to be "black" patterns and styles of discourse with black friends. Quite often, this is a continuation of the behavior and coping strategies learned in white suburban schools. Carl echoes the sentiments of other members of this group.

"I'm white here, or I act white here, okay? I'm black there (at home)," Carl says. "I'm black all the time, more black. I act more obviously like a black person, and everyone, I guess, has a different view of what that is. But to me, I'm more black than I act here. That's definitely the truth."

A person who adheres to the rules of discourse or of socializing keeps in mind a clear demarcation between that individual's "real" personality and his or her "work" or "school" personality —a personality that the adults tend to express in racial terms. But someone who rejects those white rules usually thinks of him- or herself as an outsider. This is true even when he or she is successful professionally. Thus, it would be inaccurate to say that this group, whose members understand the white rules of behavior, is more likely to camouflage behaviors that they think or suspect others might associate with being black. What is generally true is that this first group of respondents still sees a line between the "white" world of work (or of a college class-room) and the usual, predominantly "black world" of social and family life. Members of this group cross that line with frequency and seeming ease. The line is neither threatening nor limiting. But they do see it quite clearly.

There is a second, much larger group—more than two-thirds—for whom the line between black and white is blurred and for whom the worlds overlap. For this group, "comfort" requires more than familiarity and knowledge. These adults also feel comforted by the familiarity of white settings and their grow-ing understanding of the unwritten rules there. They, too, char-acterize the "white rules" in similar ways. But in contrast with the first group, their comfort comes from ease with *expressing themselves as black people* in white settings.

Members of this group usually see familiarity and getting accustomed as the first step in feeling comfortable. But after this stage, these post-METCO adults build on this comfort by con-sciously expressing their identity as blacks. What might be de-fined as distinctly "black" to one person might not be defined that way by another. Amid varying modes of expression, though, what is similar among the adults in this second group is their effort to meld black and white worlds that had been separate. One woman, in explaining her expression of black identity, pointed to her African-style clothing and her Martin Luther King and Malcolm X posters in her cubicle; her attempts to get white co-workers to accompany her to jazz clubs; and her consistent "speaking out" about the need for more training to help "upper management" be more sensitive to "race and sexism issues."

Thomas Mitchell, who graduated in the 1980s, said the most valuable aspect of METCO wasn't that it merely got him "used to being around white people," but that it compelled him to begin a search for strategies that allowed him to comfortably express his black identity in such settings. This was a common finding among the post-METCO adults, many of whom, like Loretta Yardley, stress that "feeling comfortable around white people is impossible to do unless you go through that process of learning how to not be white like them, but [how to] be black, be true to your blackness when you are around [whites]."

Jeremy Shepard, for example, characterizes his METCO experience as "very, very negative." He recounts incidents of overt racism and exclusion. Nevertheless, he believes that because his original coping strategy during METCO was unsuccessful, he developed another, "more honest, genuine" one as an adult. During METCO, Jeremy reacted to a racist environment by "hiding my blackness" as he tried to "be more white" by "talking how they talk, exactly how they talk, by doing what they want to do, listening to their music, dating white girls. You name it, I did it." Jeremy believes this strategy won him a bit more acceptance in the short term but "left me empty and hollow inside," leading him to withdraw and feel uncomfortable in both white and black settings. Like many METCO participants, Jeremy later reconsidered his METCO strategy and reworked it until he felt comfortable. Today, more than a decade after METCO, Jeremy has a high-level position in business and is supervisor to a mostly white staff.

> Now I really want people to know I'm from the city. I don't push street talk on them in a meeting or something. But I'll make allusions to my roots, or [when] they're talking about their music I'll make comments about jazz. Or I'll mention the church we go to. I'll do things that remind people that they are dealing with me, and I have a strong sense of being black and the pride that goes with that. So they know they need to deal with that side of me too, that I'm not going to just cancel all that stuff out to be accepted. We all do that presenting of

ourselves to others and that's how I present myself. Some people say, "Deal with me as a man, not a black man." I don't agree. I say, "I'm a black man, deal with it." I didn't always feel that way, and I don't know if I could go through METCO again, but I do know I'd still be testing the waters around here. I probably wouldn't even be around places like this.

Members of this group acknowledge that METCO, in part, helped them achieve more comfort in white settings than they would have had otherwise. Still, they view their acquisition of comfort as a work-in-progress—something they are clearly heading toward but don't feel they've achieved completely.

But how do adults link these current attitudes to educational experiences that they had as many as twenty years ago? After all, as we know from chapter 3, only rarely did these students achieve such culturally expressive comfort within the METCO setting. While they may not have achieved adequate levels of comfort in middle or high school, in METCO they did begin to learn that, in order to be healthy and happy with themselves, they would need not only to succeed in predominantly white settings, but to find their own identities as blacks and to express those identities to some extent wherever they are.

It is difficult to know for sure what causes the two varieties of the concept of comfort, one of which derives from understanding the "white rules" and the other of which derives from free expression of black identity. But there is a plausible explanation. The second group of former students somewhat more frequently remember that parents stressed the importance of maintaining connections to black culture and history and/or discussed openly issues of racism and the need for their sons and daughters to take pride in being black. But in addition to this parental support for cultural connection and black identity, members of this group also recall that their parents were supportive of their

children's activities in suburban schools. This support went beyond academic concerns. Their parents expressed approval of
their children's new interests in hobbies, sports, or social relationships that the children might not have developed in an all-
black community.

For example, Wendy West, like other former METCO students, remembers her mother and father stressing that Wendy
and her siblings should be proud to be black. At the same time,
Wendy said, her parents encouraged her budding interests in
typically suburban activities even though Wendy says her mother
had understandable reasons to be apprehensive.

"They weren't belittling me because I was involved in
things, like I wanted to take [horseback] riding lessons, I wanted
to take gymnastics, like the kids in [town] did," Wendy remembers. "Whereas there were other METCO parents who [said], 'You
aren't doing that. That's for them. Not for us.' There were never
mixed messages about what I was doing, even though my Mom
grew up in the South and cleaned houses for the Ku Klux Klan
grand wizard and certainly had a lot of prejudices against whites,
I am sure."

In the smaller, first group, it was more common for the
former students to have recalled that parents expressed ambivalence or disdain for white people or activities and lifestyles they
associated with being white. Conversely, a few members of the
first group recall not so much that their parents disliked or feared
whites, but that they seemed to view white culture and white
communities as superior to black culture and black communities. These manifestations of what scholars term "internalized
racism," in which blacks find validity in negative stereotypes
about blacks, were not nearly as common as expressions of ambivalence toward, or distrust of, whites.

As for increased comfort in white settings, the adults attribute that gain directly to METCO, pointing to the interaction
the program required. Necessarily, the adults also consider the

program's impact in relation to other influences. Thus, to the adults, it was the powerful combination of parental support and exposure and interaction through METCO itself that increased their confidence and steadfastness in predominantly white settings.

It would be inaccurate to say that METCO cured participants of race-based discomfort for all time. More accurately, adults' survival in METCO is for the vast majority of them reliable evidence that they can, in fact, find peace of mind and ease within settings where there may be few or no other blacks. Even so, they quite commonly continue to breathe sighs of relief when they get time away from white-dominated campuses and workplaces. Michelle Parker, a METCO graduate, expresses this view: "It's not [as though] you do METCO and then bang, you are just so perfectly, completely comfortable wherever you go as the only black person and you've got no more need to hang with just black people. This is still America, you know, and you are still black and that's not going to change as far as I know: 'Do they think I'm qualified? Are there any racists? I better watch what I say.' And inside your brain, you're thinking, 'I better watch what I say, too, because I don't want to come out of here not being black anymore.' So, it's there, the race thing."

Characterizing METCO's role in abating the overriding role of race, Michelle continues:

> But METCO's there, you do think about how you survived that. We [other friends from METCO] talk about this a lot. I didn't like everything about [the town where I went to school] and there are still a lot of people I'd like to go in and have a word or two with. Not all nice words either, I should say. And for me, to just end the week, go out with my girlfriend, party at a place where you see black faces, black faces. This is rejuvenating, I have to say.
>
> But that doesn't take away either from your experiences. [METCO's] something you look back on, that you

did, you went into this new place and you made it okay
and, you figure, it'll be okay next time, too.

Class Comfort

Post-METCO adults also report feeling increasingly comfortable
with class difference and describe with some frequency an ease
working with colleagues and privileged clients. Most of the past
participants who are middle-class speculate that this comfort is
principally the result of the economic success that they, themselves, have achieved. But still, many say that because METCO
provided early exposure to wealth and privilege, intimidation
was less of a problem for them later in life.

Bruce Paynter, who attended an affluent school, finds some
benefits from this learned ease in his current life. Like many
other METCO graduates, he finds he has more confidence dealing
with wealthy clients and work acquaintances, in part, he says,
because of his schooling in similar circles. "It was something that
was, in some of those years, very uncomfortable: just not being
sure about how to act all the time," Bruce says. "And for me, it
wasn't really about changing so I could fit in, but just getting
used to wealthier lifestyles, being around people who had a
certain level of power because of their wealth. This was important because I can enter these situations with a level of confidence I don't know if I'd have [without METCO]."

Nathan King, whose work requires movement in circles of
wealthy businesspeople in addition to builders, contractors, and
plumbers, has similar observations. "This is what my work requires me to do," Nathan explains. "It's just like what METCO
required me to do. And so, I've got that mix. From Boston, from
living where I lived, I have a sense of people that's important,
too. And from [the town where I attended school], you learn a
lot too, you learn how to move in these places and how to just go
in there as yourself without being overly conscious of yourself, to

read the situation and talk to people like you've learned how to talk to them. So, you take a lot from both situations."

This acquired comfort around prosperous people seems especially salient for the roughly one-third of the students who attended a particularly affluent suburban school; they usually bring up this subject without prodding. Students who attended schools that were mixed socioeconomically still recall being exposed to concentrated wealth, but it was a comparatively less important feature of their METCO experience.

Grace with Difference

Nick Marshall is the youngest professional in his division of an investment firm. But his colleagues refer to him as "the grown-up." "It comes from one incident," says Nick, who graduated from a suburban school in the 1990s. He explains:

> There was speculation that I got the job because I was black. And it was interesting, because, actually, the reason I got this job was the same reason most white people get their jobs. I am smart. I know what I'm doing and I did have a lot of experiences that people my age don't usually have, internships and such that were relevant. But I knew someone who knew a vice-president. Everyone involved happened to be white, all the contacts I had. One was my professor, who had been pushing me to go for an MBA, and he knew people here and hooked me up when I said I needed to earn some [money] before going to school. So I heard about these comments and I wanted to clear the air. So I call a meeting. I get the supervisor's support. I confront it. No big deal. ...sed to this, right? You could cut that tension. But ...iter, I have people saying to me, "Man, th⸱ ...⸱⸱⸵ ...t experience of my life." One woman was crying ⸱ecause she felt bad, she hadn't said anything. She

was just really personally moved by it. And it's all been said. No big blowup. I just wanted to get it out, deal with it. Act like adults. So they call me the grown-up.

Nick hadn't always been adept at confronting explosive racial issues. This skill took practice—a lot of it. As a METCO student, in fact, Nick remembers initiating race-related discussions only twice. And both attempts were, as he describes them, "total, utter disasters." As a black child and then teenager in white suburbia, though, Nick realized the power—both positive and negative—of racial difference. He says he learned "anything people aren't really talking about doesn't mean they aren't thinking about it." After METCO, this enforced silence resurfaced when Nick went to a predominantly white college. There he found more silence, more awkwardness, more of what he terms "forced politeness."

In college, Nick took two actions that were typical of many former METCO students. First, he got involved in an organization focused specifically on increasing the visibility of African-American political issues and cultural contributions at his predominantly white campus. Soon after he joined, the group selected Nick as its representative to the college administration and student government. In this position, Nick presented position papers and negotiated various matters with the mostly white administrators and student government leaders. He worked with black students, representing their opinions, contributions, and complaints to white administrators. Then he relayed the discussions with white administrators to the other members of the all-black organization.

Peter Quint, another 1990s graduate, had similar experiences in a black student group on his predominantly white Catholic school campus, where he now works as an administrator. "They really needed someone who could move in between both worlds and I gave them that and I think the group was very effective, in part because of that," he says. "I think it helped that

I could reach out, that I had those skills of reaching out, nego-tiating, of understanding both sides, that I was successful in that role."

The second action Nick took was less conspicuous and was also common among fellow METCO students. Nick began talking "in a playful way" about racial differences and stereotypes to "lighten up the atmosphere, to break the ice." Nick recalls a fall evening when students on his dorm floor (Nick was one of two black students in the dorm) were trying to decide where to order take-out food. The choices were between a pizzeria, a fried chicken fast-food restaurant, or a Japanese noodle restaurant. Nick remembers saying, "My vote's for the Japanese place. I love sushi." One young woman, Nick remembers, said, "Really?" Nick replied, "Really."

> And then, I say, "Hah, I surprised you all, didn't I? You were all expecting a strong fried chicken push, weren't you?" And they all say in chorus, "No, no, no." Then I saw how defensive they were, and—I know it sounds like it's not much—this started, this discussion about Southern food and how those traditions carry on in African-American families, but that it doesn't mean I'm going out and eating ribs every night. And it turned into this great discussion, just about cultural attachments people get to their food. We even got into how confident we are about the way things are supposed to be cooked, you know, just because our mothers cooked that way. And you start to see how cultural things affect everyone, and this includes even people who don't think they have any culture [and] who say that they are American.

Nick's stories are typical of those of other former METCO students who greatly value their gracefulness and adeptness in dealing with difference. The post-METCO adults see this grace as a learned skill that places them in roles a few described as "a bridge." In the adult lives of former METCO students, bridging takes primarily two forms, one public and the other more personal. Publicly, many METCO graduates often act as bridges in the workplace. Many former students have jobs that require them to work within both predominantly black and predominantly white groups, for example, through social service agencies and foundations or as educators in diverse institutions, college recruiters, job counselors, or members of an elected official's staff. Or, if they work solely in predominantly white settings, colleagues and supervisors often look to these adults to be leaders in improving race relations and increasing racial diversity within the workplace.

Jane Staunton, who graduated in the 1980s, has a job that requires movement between white and black communities. Through her work, Jane meets frequently with state legislators, most of whom are white. But she also works directly with clients for a social service program, of whom disproportionate numbers are black. "It's back and forth, back and forth, [and] it's that back and forth that brings me back to METCO," she says. "You are not facing reality if you think you don't have to be articulate and dress well and be in touch with the attitudes of the legislators, be able to speak their language. But then, I think of some of those white girls in [the town where I attended school] and I try to imagine them trying to help some of our clients, and the idea of it is just too funny. I do feel like I have the upper hand."

This feeling of "having the upper hand" was echoed in various forms by many of the respondents, who, although they felt out of place, awkward, even less intellectually able than their white counterparts in their suburban METCO schools, quite often speculate that they are *better* prepared for post–high school life than their white suburban counterparts. After all, most of the past participants feel they can enter, move in, and succeed in both black and white environments—environments that remain separated for most people.

Those who practice this more public, formal form of bridging are more likely to have attended college. Most of them remember that race-related issues were discussed and debated regularly on campus. Race problems were not always resolved to these students' satisfaction. But such environments, especially when the students were involved in distinctly black organizations, provided black students with even more sustained practice in bridging black and white communities and in broaching and analyzing race-related matters.

A second form of bridging was practiced with equal frequency by the adults who attended college and by those who did not. These adults don't necessarily take on public bridging roles, but they challenge racial stereotypes and discrimination and try to make racial and cultural exchanges into enriching rather than threatening experiences. For Thomas Mitchell, who graduated in the early 1980s, this translates into "just joking. It seems like joking but it's an important thing." In his workplace, Thomas asks questions about Jewish holidays and recalls out loud the ways that some of his former suburban classmates celebrated those days. He also talks about how his religious celebrations differ from his colleagues'. And he talks about visits to mostly black dance clubs and parties, describing the atmosphere and urging white colleagues to join him. He recounts light-hearted exchanges such as this one:

> I tell one guy, "Joey, you need a little black in you." And he says, "Yeah, yeah, I know. I'm working on it." And I talk to this one Jewish guy all the time about his grandmother and he tells me that maybe I should come by to meet her, that she'll try to make me Jewish. And I tell stories about my family in the South and their history. And we were joking yesterday [with] this one guy [who] has relatives who live in a trailer park. I said, "Black folks don't live in trailer parks." And this turned

into a funny conversation, nothing serious, just questions about whether that's true and such and maybe if it
is, then why is it true? It's just an open atmosphere.

Nearly all of the many former students who adopt such
bridging roles say their METCO experiences helped them develop
such social skills. But the adults did not develop such grace
during their school years. In fact only a small share of adults say
they did. Rather, their early, sustained experience and their day-
to-day practice of bouncing between two worlds enabled them
gradually to navigate comfortably and competently in both arenas. Some students, whether they went to college or not, simply
found that, as incompetent and awkward as they might feel discussing race, they seemed to be miles ahead of almost everyone
else—whites as well as blacks. This realization gave many of
these adults the confidence and, as graduate Sheila Leonard calls
it, the ability to "step into the gap."

Sheila explains, "You are ahead of everyone else on this issue
[race] even though you feel confused inside about it. You're
forced in METCO to think stuff through. So you get out and end
up having to explain things because I didn't want to just let this
ignorance go on. You figure out how to handle stuff."

Sheila is a manager in a small business that "is becoming
more racially diverse each year." She recalls that tension built
up between black and white employees over a comment a white
employee made. The comment, Sheila explains, wasn't meant
to be hurtful, though she thinks it was misunderstood by some
black employees. Sheila, who had friends on both sides of
the dispute, found that "people who needed to cooperate so
we could do what we had to do weren't working together at all—
like not even speaking." And "people were just grumpy, people
who had been friendly. No one trusted the other side." "As
usual," Sheila says, she was "caught in the middle." And she
intervened.

It was something about the stupid O. J. [Simpson] thing, something about Johnny Cochran [Simpson's attorney] arguing that you can't tell whether a person is black from a voice over the phone, something related to that. Anyway, the comment that this person, the white person made, it was in reference to that, and [although it] wasn't meant as a negative racial comment, you could see how, being a black person, that you would take it in an offensive way. The blacks thought he was a racist. And the whites thought the blacks were making a big deal over nothing. And it took hours, over this stupid thing. But I did help them see each other's side a little, that you gotta go over to the other side a little, try to see their side. But it's like people can't even start, [one side says,] "You're a racist" and [the other side responds,] "No I'm not. You're an asshole." This is not getting us very far with that being an example of the best discussion people can have. Because of the METCO thing, I feel like I have to step into that gap a little.

After high school, Sheila said she was pleasantly surprised to find use for the navigation skills acquired from her unusual educational experience. She explains:

I just always felt different, weird in a way. And it was just not the way that many other kids went to school. And so, it turns out, what you think is so weird—you know, you have this experience most other people don't have— turns out that people want that skill. People don't know how to talk to each other, they are frightened of each other and so, that fact that I can do it, it's like: "Wow, you have excellent interpersonal skills!" It's scary how separate we are, and I don't know what'll come of it and I think it might be bad. I never really realized til' I got out [of METCO], I think, how separate everyone else is—

I mean how blacks are separate from whites and whites are separate from blacks. So, how are we expected to come together, to work together, really?

The ability to bridge has helped past participants in concrete ways. For some, it has led to leadership positions both in college organizations and, more informally, in the workplace. From the perspective of past participants, this skill also enhances their productivity at work and fosters comfortable working relationships with colleagues. Many post-METCO adults found their skills working in and communicating with people from diverse backgrounds to be in demand increasingly in the workplace.

Knowing What You Need to Know

When Dwight Stephens thinks of his suburban high school, one of the first things that comes to mind is that "people were on your back all the time" about deadlines and requirements for college. Dwight describes the incessant talk about deadlines, tests, and requirements as "being like the scenery out there." Important information—a key to gaining opportunity—came, Dwight remembers, from friends, sports teammates, teachers, posters, parents of acquaintances, in hallways, locker rooms, study halls, classrooms, official meetings, weekend sleepovers.

"It was just part of the scenery out there, like the trees. You see a tree? You see a poster about when you are supposed to take your SATs," Dwight recalls. "And then you're getting ready for a game and people are talking about it, it's what they talk about. It's one of the main topics of conversation, which then I found really pathetic. But you're swimming in it. Then you go back to Boston and it's tenth grade and your friends are saying, 'What's an SAT?' In tenth grade? Not knowing when the SATs are, what they are? That's sick."

There were two distinct channels of information, as these

adults remember them. The first type might best be described as "formal." This stream of information flowed primarily from representatives of the school or the suburban district. The information was conveyed at college fairs, schoolwide information sessions, METCO-organized college information sessions, college tours (usually organized by the central office of METCO in Boston), formal meetings with guidance counselors, teacher reminders, and prep courses offered at the school and advertised and promoted extensively in school.

The second information stream flowed from more informal sources, usually from within a social network of friends and acquaintances and from the general school environment. These included conversations with friends and their families, information received from METCO parents and fellow students, and, even, overheard conversations that were part of the ubiquitous talk about college and career goals. Generally, when the adults refer to information, this includes appropriate high school course selections for college preparation, SAT preparation and related deadlines, internship opportunities, college application and financial aid deadlines, and procedures and protocol for visiting colleges.

Former METCO students generally believe that attending a suburban school provided them with more information about academic opportunities than they would have received if they had remained in the city schools. As with other facets of school life, it is impossible to know whether this perception is accurate. However, ignoring it would mean discounting an important part of the post-METCO adults' educational experiences as they understand them. The adults' perceptions do grow out of significant bases of comparison. First, the men and women compare their knowledge about college and their planning efforts with those of friends and acquaintances who attended city schools. Second, adults who had at least some experience in the city schools prior to METCO recall that they were more likely to receive important information in suburbia, both formally, from the school, and informally, in an environment where talk about educational opportunity and aspirations is a staple of school culture.

For example, Kevin Tyler, in describing the formal sources of information in his suburban school, recalls, "I didn't even have to know what questions to ask," which, he adds, "was a good thing, because coming from a family with not a lot of experience in these things, I didn't know what to ask. I needed to be told from square one."

One might expect that in schools where many parents are steeped in college applications and selection processes, school personnel would see little need to inform students about such matters. But former METCO students suggest that this was not their experience. They recount numerous examples in which they were provided crucial information from counselors and teachers in plenty of time to meet deadlines. It is also true, however, that for several students, the METCO office served as a backup provider of information or check on mainstream channels of information. Arlene Staples' characterization of the "chain" of information in her suburban high school is typical of the way other METCO graduates perceive this information.

Arlene explains, "METCO's like the beginning of the chain. It gets you on the first step, it's up to you to climb the other steps." "It's like a boost up. You learn what you need to do, when you have to do it. It can be like a weapon, just these things that seem so basic—like, what's this requirement, what's that [one]? This is what you need to get onto the next level. People can take that for granted, and you do until you see other people who don't have a clue. You realize the boost up you got there."

Bethany Cross makes a similar observation:

> You get in and there's a constant going around of information about what you're supposed to be doing, exactly.
> I mean, exactly. And you don't really think about it too much; it's just the way it is in this place, the way that life

is there. And then you see [Boston city high school] kids who, are seventeen years old, and they don't have [this information], never get it, maybe there was an expectation that they couldn't use this information, and you think, "My word, what if I never learned these things?" These are small things to you when you're out there, because it's like the every day. But you wonder what would have happened if [you] didn't have that information at the beginning, how easily you miss these things. The way I see it, it's like putting your car on the right road for you. It's up to you to steer.

This continual flow of crucial information was especially helpful for students going to college directly after high school. But information was also important for young people who went on to work or a training program after high school, although several graduates said that information about work opportunities was more difficult to obtain. For example, Thomas Mitchell, who sought work after high school, said:

I'm glad I had that exposure, [but] it wasn't completely geared for me. There was focus on college and I wanted to work with my hands. I didn't feel they had that information right there, but they did get [the information]. It was like a snap of the fingers, and they did really do their best to set me up and it was, I guess, a combo, of me working through METCO counselors and the guidance counselors that I figured out what to do [after high school]. I was not academic, not into academics, but I was a good kid and I think they didn't want me just falling through the cracks, like I probably would have done in Boston.

Alicia Holmes, meanwhile, transferred to a suburban METCO school in ninth grade and said that all the talk about college and the "hoops you needed to be jumping through" were new to her when she reached suburbia. When Alicia began high school in her suburban town, she hadn't yet thought about college, though her mother had talked about it "in vague ways, like it was a dream." Alicia's mother wanted her daughter "to go to college and figured maybe METCO was the way."

Alicia said she was "shocked" that she was supposed to have taken certain classes in ninth grade so she would be "on the college track." Her counselor explained this but didn't encourage her to sign up for these courses. It was pressure from other students and the feeling "that I wasn't doing what you were supposed to be doing, what everyone else was doing," that made Alicia reevaluate her original course selections and switch to more advanced math and English offerings. Alicia did attend a four-year college, following two years of "straight A's" at a local community college, and she may attend graduate school to become either a social worker or teacher at an inner city school, where she hopes to "hook kids up the same way I was."

"You get this panicked feeling [when] people start saying to you, 'You gotta take this for college.' I thought I wouldn't be worrying about that til' senior year. In Boston, going to college just wasn't in your face all the time," Alicia recalls. "There were [some] kids who went to college, but in [my METCO school town] it was in your face, just a different environment. Everyone was going to college, it was weird if you didn't. Where I came from, you could go either way."

Despite the fact that Alicia is thankful for METCO in that it "got me into this environment where achievement is just what you do," she also describes a commonly described contradiction. Many former METCO students, mostly those who struggled academically, felt that white guidance counselors had low expectations for them. Nevertheless, peer pressure and even casual conversation in a competitive academic environment often led the students to get needed information about courses, financial aid, and entrance exams to prepare for higher education. Alicia recalls:

> On the one hand, it felt like [the counselors and teachers] didn't expect a lot from METCO kids, but on the other hand, it wasn't right or something if you didn't know about this stuff. Someone was banging it into you. You couldn't get away from it. You say, "Well, I'm not so sure I wanna go to college." [They say]: "Whoa! What?" Not the counselors so much, because I felt [that] they don't think I can go to college anyway, and my grades didn't always show off my brains. I'm talking more about the other kids who thought you were some kind of strange person not wanting to go to college.

Marquise Bell also remembers "being completely ignorant, still, in ninth grade," that he had to "take a test" to qualify for college.

> I get there and these white kids are talking about the SAT like it's something they've known about forever, like they learned about this in kindergarten or something. And people are taking these prep courses? I'm thinking, prep courses, for one test? And the METCO counselor tells me, "Damn right. I signed you up." I just remember feeling like I was just a person standing there while they guided me here and there: "Here's one requirement. Here's another. Do it. Okay, now. Do another one. Okay? Here's this form. Fill it out. Okay, get your mother to sign here." And then they're on you: "Where's the form? What do you mean you lost it?" Stuff like that. And you get the hang of it and it's cool, because now, I pass that stuff on, you know, to other kids in the neighborhood. I check with them and with my nieces [saying,] "Stay on top of this shit." And I'm talk-

ing to my sister, telling her, "You gotta get her into a prep class for the SATs." And my sister is saying, "Yeah, yeah, whatever." And I tell her where to call and just that reminder, you know, like I got [when I was in high school], it gets her paying attention and [now] they're signed up [for the preparatory courses].

Social networks usually worked as secondary sources of knowledge but were terribly important when students either hadn't received adequate or timely information from the more official institutional sources or had forgotten the information. Samuel Dean, who attended Boston schools until he began high school at a suburban METCO school, said that it wasn't until he came to suburbia that he learned about the entrance requirements for college. Samuel credits friends (mostly a fellow METCO student) for reminding him of requirements and deadlines.

"It's weird, I think, for me to have five older brothers [who did not attend METCO] and not know about the SATs until I get out to [the METCO school], there's something really wrong," Samuel says. "Mike would help me out, Mike and his Mom let us know when things had to be done, and if we had questions, we knew we could call over there."

The Power of Association

Sandra Robertson graduated in the early 1980s from a suburban high school in an affluent town west of Boston. She recalls being forced to attend METCO by her parents and speculates that she might very well have received a higher quality education had she enrolled in an advanced placement program in the city schools. Nevertheless, she has had clear practical advantages stemming from her attendance at a prestigious suburban school, even while she realizes that prestige may not accurately reflect educational quality.

"Truthfully, I'm not so sure I did get a better education," Sandra says. "But other people think I did and that matters. It's right there on my resume and people say, 'Oh you went to [that] high school? Oh, really? Great. Great.' So, if I went to South Boston High, you think anyone would be saying that? No. The way I look at it, there's more of a chance that people who are in a position to get me jobs are familiar with [my] high school. Or, maybe I should say, they are familiar with the good reputation of the high school. So, yeah. It makes a difference."

Many of the former METCO students share Sandra's perception that mere association with a prestigious suburban school has helped them win opportunities and improve their chances for success. The adults recall most commonly dropping the name of their suburban high school during interviews at college admission offices and with prospective employers. On résumés, the adults highlighted their METCO participation, even long after high school ended. The former students often recall, as Michelle Parker does, the interviewers' "faces lighting up," or as Shirley Rogers characterizes it: "a shift in their mood, it's like all of a sudden, you are one of the gang. They think they know where you're coming from." During one job interview, Sheila Leonard even reminisced about familiar suburban landmarks with an interviewer who grew up near the town where Sheila had gone to school.

It sounds nuts, I know. But there was this rapport. Like, "Yeah, sure. I know where that ice-cream place is. You hung out there? I've been there." I'd say stuff to break the ice, like, "Maybe we were there at the same time. I stood out. I was the only black face there, or whatever." And we'd talk about fields, sports fields and some things that were in common. And there was a very strong, sort of immediate rapport that developed. It's like we were from the same generation, she and I. But that wouldn't have mattered, you know, that ability to talk things up, to schmooze around about common things I wouldn't have had [if not for METCO]. And you know, she was impressed with the fact that I came from her world, like I could graduate from that high school, hang out, and do things she had done and go on from the suburbs, survive fine and do well. The high school name [was] something that stood out [on my résumé]. She noticed that and it did, I think, get her to see me in a good light and then, I could take it from there on my own.

Michelle Parker used to "think sometimes about just leaving METCO." But in later years, she, like so many others, began to see years that had been "hardly all positives" begin to "pay off." She recalls visits to admissions offices at some competitive colleges in New England:

It was like their eyes brightened up, their faces were all lighting up when they saw the transcript. And they smiled and nodded and said, "So, you're graduating from [that high school]? I hear that's a great school." And then, they'll go into talking about their friends and this and that—who went there or who had boyfriends at my high school. And they always say things like, "We've had success with students from [your school]." And if I had gone to Dorchester High or someplace, I know I would not be having this conversation. I felt like they were [saying] something that was not explicit. But it was still really clear anyway: it's like saying, "Okay, you're accepted as a member of this club."

Michelle earned good grades in high school and was often angered by what she felt were white suburban teachers' low expectations of her intellectual abilities. But like many other METCO graduates, she said she is not resentful that the mere mention of her suburban high school wins her recognition and perhaps even special opportunity.

"Did it make me angry? No," Michelle insists. "I guess you could complain [that] they weren't really seeing me as a person and only seeing this institution on the paper. But it was more like the whole point of METCO was kind of made clear to me once I started going around and talking to these [admissions] people. Before I didn't know really if I was going to get anything out of what was day to day like a kind of torture. What would have made me mad was if they didn't notice where I went. It was like a payoff."

Kevin Tyler, who says his METCO years were "a mix of good and bad; I have to say I'm glad it's over," often wanted to "just get out of there," as a teenager in suburban schools. Some nights, Kevin recalls, "I just went home hating the place, feeling very angry about the advantages those [suburban students] had." But soon after high school, Kevin began to see "results—concrete reasons for having gone there that I didn't see before."

Kevin's anecdotes are strikingly similar to those of other past METCO participants who found people in the real world impressed by educational credentials from suburban schools. Like many others, he first realized the power of suburban association in a college admissions office. Kevin recalls his visit to the college that is now his alma mater.

I was very conscious during that time of being black, like, "Don't look at me the wrong way, okay, or you're going to pay." That sort of thing. No fighting or physical aspects to it, just an attitude, and it didn't take me much to mouth off. So, I was ready to be treated in a certain way. I was looking for evidence that they were going to be discriminatory. And my father's saying, "Stay cool. Stay cool." And I go in, and they ask me to talk about my high school, and it doesn't say METCO on the transcript, I don't know, in my years it didn't. So I didn't explain the program, really. I just talked about the school and the rigors and such and this person was very impressed. And he said that he had relatives who were moving to [that suburban community] because of the schools. And so, me and my Dad, we talked to him a lot about the schools and what we thought was good about them and he asked if it was okay for him to share it with his cousin and we said, "Yeah. Sure. Here, take our number." He didn't, but it was [something in] common, like, you understand the positive reputation of a place, you ask about it, it's in your world.

Years later, after gaining admission to this college, Kevin wanted to enroll in an honors program there. The admissions process to the program required an interview with an academic dean. Again, Kevin believes the reputation of his competitive high school, while surely not the sole factor winning him admission, seemed to please the interviewer and make "the process go more smoothly."

The guy was really impressed with this. He said, "This system has a national reputation." And [he looked] at this history course that I took, I was really into history at that time and I wanted to major in it. And it was a special kind of honors history course that was offered at [my] high school, and I got an A in it. So he was asking me about my experience as a METCO student too, and my experience in this school and was impressed with how well I did in this school in particular. And it was a bigger deal, I think, doing well in the school where I went than if I had done well [in a city high school] where I would have had to go if I didn't do METCO. My grades were okay. Not great. But it was the school that got him impressed. And at the end of the interview this dean told me he'd advocate for me, make sure I got a good chance on things. And I did get into the program, and it's not that that's the only reason I got in, but [attending that high school] always worked as a little benefit, an added little thing.

If the post-METCO adults remained in the Boston area, for either college or work, they often continued to bring up the name of their high school intentionally when talking with professors and instructors, when meeting new clients on the job, and in discussions with supervisors and colleagues. To past participants, the purpose of this name-dropping was usually to impress whomever they were talking with, especially if this person had opportunities to offer. As one respondent put it, "it opened up doors pretty wide for you." Several adults said they dropped the name of their high school not only to impress, but also to "surprise" the whites they were talking with. As Kim Peters, who graduated in the 1970s, explains, name-dropping, in addition to helping her win opportunity, "also shocks some of them, because a lot of people, they see black skin, brown skin, tan skin, they think, 'She's never been out of Roxbury.'" The former METCO students acknowledge that their association with a prestigious suburban school might not be the only or even a deciding factor that has won them opportunity. But name-dropping will, as graduate Thomas Mitchell sees it, "put you in their world in a more definite way. You can start to see them seeing you as one of them."

"White People's Affirmative Action"

One of the most powerful theories that speaks to the potential for racially integrated schooling goes like this: In American society, middle-class whites, because of historical advantages, are, on average, better connected than blacks to job and educational opportunities. Then, when whites associate with each other they connect one another informally to opportunity, through social networks that include powerful people in positions to grant opportunity. This association thus enhances whites' chances for learning about job openings and getting hired. This unseen structure of opportunity includes word-of-mouth information about job opportunities and personal connections that might give a job candidate special consideration. Thus, racially integrated social institutions might level the playing field in this regard.

Some former METCO students would probably say this theory is correct, though they would offer some important caveats. They report using the interpersonal connections and relationships they formed during METCO to get opportunities. There are several dozen clear examples of making use of such connections. But interestingly, the black students and their families far more commonly made connections with other blacks associated with the METCO program, rather than with suburban whites. These included connections made with METCO directors who worked at suburban schools and connections made with black staff members at METCO's central office in Boston. But most powerful and common were connections made to mothers, fathers, and, in some cases, older siblings of other METCO students. These are the networks that regularly connected students to job, internship, and college opportunities.

As Nick Marshall recalls:

> I would say there was a network there, sure, but it was the METCO network helping each other get hooked up to stuff and stay on top of what kinds of opportunities, scholarships, and what have you. There were the phone calls back and forth between all our mothers, talking about colleges and what colleges were good and places where admissions offices had people of color who were willing to help out African-American students and who

could answer questions that young African-American students might have. And there were the carpools and such to go check these places out. And my mother knew a lot about camps, educational-related camps that were good for keeping up the academics during the summer. She knew people who worked and she helped get kids in and there were things at these places you learned about, like [camp] counseling jobs, other businesses and such where you could get in and they'd set you up with things that related to your interest, different opportunities for African-American youth that a lot of us got into.

And many former METCO students recall that there was a kind of safety net, with METCO parents watching out for each other's children to ensure that the students knew about various opportunities. For example, some parents had more information about college than others, Jeremy Shepard recalls, while other parents knew about scholarships and loans. Jeremy describes the sharing as "straight out." "Somebody knew something? They were going to pass it on."

"My mother didn't go to college and my father started but quit for money reasons and so this was foreign to them, all the different requirements," Jeremy recalls. "But other parents really made sure we checked out all our options and knew about money sources."

Cherisse Clarkson remembers most clearly a black METCO administrator who "went totally out of his way for me."

My family was supportive of our education but it wasn't like they knew exactly the right things to do all of the time, do you know what I mean? My mother was always on us, telling us to do our work, using threats to get us to do it and things. But this particular man knew exactly what to say that would keep me working. He was always getting me into projects and programs to help me just get more out of things and so I got into different programs that got me thinking about reading and writing and what I wanted to do. And he seemed to know everyone somehow and so I could rely on him for passing on a good word to people about me. People around really trusted him so, you look at it now and you think, "He led to this, which led me to that, which put me in a certain state of mind about my education and my brains and what I was capable of," and you realize this was an important contact in my life.

There are also many anecdotes in which black students made connections with powerful whites and were provided opportunities as a result. These stories often involve host families or parents of good suburban friends. For example, Sheila Leonard won a coveted internship position in the business office where her host mother worked. And in the summer before his senior year of college, Cliff Porter worked in the financial office of a public relations firm where the father of a suburban school friend worked as a high-level executive. From there, Cliff made connections through which he learned of available jobs in finance-related areas. A suburban white family used their connections to help get graduate Nathan King scholarship money. Mara Taggart's host mother, with extensive contacts in the legal community, helped get Mara paid summer jobs at law firms, where Mara made her own contacts who led her to other jobs after college graduation.

Mara remembers that she "had to take a year off [from college], somewhere in there, I don't remember what year. But I knew I'd just call [my host mother] and she'd be there, working the phones for me. I called one day, told her I needed to make money. Two days later? I've got an interview. A week later, I've got a job."

It was common for young people, long after METCO ended, to

begin to understand that part of METCO's function was, as, Shirley Rogers describes it, "to put me in the white world, into this place where the power was." Much as the students in chapter 3 recall analyzing the intersection of race and class in society, the adults began to see, with sharp clarity, that a social network that includes some whites is necessary because whites are generally better connected to power in society. This was especially true for students who went to college and then got professional or semi-professional jobs. They developed a keen sense of the need to develop professional networks that include some whites. This is true even of the past participants whose close friends and social groups outside of work include only blacks.

As graduate Trevor Baron explains, he realized "who you know" can be the key to acquiring success and winning opportunities on the job.

"When you get into these circles, you start to see it, how people fill each other in about opportunities, about jobs, new openings, different things," Trevor says. "And one phone call can make a difference for you when you apply for a job. And you start to say, 'Hmm, okay. This is how it works inside here.' It's who you know. And this is how I look at it now: Networking? Networking is white people's affirmative action."

In much the same way that former METCO students perceive the program helped them become comfortable in white-dominated groups, they also believe that METCO enabled them to develop networking skills—skills that require a prerequisite confidence within white settings. As Cliff Porter, a former financial advisor now pursuing graduate studies, describes it, "It's an air you put on when you network, just this air that shows you assuming that you're in this circle now. And you gotta learn this, you pick it up over time. You can't be this hesitating black guy begging around for crumbs. I play golf; sometimes I play with an all-black professional crowd, these are more people who are my friends, and sometimes I play with a white professional crowd, friends of friends, people I work with. And with the whites, you wouldn't believe the contacts, the phone numbers that get passed around and how many clients you can pick up this way."

Despite METCO's perceived role in helping its students develop skills for networking within powerful white circles, the participants did not commonly form networks of powerful whites while they were in METCO. Rather, it usually was not until after high school that the students, looking back upon the utility of their METCO days, understood the value of such networks. Skills and confidence learned in METCO did indeed help these students form and maintain their networks. But contacts usually included people the adults met in post–high school workplaces and learning institutions.

METCO's Interventions

Most of the former METCO students believe that the program gave them access to powerful educational institutions that helped them gain opportunities in their adult lives. The power of the suburban school wasn't merely that it had a more advanced curriculum and more demanding teachers. Nor was entry to suburbia powerful only because it got black students personally accustomed to life in a white-dominated world. From the perspective of these adults, METCO's power also came from its ability to intervene in a structure of opportunity that would normally provide advantages only to suburban students, most of them white. Once they finished high school and moved on to college and careers, the former METCO students capitalized on the prestige their suburban schools had in the real world. While it does appear that the students gained some opportunities from connections and social networks they developed in METCO, those networks were not predominantly white. Still, it's likely that the METCO program itself, by bringing together determined black parents with ambitions for their children, forms a powerful network whose members assist each other. Likewise, the institutionalized METCO program and its mostly black staff was an obvious network of information and connection to opportunity.

Adults do recall getting important information about higher education from the adults in their school who had the explicit responsibility of providing that information. But it also came in casual, even unobserved ways, through conversations, including those overheard by METCO students. To many former METCO students, such information seemed to permeate the environment of the suburban schools, reaching METCO students even when they weren't sure themselves about whether they needed or wanted the information.

For the vast majority of the adults, METCO is one important and lasting influence that helped them achieve whatever success, peace of mind, and interpersonal skills they have in their lives. But of course METCO alone was never the only factor—and hardly ever the primary factor—influencing the direction and content of their adult lives. After all, METCO couldn't alone provide benefits if students didn't do their parts. They needed to work for good grades and, after high school, get the money and make the connections they needed to take advantage of the opportunities they wanted. And most important, METCO's past participants point out that the program wouldn't have had a chance to benefit them at all had their parents not been supportive of the program and, in many cases, forced them to stick with it.

It is quite common for former METCO students to say things such as: "If it weren't for METCO, I wouldn't have gone to college," or, "If it weren't for METCO, I'd never be able to work here." But as the conversation goes on, the adults usually give first credit to their supportive parents for allowing them to take advantage of the METCO program. Even acknowledging the crucial role parents play, the post-METCO adults still point to benefits and experiences that their parents could not have provided on their own—practiced interaction across the racial divide, exposure to an unfamiliar culture, and daily immersion in a competitive academic environment. These are gains they attribute directly to the difficult experience of being black city children in white suburban schools.

But some of those characteristics that adults today count as METCO's positive attributes have negative sides to them. For example, as former students talk positively about their roles as bridges between seemingly separate black and white worlds, some feel burdened and exhausted by such roles. The following chapter weighs the post-METCO adults' perceptions of the positive long-term benefits against their perceptions of the program's longer-term negative aspects.

5

The Resolutions

The Costs and Confusion of
Suburban Schooling and Making Up
for What Was Lost

The young black students in METCO learned to survive simultaneously in black and white worlds, but they often felt fully accepted in neither. Many of the former students who believe that living in both white and black worlds paid off over the long term nevertheless associate confusion, longing for a sense of community, and loneliness with their schooling in white suburbia.

Adults recall these feelings vividly because much of the alienation and searching they link to METCO experiences get re-ignited during ordinary life in white-dominated America. The painful searches for belonging that began in METCO didn't cease when the program ended. The resolution of these conflicts continues years, even decades, after their bus trips through the invisible but tall barrier dividing black and white communities.

While this chapter focuses principally on the longer-term negative aspects of the METCO experience, it examines not simply loss and confusion, but also the processes of resolution and change adults experienced after high school. By understanding these processes—which include identity development and reconnection to community—one appreciates the complexities, even the seeming contradictions inherent in the METCO experience. The negative aspects, such as alienation and confusion over identity, were quite often transient and resolved to good effect in later years. There is far more hopefulness in these stories than feelings of victimization and sadness.

Some of the adults place partial blame on METCO for their alienation from old friendships, from some family members, from black culture and history, and from predominantly black communities where they grew up. From the adults' perspectives, their suburban school days did intensify or otherwise affect their sense of themselves and contributed to their later reconnection with what was lost during the METCO years.

Even some of the adults who today credit METCO with providing priceless skills still feel lingering ambivalence about their early immersion in white suburbia as they question whether they missed out on a valuable experience by not attending predominantly black high schools or colleges. Some of the adults who believe METCO enabled them in later years to communicate across a racial divide feel exhausted from repeatedly employing this skill, which few other whites or blacks seem to have. Finally, there is a disappointment among many of the post-METCO adults who discovered that, although they had learned rules of the so-called white world, they were still often judged and categorized by the color of their skin.

Do I Still Belong Here?

Life is going pretty well for METCO graduate John Johns, and he appreciates it. He's got a good job, a loving fiancée who shares his passion for folk art and jogging, a circle of close friends, both black and white, and a condominium in a racially diverse neighborhood full of working professionals in Boston.

"Sometimes, I feel I am just skating through my life; it is almost too perfect. I need to pinch myself," John declares over coffee in an upscale café near his home. John is proud of his life, but "in a strange way," he explains, "I don't feel right bringing this back home all the time." There are "certain times," John says, that he feels a familiar kind of "kick in the stomach."

"It's a feeling of discomfort kind of laid over right on top of all that stuff that feels so natural," John says. "Like, I belong here, yes, but I am different. And METCO starts you off on that stuff. I mean, it's not like I'm not used to it. That is one of the difficult things I would say that comes from that; it is this feeling like you can't just completely step back into this life. You've had more opportunities and that's a good thing, but something for me is gone and you can look at your life and see all the good of it but then, I tell you, it's like a kick in the stomach. Like, boom. Telling you, 'Remember where you come from, son.' "

John's story of intrusive discomfort resurfacing in an otherwise good life is a common one for many past METCO participants who feel uneasy and a sad alienation among old friends and acquaintances and certain all-black groups. It has been years—in some cases, decades—since these adults struggled with the challenges of living in two worlds. So how is it they can so certainly ascribe their adult alienation to suburban school experiences?

Adults generally associate these alienated feelings with their previous METCO experiences in two important ways. A large group of post-METCO adults say they remain overly sensitive to feelings of alienation precisely because these adult experiences evoke memories of feelings they had in suburban schools. Second, the adults commonly view METCO as at least the symbolic beginning of their journey into a white world that made them confront feelings of separation and address questions about where they belong. If not for METCO, then, they might have altogether avoided deep immersion in the white world—an immersion that evoked identity conflicts and forced them to struggle with questions about the role of race in their lives and in society.

Three different forms of alienation, experienced in varying degrees of intensity, remained salient in the adult lives of former METCO students. The first is alienation from relationships that are or had been sources of comfort and belonging. The other two are alienation from community and from a common black history or culture.

Withered Relationships

Post-METCO adults often tell histories of damaged relationships with old neighborhood friends. The adults offer dozens of similar stories about friendships with black friends that faded or ended during school-age years. Some managed to hang on to one or two of these old friendships, but by middle school and high school, their interests usually diverged from their friends', and the lack of daily shared experiences put distance between them. Such shifting friendship patterns may, in fact, be universal but for the young black students, the loss of friends often was tangled with deeper questions about belonging and racial authenticity. Indeed, today, post-METCO adults look back upon the familiar taunts of "white boy" or "white girl" as symptomatic of the increasing disconnection between METCO students and their neighborhood acquaintances.

Bruce Paynter reconsiders the once-"devastating" taunts from neighborhood friends and finds that, these days, more than a decade after graduating, he can analyze the teasing with dispassion.

> Back then I would never have thought about this in any kind of analyzing way. But I can now see that it's like,

"Shit, he's not really part of the scene anymore. There's something a little different about him." I'm talking now about the Roxbury kid looking at the METCO kid. And he's feeling probably a little afraid, kind of threatened by the METCO kid. And so, it's this distance that starts up because you're not spending all day with [the black young people in the neighborhood], and so those changes are probably threatening to those kids who see them happening to their friends, they see people slipping away, and so they punished them for it.

A small group of post-METCO adults—fewer than a dozen—report no changes in the character of their neighborhood friendships over time. Most, though not all, of these adults attended METCO schools relatively close to Boston. Today they recall that their friends and their friends' families supported them, even when these old neighborhood friends didn't attend college. For example, some former neighbors sent book money to one teenager's college campus, and some former METCO students got frequent encouraging phone calls at college from old neighborhood friends and their families. But these were exceptions. Usually, friendships ended. And adults see meaning in these losses, viewing the broken bonds as symbolic of their early disconnection from a community and a way of life. No one reported longing to reconnect with specific old neighborhood friends. But many either long to or have rebuilt relationships specifically with other blacks so they may reestablish the safety and enjoyment provided by earlier neighborhood friendships.

Alienation between family members, while rare, was particularly painful over the long term. Post-METCO adults usually view the withering of such relationships as consequences of their own personal progress—progress that other family members could not experience. Following high school, the adults tried, and frequently still try, to maintain or rebuild their weakened family relationships. Alienation from family members most often occurred between extended family members, including cousins with whom a young person had been quite close, or other close friends of parents whom the student had considered family and, in some cases, even called "uncle" or "aunt."

April Patterson, for example, who graduated in the 1980s, still longs to have "an easier time" with some members of her family, mostly cousins and two siblings who did not attend METCO. As she first did in METCO, April now moves between a well-educated, largely professional, predominantly white world where she found career success, and a "close-knit," all-black family life in the neighborhood where she grew up. April recalls a holiday visit back "home" that characterizes the internal struggle typical of past METCO participants who still find themselves moving between two worlds.

> I'm tired, I step off the plane, finally hail a cab, and I am on my way home, or so I think. I'm coming from my job, where I'm around white people, only white people, all the time. And, not that that's an all bad thing, but I was looking forward to getting back where I really felt like I belonged and I guess I had this visit all up in my mind.
>
> And I get there, and I'm looking good, right? And it's not like people aren't happy to see me, but it's all my cousins talking about stuff they'd done together and my brothers and my sister talking about people they know. And I feel a type of comfort, but I'm out of place. You know, I'm treated warmly, my family, all of us, we are very warm people, a lot of hugs all the time. But it's coming back to me, the memories of trying to step back in at the end of the week at METCO. [It's] like, "Here I am, take me back now." And all during it and after I left, it was just this kind of sad thing and I find I'm looking forward to getting back to my other life. And I'm really

confused at that point, because at my job, I'm counting the days I can come back to [Boston]. So, it's strange. Really, I would cry about it, too. I mean, really cry.

Among the adults I spoke to, none felt alienated from parents, and perhaps this is because mothers and fathers had clear goals of social mobility for their children and even initiated contact with METCO. Likewise, METCO students were less likely to feel alienated from siblings than from cousins, aunts, uncles, and close family friends. In the several cases in which adults believed that sibling relationships withered because of METCO, the students' brothers and sisters either did not attend the program or dropped out. The adults' relationships with non-METCO siblings did, generally, become close again over the long term. But these respondents say that because they were more focused on college and later on professional careers, bonds between brothers and sisters weakened at least temporarily. In this case, then, the former students don't view METCO as the direct cause of weakened relationships. More exactly, they see METCO as a catalyst for new goals and priorities. The new goals and priorities, then, weakened the relationships.

In the METCO years, feelings of not belonging came out intensely at large family gatherings and in encounters on city sidewalks, apartment building steps, basketball courts, and homes of neighborhood friends. The vast majority of the adults I talked with report post–high school feelings of "being out of place," "not fitting in," "not feeling like I could be myself," "being afraid of sounding different," "[not] really able to go with the flow of what was happening," and "feeling separate from my body, almost feeling like I wasn't there." The examples below show the range of intensity with which adults experience such alienation and confusion. While some adults experienced intrusive physical symptoms of anxiety and depression, others felt mildly annoying awkwardness and uncharacteristic timidity.

Following a college graduation ceremony at which "my aunts, uncles, cousins, everyone, was incredibly proud—you could tell by reading their faces it was genuine," Mary Carson nevertheless remembers "feeling left out and very, very depressed." She was the only one in the family who had attended college. Two of her brothers were in college at the time and though most of her cousins, like her parents, aunts, and uncles did not attend college, "everyone read in those households and encouraged me and wanted me to succeed." Even so, Mary recalls:

> It was horrible. Like I just saw this world as not really mine even though the closeness was there. It wasn't the education thing, it was more like in their responses when I said I wanted to travel here or there and they're like, "I wouldn't go there." You know, assuming that everywhere I'd go—I don't even remember where I said—I'm going to get beat up because of my skin color? And I'd mention friends, you know, white friends, and it was dismissed or ignored. There was this unsaid kind of disapproval that I felt for that [having white friends]. After that I sunk into a big depression and I was really almost physically sick over it for a while.
>
> I did talk with a counselor. An African-American counselor, a woman, in fact, and she did help me see it does go back to METCO. Like you feel pushed to succeed in this world and then, it's kind of, "Who are you when you do [succeed]?" And so I'm still dealing with it I guess. But a lot less than I used to, I think.

Marquise Bell also had "some feelings of not belonging" that surfaced "during times when it was supposed to be celebration[s]. Everyone was together, having fun, and I couldn't relax." Marquise explains that he "felt out of my element." But, over time, he says, "I learned to hang back and enjoy what's there, and so, just now there are little feelings of being awkward, like in these relationships with people who are my family, you know, a lot of these relationships that used to be easy, you know, sort of second nature? They got to be more difficult all of a sudden."

It wasn't only changing relationships that made many of these adults feel lonely. Adults also associate METCO with their long-standing feelings of being separated from a community of other blacks.

Community Rediscovered

In the eyes of many adults, a second type of alienation stemmed at least in small part from childhood disconnection from predominantly black communities. This group, about four dozen, recalls that for just a few years after METCO, they longed to create or to reconnect to a predominantly black community. Generally speaking, these adults viewed "community" as a physical place—a center of activity where other blacks made decisions together, helped each other, enjoyed each other's company. More than half of the adults recall that, as young people, they participated in METCO while managing to stay involved with black communities. These attachments quite commonly involved the church, or all-black weekend and summer youth activities, often focused on the arts. A second, smaller group, less than one-quarter of those interviewed, said they had witnessed such community arrangements in their neighborhoods and churches and felt disconnected from them because METCO had displaced them physically and took up their time. A third group, however—just a bit larger than the second—never did experience such community life while growing up. Regardless of METCO, these adults recall their neighborhoods as fragmented—streets and buildings populated with people not joined by common goals, lifestyles, or social activities. Even the former METCO students who fit into this category nevertheless recall a post-METCO longing for an ideal community where other blacks would come together to work and enjoy one another.

As Bruce Paynter, who graduated in the 1980s, says, "It's not like I saw other black people doing this and thought, 'Damn! I'm missing out on this. That damn METCO's makin' me miss this.' That's not what it was. This was an ideal kind of thing I had in my head, like I had this idea of black people sitting around holding meetings and doing things for themselves and it was like, for me, going to METCO made me want it even more than I normally would have. It was just this need to bond to people with a common something. It was always a need I felt in a very, very strong manner. I did always feel that there was this hole there without it."

Most METCO students still occasionally feel out of place in some all-black settings. Notably, such awkwardness is most commonly felt by those who graduated college and perceive themselves as members of the middle class, but whose parents have more modest incomes and less-prestigious jobs and did not attend college. Nearly always, the post-METCO adults' feelings of awkwardness manifest themselves during social encounters with blacks who are working class, who did not attend college, or who are poor. This discomfort, then, does not appear to be related to race and culture alone, though it is described that way initially. These feelings seem to be more directly related to class mobility than to any shift in racial identity. These men and women usually don't identify their discomfort as based on class or education level until they acknowledge that their primary social group is either all black or nearly all black, and that they generally prefer the company of other blacks to the company of whites.

For example, Mara Taggart, most of whose closest friends are black and who by choice spends most of her social time in all-black-settings, describes her feelings of being "unconnected" and "apart" from certain types of all-black environments.

I would have to say that there is one thing that makes me very sad and feel very guilty even to this day. And it is coming from METCO, I think, because it has been going on since then. And that's that I just can't fit in all the time when I am in a place with all other blacks, in all-black communities like Roxbury or parts of Dorchester. This is in certain places. It's like I feel almost ashamed for who I am, like I don't really belong here anymore. It's like feeling you are totally unconnected and apart from these places. It's when I'm around people [who] aren't my friends or anything, just people talking to you, even in a store. They assume I'm just like them, and I feel a lot different and I look like they do but I'm sticking out. I'm fooling all of them and then comes the guilt thing.

But once Mara acknowledges that she essentially does have her own all-black community, she considers that her awkwardness may not be related only to race.

It is true that I hang with my friends, with my black friends. And I do have white friends, it's just that, the getting to know part, I wonder if it takes a little longer. In some instances it does. But I would say for the most part, I have black friends and we do okay. We do black kinds of things. Is this a racist comment? I don't know. But we mostly do things, go to parties, clubs, whatever, where there are other black people.

But it is different I guess because of the interests, like maybe I feel guilty because from a money stand-point? Being a single woman? Educated? I'm not hurting for money and so neither, really, are my friends. We are all in this same kind of situation, economically and educationally we've been exposed to certain things educationally. And that is important to me in my friends, and we share this. We can travel together, share that and talk about this book, that book, or really do a lot of cultural things. And it's just a weird feeling to go back to where you're from and see, okay, I've grown, but I don't want to be thinking I'm better than these folks, and you worry people are thinking that you think you're better. Because that's what you always heard in METCO. And so maybe this isn't a black thing so much.

As revealed in chapter 2, some METCO students did develop negative feelings about their communities during their school years. These negative feelings usually stemmed from comparisons of community conditions—the poor city roads compared with well-paved suburbia or unemployment in the city compared to the seemingly well-heeled, gainfully employed wealthy parents of suburbia. Jackson Xavier, who lives in a racially diverse section of Boston, for example, said he often made comparisons between the physical conditions of his urban neighborhood and his suburban school community. He explains that his initial impressions changed over time.

"You think this way when you are young," Jackson says. "Why is everything such a mess here? Everything, all your questions are very simple. There aren't any gray areas. So what you're thinking as a young person isn't a permanent state of mind. You adjust that as you learn more, you read more and think more." As Jackson says, he adjusted his attitudes as time went on. This is certainly true of the past METCO participants who recall such sentiments and who, in so many cases, are both living in and deeply committed to all-black communities and neighborhoods. But for some—just less than a quarter of the respondents—guilt about old opinions lingers and exacerbates feelings of alienation from the once-familiar.

For example, even though Paul Hammond today has a strong sense of "being firmly committed to a black community," he nevertheless feels "haunted sometimes by how I remember feeling when I was younger, just that feeling like I was better than this place, that I was going to escape it because it wasn't good enough and it wasn't like the stuff I was seeing where I went to school."

Similarly, Cherisse Clarkson, who is heavily involved in her black church and who sits on the board of directors in her predominantly black housing development, imagines she will "always be living among black people." She adds, "Being surrounded by that culture and immediate understanding grounds me as a human being."

Despite her commitments, Cherisse harbors guilt about long-gone fantasies that her family would move to the wealthy suburban community where she went to school. "A big yellow house, I remember, is what I wanted. In [my METCO town]. This was what I thought would make me happy. To get out of Boston. I think part of that was a kind of racism, you know. This feeling like white people have a better way of life, which isn't true, which I realized when I grew up."

Quests for Culture and Common History

A third form of alienation relates to history and culture. It is common for the former METCO students to suspect that they were deprived of learning about black culture and black contributions to history in their all-white schools. Many feel that because they went to nearly all-white schools, they never had the chance to develop an interest in these subjects. Jackson Xavier, for example, recalls good and bad parts of his METCO experience. But the "most damaging" longer-term negative effect, Jackson says, is "the fact that I never learned my history. I had to make up for that later, and if you don't know your black history, you are missing knowledge about yourself."

Jackson's comments are similar to those of most interviewees (more than two-thirds) who complain that the suburban schools did not offer comprehensive black history or even discussions of black contributions to American culture. Post-METCO adults commonly describe a cluster of feelings: "disconnectedness," "being lost," and "out of touch," which emerged from "complete ignorance about the history of blacks," of "knowing nothing about the history of black people in America, other than what my parents told us," and of "being left out of the story," and "missing the story that connects all of us." This cluster of reactions was discussed most by college-going METCO graduates, though a few who did not attend college report similar feelings. For example, Thomas Mitchell, who did not attend college, was "frustrated, even as a little child," that discussion of black achievement and history was so limited in his white, affluent suburban school.

"You know, they do the slavery thing: 'Oh, bad. Bad, that was very bad, children. Slavery was bad,'" Thomas recalls. "Okay, so then you might do a little Frederick Douglas, but no civil rights movement, no art, no Malcolm [X]. And there was Dr. King thrown in there, here and there. And there were posters of him. But I had to ask my girlfriend [who attended an historically black college] for deeper stuff. She got that where she went. So, that was maybe one of the more negative things about that experience, that we didn't get the full story."

Students who never attended predominantly black city schools of course could not know whether black history was taught more frequently and thoroughly in majority black schools. Regardless, it was common for the adults to point to METCO as one impetus for a post–high school craving to learn about black history and culture, and to understand how various political issues and problems affect blacks in particular. The following sections turn to narratives of post-METCO graduates' personal journeys that helped resolve conflicts and rebuild what may have been lost during years in white suburban schools.

Understanding the Search for Identity

Few teenagers—white or black, segregated or racially integrated —are strangers to the conflicts that accompany personal searches for identity. Few are immune to the incessant self-inquiry that intensifies in adolescence and often continues into adult years. Of course, virtually all teenagers and adults struggle with questions that go to the core of who they are as human beings— questions about where they fit in relationship to their families, social groups, communities, and the larger society. Even so, scholars who study American blacks identify a process of racial identity development specific to this group.

It's necessary, then, to distinguish between specific longer-term reactions to the METCO experience and the typical confusion and stages of change associated with racial identity development among blacks. Two questions that need to be answered are: First, to what extent and in what ways does the process of racial identity development, as outlined by scholars, either reflect or deviate from explanations and recollections of post-METCO adults? Second, how do these adults, themselves, perceive METCO's role in their development of racial identity and related efforts to cope with and resolve their feelings of alienation?

Psychologist Beverly Daniel Tatum suggests that racial identity development can best be understood within the context of the larger society. That is, the way people think of themselves in terms of race is related to the messages that the larger society communicates about their racial groups. Thus, the reason black adolescents and adults think of themselves in terms of race, while whites generally do not, is because the larger society defines blacks by race or by racial difference while seeing whites as the racial norm (Tatum, 1997). Thus, Tatum explains, research has found that people of color are far more likely than whites to actively explore their racial or ethnic identities.

In psychologist William Cross's model of racial identity development, there are five stages that continue into adulthood (Cross, 1991; Cross, 1995). Cross refers to the first stage as *pre-encounter*, as black children may begin to highly value the standards of beauty and lifestyle as expressed by the dominant (white) culture as opposed to those standards defined by their own racial group. Picking out the white doll in a toy store display, as one respondent recalls doing, might reflect this stage. During this time, a young child may hardly comprehend the social significance of her race. In the second, or *encounter stage,* young blacks typically face instances of racism or racial difference that cause them to realize that belonging to a group will subject them to discrimination. Tatum's own studies of young blacks who live in predominantly white communities suggest that encounter stages can begin as early as middle school (Tatum, 1992; Tatum, 1996).

As racial identity development continues into young adulthood, blacks surround themselves with symbols of blackness. Cross terms the third stage *immersion.* They may socialize exclusively with black peers and make deliberate efforts to learn about black culture and history. In the fourth stage, *internalization,* a black person develops a sense of security about his or her racial identity and thus becomes willing at this time to develop relationships with people from other racial groups. In Cross's fifth stage, *internalization-commitment,* blacks use their own healthy racial identities to act upon their commitments to specific issues or causes that affect blacks as a group (Cross, 1991; Cross, 1995).

Though I offer these stages here in conceptual progression, scholars such as Tatum and Cross stress that the phases don't necessarily unfold in an ascending order. Rather, the phases are circular: even adults in the internalization-commitment stage will probably run into conflicts and questions similar to those faced during the encounter or immersion stage (Tatum, 1997; Cross, 1995). As we see in the following section, the cyclical nature of racial identity development applies well to former METCO students who still struggle with questions they first faced as adolescents. In this section, adults speak further about the alienation they felt from relationships, culture, and community and the process of developing racial identity that helped ease their discomfort.

Searching for a Place

Post-METCO adults commonly perceive that years living in white and black worlds made the normal process of racial identity development more confusing, complex, and intense than it might have been otherwise. Surely, they say, they were forced to understand the social significance of race earlier and confronted it more frequently than city peers who remained comparatively insulated in black communities. The program forced young people to live in two worlds, each of which sent negative messages about the other. Years of bouncing between worlds and trying to function in both and survive intact required students to discard the negative messages over time so they could develop their own healthy racial identities and independent definitions of what being black means.

For a former METCO student who attended college, the immersion stage of development was characterized by deep involvement in campus student groups and in organizations specifically concerned with political and cultural concerns of blacks as a group. These organizations included cultural, academic, artistic programs, student government, support groups, community volunteer groups, and political activist organizations. Many of the former students held leadership positions in such groups, even if they had not been particularly active in organizations during their METCO years. While such groups focused on black concerns, these men and women, as leaders, were required to move frequently between white campus groups, white officials, and white students, and black group members and black student constituents. For these students in the immersion stage friendship groups were not always exclusively black; it was remarkably less common for these black students to have exclusively black friends than it was for them to have a racially diverse social group. But nearly universally, once at college practically all of these students expended great effort consciously seeking out black friends. During this stage, the college students, having left behind nearly all-white high schools, often piled on African-American studies courses. Some even elected to be Afro-American studies majors, which they usually changed by junior year. Several minored in African-American or Black Studies while majoring in other fields.

Arlene Staples, who attended a liberal arts college after spending three years in low-wage, temporary secretarial jobs because she needed to earn money, found the intellectual discoveries about black history, culture, and especially the visual arts "completely transforming and empowering for me, as a person, as a black woman." This is a common reaction for the college-going METCO students as they discover, usually for the first time, the breadth, richness, and complexity of black history and cultural contributions.

For Arlene, like many METCO counterparts, her immersion experience in college is still vivid many years after it ended:

> I'm in a classroom [that has] maybe four white students and the rest all black students. And I had been working to learn some of this material on my own with help from a cousin. There's a dynamic black professor there, a very academic type, and I was on the edge of my seat. It's all I wanted to do, go to this class, learn from these people. And I'm supposed to be studying accounting, right? There was a long study of the Harlem Renaissance, and we read Jean Toomer and studied [Romare] Bearden and all. It wasn't just the basics, like, this is Malcolm X and Dr. King and throw in some James Baldwin here, okay, good-bye. The classes were really

intense, very rigorous, talking a lot about what we could learn, too, about history and black position in society through the arts. And a lot of us had been to white schools, the students I mean, and this was a white college. And so anyway, it was a very consuming experience. For me, the [Afro-American studies] department, what I got from it, it was completely transforming for me, empowering for me, as a person, as a black woman.

It also was common for former METCO students to recall their desire to attend historically black colleges. The adults frequently recall, for example, "just wanting to get away from white people," "a desperate need to be with all other blacks," having "a strong desire to be totally all-black in an all-black place" and "[wanting] to see only black faces for awhile after what I had been through." Although graduating METCO students commonly gave serious consideration to all-black colleges or universities, fewer than 10 of 65 respondents actually went to such schools. Only one stayed to graduate. Most often, the students transferred out of the southern campuses and attended and graduated from urban colleges closer to Boston. There was a range of reasons for the transfers, including financial problems exacerbated by plane fares home, ailing parents or relatives in the Boston area, and personal discomfort in a southern or an all-black educational environment.

The METCO students who did not go to college found greater difficulty immersing themselves intellectually in black history or culture, though a few did find ways to do so independently. Since specifically "black" organizations weren't ready-made outside of college campuses, these young people rarely joined black groups, at least not right after high school. Nevertheless, the terms with which this group of adults describes their immersion in racial identity are similar to those of the college-goers. In fact, many of these men and women recall immersing themselves by wearing symbols of blackness or black solidarity, including South Africa's African National Congress flags, buttons, and African-style clothes, and by involvement with political causes, such as divestment in South Africa. Following high school, many developed affinities with African-American political and spiritual leaders, both locally and nationally, including the Rev. Jesse Jackson, Louis Farrakhan, and others.

This stage, termed *immersion* in Cross's model of racial identity development, is typically experienced by young blacks in general, not only those with early racial integration experiences. But METCO adults offer two divergent assessments about the program's impact on this stage. A small group of post-METCO adults perceives that the program had no effect on this stage and that all manifestations of immersion stemmed from other experiences, such as personal psychology, disposition, and family-related matters. A larger group—more than two-thirds—perceives that METCO might have made the desire for immersion more intense, and as Nick Marshall, a recent college graduate, terms it, "more desperate."

"It's different I think for some of us coming out of really white schools, it's kind of like if you weren't going to get more black in your life, you'd curl up and die," Nick says. "It was an all the time thing for you."

It was common for these former METCO students to feel intensely driven toward black culture. From their perspectives, they were trying to fill a void in their lives, an emptiness. Again, Nick Marshall recalls events and feelings similar to those voiced by other past METCO participants:

> It was all you did, really, everything was black, black, black. For me, I could not get enough of it. And it wasn't really [as] exciting for me [as] I think it was for other young blacks from more urban schools. For me, it was like, "I have to have this, or I will die." And I had this

fear of not being accepted by [other black students]. Like black is all you are? Of course it's not but you are in this place all through high school where you can't express yourself in a cultural manner and then so you spend a lot of time looking for a place where you can do that. It's not really all fun either, it's sort of like an uncomfortable thing, like you are figuring out how to do something that seems natural to everyone else.

Kevin Tyler has a similar account:

It's like a big candy store; you realize there are books on this subject. And thinking back now, about how ignorant I am. I have to say this makes me a bit ashamed.

Really, though, it's amazing coming out of that world, out of a very white, very suburban place and there's a bit of an anger that comes out. How come no one ever told me about this? And it was like a conversion for me, the closest kind of religious conversion experience when I began to feel free from white people and their knowledge. I would describe it as a thirst. You hear the term all the time, "a thirst for knowledge?" And you don't really know what that means. For African Americans who have had that experience, lived in this very white culture and had to learn what was given to you, when you are exposed for the first time to the fact that there is more knowledge out there, about your people and where you come from, you really do, you understand what that means: "a thirst for knowledge." I was. I was so hungry. There was this emptiness that was basic to me.

The young adult experiences of former METCO students seem to differ in another way from the typical course of identity development as laid out by scholars. As Tatum, the social psychologist, explains, young blacks in their immersion phases often see white people as "irrelevant." That is, blacks don't see whites as enemies, but simply as less important than other blacks. During this stage, Tatum and other psychologists have observed, young blacks are less likely to form relationships across the race line and more likely to stick exclusively with other blacks (Tatum, 1997). This was not typical of the adults I talked with. Although some students report having had black friends exclusively during college or in the years immediately following high school, the post-METCO adults usually formed and maintained cross-racial relationships and took on roles requiring them to move socially between black and white groups. The former METCO students did indeed view these cross-racial behaviors as dissimilar to the experiences of other black peers who, they perceived, had less to do with whites. Because the sample includes various ages, all the later phases of racial identity development are represented. In the internalization stage—the phase in which blacks become more secure in their racial identities—former METCO students commonly adopted independently formed definitions of what it means to be black. Prior to this stage, usually in high school and in the years following high school, these men and women had accepted cues and instruction from peers and the popular media about what "black" means. The type of peer-defined, authentically black speech patterns and dress that adults spoke of in chapter 3 are examples of imposed definitions of blackness. In some cases, though, parents and other family members subscribed to other meanings of blackness, which included emphasis on the arts, history, academic achievement, and cultural contribution. These men and women usually incorporated such definitions as they formed their own black identities and shed, to varying extents, the stereotypes imposed by forces of adolescent culture and the society at large.

Though generally secure with their own definitions of what it means to be black, the post-METCO adults are often particularly sensitive to teasing and criticism about degrees of cultural integrity. This is true even when criticism comes from people they believe have incorrect notions about "blackness." Because the students so often were called "white boy" or "white girl" in their METCO years, criticism, even if patently ridiculous, still stings.

One METCO graduate, Donald Isaac, can quite clearly outline his own process of developing a strong and consistent black identity with which he is comfortable. He is committed, through work and volunteerism, to improving predominantly black communities, and he speaks out against racism and discrimination when he sees it on the job or in other facets of his life. Economically successful, Donald says he could "afford to live anywhere," but made a "conscious choice" to remain living in a predominantly black community. Still he, like so many other former METCO students, says he feels sensitive and angry whenever blacks judge him or other blacks on a misperceived degree of cultural integrity.

> And sometimes now, you hear black people judging other blacks on how black they are, so to speak. It's really difficult for me to hear that talk and it gets me angry, too, to hear it. It's frustrating for me being around some black people who say I talk like I'm white. I mean, I know it's a joke, but it's not funny. I want to say sometimes, "Hey. I coach little league in the city. I don't have kids of my own, so I don't have to do that. I mentor a kid who lives in the city. I don't have to do that. I live here, in the city. I don't have to do that. I want to do that." Sometimes, I think about all this crap, and I think, "Hey, why don't I leave?" That's the quick reaction, to just leave. It's tough. And it's sad.

Likewise, April Patterson, who until recently worked for an organization fostering relationships between older and younger blacks, has struggled developing her own black identity. April says that she once believed neighborhood friends who told her "that being black meant walking with a certain stride, you know, listening to a certain type of music, thinking white people were scum and saying it. None of these kinds of 'Screw you, White People' things were allowed in our home growing up. We were very traditional, pretty conservative growing up and all. So, fine, I guess for awhile I thought that I wasn't really black."

April, who believed into her college years that she "wasn't quite black," eventually shed the standards placed upon her by neighborhood acquaintances who called her "white girl." She incorporated many of her family's values with her own and developed a secure black identity. Still, years after high school, the taunts of "white girl" echo.

> Ugh. I hate it. I hate it. I hate it. I mean, I really can't stand to hear it and just seems it's getting worse. My relatives do it to me, you know, making fun of my speech, my girls' speech. These are grown women I'm talking about here. Women in their 30s and 40s, saying, "Oh, listen to this one, she thinks she's white." Talking all this shit. Please, grow up! I'll do anything to protect my girls from that crap, that you-wear-this-or-you-ain't-black-girl crap. It's crap, like, you think O. J.'s guilty—and I do, by the way—oh, look out, you're gonna get it. Like, "You call yourself black?" Excuse me, since when is blackness about supporting a guy in a mansion? Like I can't have an independent mind? If I do, I'm white?

If sensitivity to taunts about cultural integrity lingers into adulthood, so too does a need to connect with predominantly black communities and to commit oneself to organizations that serve a significant share of blacks and issues affiliated with blacks as a group. This is a significant point because one of the most prevalent criticisms of urban-suburban programs such as METCO is that they will tear black children away from urban neighborhoods as they aspire in adulthood to white-oriented suburban values. Interviews with the METCO adults suggest this is far from the case, as many of the respondents say that early immersion in white communities may very well have been a contributing factor to their current need to remain strongly attached to predominantly black communities. It was far more common for the past METCO participants to be living, by choice, in either predominantly black or racially integrated communities than in predominantly white towns of the type where they had traveled for school.

In addition, former METCO students commonly either have professional jobs that fulfilled such commitments to black communities, or were moving toward such jobs. (More than 60 percent fit this description.) Such jobs included social work; public health administration; working for progressive foundations; administrating, counseling, tutoring, teaching, and teaching aides in inner-city and racially diverse schools as well as for other educational programs for blacks and other racial minorities; administrators for mentoring programs; owning businesses in predominantly black communities; fair housing advocacy; providing child care to the poor; and public advocacy lawyers. Among this group were several men and women who had changed careers in order to work for these organizations. Some of these men and women had done work that was not associated with black issues and that did not serve large shares of blacks. But they had either gone back to school for degrees that allowed them to switch careers or changed careers with little to no extra training. The men and women commonly had taken reductions in salary to fulfill their new commitments.

The former METCO students also fulfilled their commitments through volunteer service. The adults did this in their communities either through youth sports (some had children and others did not) or through community improvement groups, including homework drop-in centers and teen centers. Dozens volunteered through their workplaces, including one-on-one mentoring, adopt-a-school programs, speaking at career days at inner-city schools, and organizing wider-scale volunteer programs for businesses.

Post-METCO adults with children consciously pass on lessons about black culture, history, and the importance of black communities. Thus, the adults are commonly what scholars term "race-conscious" (Tatum, 1997). They talk with their children about race and racism and offer definitions of blackness that include academic achievement, tolerance for others, and a pride in distinctly black culture and history.

Few of the former students say that METCO was directly responsible for these commitments, whatever forms they take. More typically the men and women see their commitment to black organizations, culture, and causes as the result of many factors, principally their parents. It was most common, in fact, for the former METCO students to recall their parents stressing the importance of "giving back to the community," of "giving others a chance just like I had," of "not judging those less fortunate," and of "helping your own kind" and "remembering where you came from." These messages, from parents and other significant black adults, carry on in the METCO students' lives, no matter what successes they've achieved, new interests they've acquired, or amount of time they have spent or spend in white communities. Their years in METCO didn't diminish these strongly held values, and in some cases, the adults speculate, they fortified their commitments.

A relatively small group—about a dozen—found yet another way to reduce the alienation they say was spurred to some degree by METCO. (This group includes only former METCO students who attended college and who consider themselves middle class.) They sought and found a social group of other blacks whose childhood and teenage experiences paralleled theirs in METCO. Some of these social groups include fellow post-METCO adults but others include blacks who attended traditional prep schools or who grew up in predominantly white communities. These new friendships are significant, as the adults seek out not just other middle-class blacks, but blacks with whom they share common references from their youth. Donald Isaac, for example, found solace in such a social group after years of "not feeling really understood" in suburbia.

"This is a group where I feel at home," Donald says. "And I talk with these people and it's amazing the similarities they have in their experiences and their feelings about these conflicts. They can relate. Yes, finally, I found some people who could relate. That was a good feeling. It was amazing."

For some, METCO, in making ties to community more tenuous, paradoxically reinforced their hold to black communities and culture. George Gardner, for example, speculates that his appreciation for black communities and for relationships with other blacks is stronger than it would have been without having spent time in METCO. George explains:

> You could say it's because we were away. We were in a sense away for eleven, twelve years if you started METCO early. You are away in some sense, even if you are still connected [to a black community]. For me the significant thing is that you're not sharing in something other people are, the things other blacks have in common with each other. While you're in a white town, other people are in a black neighborhood. That's a difference. So it's probably that appreciation but also this feeling that your connection is a little shaky, that you might lose it. It's not a natural, constant thing for you; you need to reconnect to it after METCO's over. It wasn't a constant thing just there for us, like it is for other blacks. Do you see what I mean? And so you see how it could slip away, for a lot of METCO kids. Speaking for myself, you do slip away a little bit and you need that connection.

Although past participants feel METCO did have some effects upon the development of racial identity, such perceived effects are not radically different from the typical patterns outlined by scholars. But of course this is not true of every post-METCO adult I spoke with. Several of the adults, whom we will hear from in the following section, are not on clear paths toward resolving the alienation, resentment, and anger although decades may have passed. This phenomenon was quite uncommon—with about 11 percent of the full sample expressing such feelings. But because their stories and opinions reveal themes shared by most skeptics of similar racial integration programs, they are worth examining.

Struggling Still After METCO

Paul Hammond has few positive words to describe the overall personal effect of his METCO experience. "Yes," he concedes, association with prestigious suburban schools might have "opened doors" for him. And he readily admits that the college preparatory atmosphere in his competitive high school "saved me, probably from a life of not doing much at all" and helped pressure him into attending college and earning an associates degree at a two-year college. But opened doors and educational advantage matter little to Paul. For him, METCO's negative consequences mattered most.

Paul says, "[METCO] screwed me up for life." "It's like taking a kid who's black, who's from someplace and saying, 'Kid, okay, this place is a garbage heap. You need to go somewhere else to learn about the real world, cuz where you're from? Where you're from is for shit.' You don't think that screws a kid up? Telling him in so many words that the place he comes from is garbage, that he's got to get out in order so that he can make it? You start saying, you know, 'Oh, I see. What he means is, I'm shit.' Try fighting against that your whole life, that's not going to get you very far."

The adults in my sample who perceive that METCO had mostly long-term negative effects hold a similar strain of resentment and anger. Unlike others who have complaints and feelings of loss but have found ways to resolve those problems, these men and women (whose ages and backgrounds vary) remain angry and bitter about their experiences and don't foresee that their pain will heal. They express two related complaints. One is that METCO greatly damaged their self-esteem by placing them in white schools where their background, culture, and community were neither acknowledged nor valued. For example, Lauren Baldwin, who says METCO did provide her some "academic benefits in the long term," feels the gains just weren't worth the cost in self-esteem. And, she said, METCO made her "angrier."

"I do think that some kids can handle it and others just cannot," Lauren says. "But I think even if they do well, and I did do pretty well, it still takes something away from those kids and that is their self-esteem. I really believe that. And they are so confused about their identity. The unsaid things that get communicated about their identity. All those things."

These former students remember that in response to feelings that their communities were not valued, they internalized negative images and grew ashamed of where they came from. A few distanced themselves from their families and communities and from their culture and never did find ways to reconnect. These graduates lament their lack of connection even though they all have jobs and volunteer positions that signify strong commitments to blacks as a group and to improvement of the black condition. Even so, they never had a chance to develop healthy black identities and wavered between being ashamed and angry about blacks' low status in the suburban schools and in society.

As METCO graduate Wanda Carter terms it, "I think that if I didn't go to METCO, I would be stronger as a black person, feel more pride about being black. METCO tells you to be more like whites."

The second complaint of the former students is that they still feel trapped into assimilating the white dominant culture although they feel hypocritical doing so. Thus, unlike other former METCO students who simply view their old opinions as transient— as "stages" of development—this group expressed self-contempt for current assimilationist behavior they say they learned in METCO and, quite guiltily, have carried into their current lives.

Wanda Carter stresses that she is "appreciative of the education she received," but speculates that she could have received as good an education in urban schools and been spared the pressure to assimilate.

"Sometimes I think that I should have, well, instead of trying so hard to be like everyone else, I should have tried to be more like myself," Wanda says. "And you know, it sounds weird, and I've never said this to anyone, but when I'm thrown into situations with people from my own culture, I feel uneasy. I'm uneasy, especially now that I see my sister who is really into her culture. So I feel bad that I am sort of ashamed of it.

Like other former METCO students, Wanda speculates that her ability to adapt to what she and others call "white" forms of speech, dress, and behavior contributes to her acceptance and success on the job. But, again, she asserts that the price she has paid is too high.

> It's not necessarily an advantage. I wish I could say, "Hey, who cares if I don't fit in." You know, this is how I wish I could be, how I wish I could think. But now, I'm so used to having that need to want to fit in that I do it anyway. There's a lot of me that I don't bring out, that I want to bring out. You know, just the ability of telling someone like it is. I still hear a lot of really ignorant remarks from people and I want to call them on it, but I don't because I really am used to wanting to be a part of something. And so, since I've always been in really white environments, that's the environment that I've always wanted to be part of.

I have a friend [who] does not give a damn, and she will call you on a lot of stuff. I wish I could be more like that. And I think people like her even more for that. I mean, my sister, she is like that.

It is unclear why there are such stark differences between the stories of people in this subgroup and the more typical stories of men and women who compensated for the losses they suffered as a result of METCO. It is plausible that the differences stem from family attitudes toward race and culture. A few of these men and women do remember their parents downgrading blacks in general, aspiring to "white" [or as one woman termed it, "mainstream Americanized"] standards, of culture and beauty and stressing that suburban lifestyles were something they wanted for their children. Paul Hammond, for example, recalls:

My mother was so worried about what white folks would think of her, you know, dressing up for school nights and always telling us we needed to behave properly, be really good and appreciative that whites were accommodating us in their school. There was no indication from her that she thought we might have some, some benefit to [offer] white folks. And you learn that your own mother thinks whites are better somehow and I did try to challenge her on it. These are not things you should say to a little black child.

She'd say, "Look around you, look what black people are doing to their own homes. This filth! I don't see none of this where you're going to school." [She was] talking like, what's that big, fat, racist white guy? She was like a black Rush Limbaugh. That's like my mama.

Previous research indeed suggests that black children whose parents display positive attitudes toward blacks and black culture, and who establish connections to black history and communities, may be less likely to have difficulties in their development of racial identity (Tatum, 1997). But because this group with problems was so small—seven of the sixty-five interviewees —I can't reliably analyze the causes of these differences in attitudes about the long-term negative aspects of METCO. Interestingly, however, these attitudes do not seem to stem from the character of a person's METCO experiences. These former students' recollections of METCO were not entirely negative, though all included negative aspects. They describe their in-school METCO years as "mixed," or "about half good, half bad, I'd say," or "not bad, it was okay." In fact, those who felt most negatively about METCO *while it was going on,* including adults who refer to the METCO experience as "day to day like a kind of torture," or "like hell, pure hell," or "the most painful thing, ever, in my life," are in the group that resolved their earlier problems and, from their own perspective, even matured as a result.

What Have I Missed?

Samuel Dean, who graduated from high school in the early 1990s, remembers visiting historically black campuses during his college years. There he experienced the strong sense that the young blacks on campus "felt like the place belonged to them." With that feeling of proprietorship, the students, Samuel said, exuded "a confidence." But Samuel, who went on to two predominantly white colleges, said he always felt like he was simply "visiting" these colleges, including the Catholic college in New England from which he graduated. While Samuel is glad he attended METCO and graduated from college, along with about two dozen other post-METCO adults, he thinks he might have drawn a deeper sense of security and "strength" from an all-black learning environment.

> When I went to [college], it was the same thing. The only black guy. You know, every year when I was at [college], I tried to go down to a black college to their

homecoming or whatever. Just some buddies and I would go down to one of those colleges. That really started to become a culture shock for me, a whole college campus full of black people. I was enjoying it, but it was a culture shock, still. The first question you ask yourself is, "Could I go to school here?" The second question you ask is, "Would I party too much? Would I not even think about school at all?" Because where I went to school, or even in [college], your social life was limited. But no way did I ever feel the way I felt when I went to one of those campuses. In terms of like, hey, it's yours. It's mine. You just feel like it's yours. There's this feeling of confidence that [the students] had.

I'll give an example: I never felt like [the college I attended] was mine. Now, [if] they call to [ask for] money or [if I] come back to a homecoming, I don't feel like [the college] was mine. And I sense that now that I'm working with other people, the school that they went to, they claim it, it's theirs. There's a security about the place. I mean, I remember walking down a campus, one of those black campuses, I remember, even though I didn't go to school there, that this is mine, it's mine, these are my people. And it was a strong feeling.

Shirley Rogers says she'd "repeat my years at [my predominantly white college] in a flash. I wouldn't think twice." But Shirley still wonders if she might have gained something important had she spent "one or two" years at either an all-black "prep-school type" high school or a historically black college in the south. Like many other former METCO students who have nagging questions about what they might have missed, Shirley speculates that she would have gathered more self-confidence and more "black pride" from years spent working and learning exclusively among other blacks.

It's a question of pride, maybe. What they call black pride. I have a very strong sense of being black, and it's a huge part of who I am, and I've dealt with a lot of the baggage issues with that, living with racism and what have you. But I think about being in a place where everyone is black, so there are black leaders, black musicians, every leader of every group, people on the student government, whatever. Everyone is black. And seeing that and getting used to it. It might make you stronger as a black person, or this is what you wonder about anyway: whether I'm missing some kind of confidence or pride or something, because I'm so accustomed to white people being in charge. I don't know. I don't know anyone who went to a black college, and there's an argument there for saying that it's not like the real world, but I don't know, maybe it would have been a good thing to experience.

Few of the adults I spoke with go so far as to say they out and out regret choosing a predominantly white campus and wish they had gone somewhere else. While some think it would have been better to have spent at least a few years in an academically rigorous all-black high school, they lament the fact that there seem to be few such places. Some of the students, such as Jeremy Shepard, speculate that once a young person is accustomed to either an all-black or a racially integrated institution, it might be "difficult to make a culture switch just like that." Jeremy characterizes this common ambivalence:

I can't say I'd do it different in looking at the options I had. If you can give me a school that's just like [my METCO town], a high school like that, that's all black? I think a lot of people in METCO would go for it because it's a welcoming kind of place, like an escape. It could, anyway, lead to feeling stronger as a black person.

But "When does it end?" maybe is the question you have to ask yourself. Eventually you are going out there, right? And so, you start in kindergarten, go through college—that's sixteen, in my case seventeen years because I was at [college] for five. But that's sixteen years for most people without dealing with white people, ever? In an academic learning context? Black males are taught in this society to think lowly about themselves, [so] it would have been better to have a balance of white and black, some years in METCO, some years in an all-black place. And this is something that's on my mind that you have to ask yourself what could have been, but that's not easy to get. You get used to one or the other and you just keep doing things that way. Human nature. You know, okay, white [high] school, white college. But these other things you want, like you think, "black college" instead of white [college] for a second and it's like, "Hey, that's nuts. I can't. Can I?" But in my case, you don't [consider that]. I think that might be how it is.

Accumulated Burdens

As discussed in the previous chapter, many of METCO's past participants found upon their entry into college and the workplace that they had a rare skill. These men and women could move with relative ease between white and black communities and white and black co-workers and acquaintances. Because few other people—either black or white—are adept at being what one METCO graduate terms a "cultural translator," the former METCO students often did that work. Generally, these men and women are proud of their abilities and believe their skills at cross-race communication—often it is more like mediation than mere communication—have contributed to their success in work and in higher education. But they also are often quite tired and frustrated by the requirement, as Jane Staunton says, to "do all the race work."

"Sometimes," Jane says. "I just want to let stuff go, you know, an ignorant comment that you can get in a racial sense from blacks as well as whites, mind you." However, Jane, like many of the other METCO graduates, feels compelled to "say something, to make some kind of positive mark on this person in terms of their racial attitudes."

> Just the other day, I'm at lunch, just wanted to eat my sandwich. And I'm with two black friends and some comment comes up about white trash, about someone being white trash and it was, "Oh, no. Here we go." Damn. Can I eat my tuna, please? Can I pretend I didn't hear this? Please, God? Please. But the Lord, sometimes it does feel like the Lord saying these things, telling me to "Keep going, girl." So, I say, "Ginny, think about what you said. This person has no money. She doesn't know about things that maybe we all learned at home, you know, from our own mothers, things about parenting children."
>
> This person had some particular problems with her child-care situation and was in the office [where my friend works] and screaming at her kids. And, so my friend [did], I think, start to think more compassionately, like the way I know she treats her own people, black people who are low income. So this is why a lot of times I will just eat alone, right here at my desk, thank you very much, because I need some peace from the racial matters that come up.

Thomas Mitchell said that in his racially mixed work environment, he occasionally suppresses an urge to scream: "What is wrong with you people? You are acting like children. Worse than children." He gives an example. "This one guy, a white guy, he says, 'Oh, you can't trust [him], you know, he's a Jew.' I'm thinking, 'Wait a minute, did I just hear this?' And this was probably the eighth or ninth time that day, in this one day that I needed to step in. And you get so sick of it. Is it doing any good? You start to say, 'Don't bother.' I just said, 'Lou, you are a real asshole, you know that? A real ignorant asshole.' So this wasn't constructive. I am aware of what's constructive. But sometimes you got to throw up your hands."

These men and women complained particularly of white co-workers and college classmates who rarely speak up in conversations others are having about racial issues. The past METCO participants say they often are the only ones in a room or at a lunch table able to broach a subject that relates even remotely to race. In such situations, they say other blacks or racial minorities might join in, and whites often remain silent. Once in a while, a white co-worker approaches one of these black men or women following a conversation and thanks them for bringing up the subject of race or for trying to settle a dispute. Sheila Leonard describes this type of conversation, which is similarly described by the other adults:

> It's a meek kind of approach, people who are usually so strong in every way [that] you wish you had some of their confidence, they come over to you, looking all ashamed, and I'm thinking, "Oh, my! What's wrong?" And they stumble [over] and say, "Oh, I just want to say, it must have taken some strength to talk so honestly like you did, about the discrimination you have to deal with." And I say, "Nah, not really." And [they say,] "Well, I found what you said really refreshing." That's a big word: refreshing. Like I'm a soda fountain or something. I know it's well intended but you want to say, "Speak up, damn it. Say something."

Former METCO students such as Sheila say they intend to continue crossing what she terms "the racial divide." But at the same time, these men and women question what good their efforts will do, since most of the other people they meet won't even, as Sheila complains, "come halfway across this ocean between us."

The Continuing Matter of Race

Whether they are generally happy or dissatisfied with the long-term effects of their METCO experiences, many of the former students do stress the program's limitations in a stubbornly race-obsessed society. While METCO's past participants often acknowledge the important personal benefits they gained from the program beyond high school, they all learned quite quickly that working hard in their suburban schools and acquiring navigational skills for white settings did not mean they would no longer be judged and treated differently from white people.

As described in chapter 4, the adults commonly perceive that METCO helped them break down structural barriers in society. But of course, the men and women concede, the program could do little to alter attitudes and behavior of white people and white-dominated institutions. A few former METCO students go so far as to blame the program and the adults in charge of it for having set up unrealistic expectations about how much blacks would be able to achieve in a racist society. But more often, they suggest shifting METCO's focus so that METCO could not only benefit black students, but also improve the racial attitudes of white students.

Former students who perceive even very substantial personal gains from METCO nevertheless complain that the program requires little or no work or effort from the white suburban students. Some past METCO participants suggest that, as a matter of course, white students should be taught about the black experience in America and should discuss, with METCO students, the divergent experiences and histories of blacks and whites. Other students suggest that because black METCO students have to learn and adapt to the habits, speech patterns, and lifestyles in white suburbia, whites should be taught about diversity and that white suburbia does not set the standard in such matters. Arlene Staples says, "It's two things. One, someone has to teach them their way of life isn't the only way of life. That white isn't necessarily right. And two. The second thing. Someone's gotta use the METCO opportunity to show that being white and black isn't the same thing; we get treated different, we have a different history and in a lot of ways we are going to see things different because of that. It's basic."

Arlene articulates the sentiments of many respondents when she says, "METCO did a lot for me, I really do believe that. But after METCO, you are still black and you have to deal with this. METCO can help all the black kids in Boston, okay? But we have another problem, people. This program helps the black children. Who helps the white children? Who helps the white children learn how to be better people?"

As Nick Marshall sees it, METCO leaves its effect on white students "up to chance." This sends the message, he says, that fixing discrimination and inequality is "up to blacks and other minorities and a matter of them improving themselves, not a problem for whites to deal with in themselves." Nick, who also believes he benefited greatly from his years in white suburbia, nevertheless complains, "Maybe there'll be a friendship out of this. Maybe there'll be more understanding and maybe a white kid, 'cuz of METCO, starts to see something differently, maybe challenges racism a little bit. But it's a crapshoot, up to chance. There's a line they say, that METCO is bringing diversity to the white schools, but it's got to be more than that. It's gotta be a kind of effort where everyone gets something. You can have these enlightened black kids who know maybe a little more about how the world works, but still you've got white kids, twelve years of being with METCO kids in the same schools [who] still don't have a clue."

Sorting Out the Good, the Bad, the Confusing

Traveling back and forth from black city neighborhoods to white suburban schools, METCO teenagers usually saw their journeys as part of their parents' practical program to enhance their children's chances for success in life. Whether or not they are satisfied with their achievements in school or career, the young men and women also were, and are driven by something besides rational self-interest. With other black children, teenagers, and adults in the United States, they also struggle not just for social mobility, but for identity, meaning, and belonging. To many of the students, going to METCO intensified and complicated that continuous struggle and confusion. Occasional bouts with alienation and questions about where one fits in haunt many of these men and women. As noted in chapter 4, past participants commonly perceive that their educational experiences in white suburban schools made them more comfortable in white settings. But having gained that, they still often struggled to feel comfortable with themselves. Long after METCO ended for many of its former students, these individuals still had to fashion new meaningful relationships with black communities, peers, and family members. In later years METCO participants most often did find the personal meaning they craved through professional, social, and volunteer connections with groups, organizations, and causes concerned with blacks as a group.

Nevertheless, long after their daily connection to METCO had ended, these former METCO students usually continued to make personal choices that replicated elements of their lives during METCO. They remained firmly connected to black communities, family members, and organizations while immersed in predominantly white settings. But many of these men and women have a lingering ambivalence about their years in suburbia and still entertain questions about whether they might have benefited from attending all-black educational institutions at some point in their lives. As many of these men and women take on roles as arbitrators, mediators, and cultural translators in racially diverse workplaces, some feel burdened by skills METCO helped them develop, but wish others also had such skills. Generally speaking, then, METCO did have tangible benefits for the adults who participated in the program. But, as the post-METCO adults learned after high school, even with the exposure and credentials white suburbia gave to them, the small program, as one respondent says, "couldn't reform the world, couldn't erase race as the thing people see about me first."

The following chapter moves beyond reflections on individual experiences, as the post-METCO adults consider whether they would place their own children on a bus to white suburbia.

6

What About Now

Balancing the Gains,
the Losses, and the Realities of
American Society

Imagine a line. Now imagine sixty-five former METCO students, each of them occupying one space on that line. The closer the students sit to the left, the more positive their METCO memories. The closer they are to the middle, the more mixed their experience. Toward the end sit former students who characterize their METCO days as entirely negative. As noted in chapter 3, about 20 percent of the respondents would occupy the spaces toward the left. Most—about 70 percent—crowd the middle. Fewer—the some 10 percent with solely negative experiences—scatter around the right-hand section of the line.

It would seem logical, then, that the relatively small number with only positive memories would be the most enthusiastic about placing their children on METCO's waiting list. Following this logic, a second, larger group might be split halfway between yes and no replies, with some members undecided. And of course, it's logical to assume that men and women with only negative memories would neither repeat their trauma nor subject their children to it.

But that is not the way it turns out. The quality of one's experience in METCO is rarely the most important consideration as a person decides whether one would repeat METCO or enroll children in it. The more potent factors to these METCO adults are the real-world experiences they had after high school. It was only then, in either college or the workforce, that they began to see clearly the reasons they were placed in suburban schools to begin with. It was fairly common for the men and women to say that if they had been asked in junior or senior high school: "Would you go through METCO again?" they likely would have answered, "no." But if you ask the same question of the same people, five, ten, fifteen, even twenty years after they're out, they most often say "yes."

The fifty-seven people who say they'd go back to suburbia through METCO and enroll a child there include men and women who had mostly positive experiences, others who had mixed experiences, and still others who had nearly all bad times in their suburban schools. In the following sections, adults speak about the reasoning and logic behind their decisions, not all of which are hypothetical. Just less than one-quarter of the people I talked with did need to decide whether to place their own children on the METCO waiting list.

Just four of the sixty-five are sure that they would neither repeat the program nor send their own child—actual or hypothetical—to a METCO school. Two others, although undecided, lean strongly toward saying that they would repeat the program themselves if they had to do it over again but that they would send their children to independent schools. And two others would repeat themselves, but in thinking about the specific circumstances and needs of their actual children, might send some but not all of their children to METCO.

Going Back

It might seem difficult to understand why Jeremy Shepard would want to repeat what he calls, "pure hell." "It was like hell a lot of the time," Jeremy remembers of years spent in suburban classrooms. "More than anything, I remember wanting to get out. And crying. I remember crying about it when I was younger." But Jeremy's reasons for saying he'd return to METCO if he could go back in time and for placing his future children in the program with "no questions asked" are similar to the justifications other people give. As Jeremy sees it, METCO, for all its daily trials and inconveniences, teaches two important personal skills "for the real world."

> You need to face the reality of the situation and that's that you can't have a separate black nation within the nation that exists right now. We have no choice. You have to integrate. You gotta know both, and the fact of the matter is that white people aren't all racists and that white people do control a lot. You have to live in this society, and it's better to do it without having to avoid white people your whole life, and there's gotta be people [like those in METCO] who learn it early, who come together and learn this, about living together in some way, that it's better to have a peace about the black-white thing. Coming to terms is important, and if you start young, you give people time maybe to make their peace, learn the ropes, [then] things will get better between the races, I think.

People such as Jeremy, who say they'd repeat METCO or put a child in the program, generally offer three justifications for going back to suburbia. Two of these reasons are related to personal gains that the adults say they earned in the program. The third justification relates to the adults' perception that METCO-like programs can create a more racially tolerant society. This last justification, however, is somewhat less common than the others and generally less important to the adults.

First, the adults quite commonly reason that because whites still control much of the wealth, political power, and status in American society, it is important for blacks to understand the nature of such communities and to overcome fear of such settings by interacting in them. Thus, such knowledge and practiced interaction will reduce fear and, by doing so, expand choices. Given such exposure, the men and women say, a person can then choose either to navigate in a white-dominated world or (if practically possible) remain separate from that world. This is a practical justification. It incorporates respondents' critical analyses of the structure of opportunity and power in society with their actual experiences in college and the workplace.

One METCO graduate, Carl Pierce, epitomizes this position:

> I used to be on a high horse. You get a lot of crap from white people, there are a lot of people who insult you. There is this resistance to seeing you as an equal and there is a threat, I think, that a lot of them feel when they meet an intelligent black person. So there has been a tendency for me to say, "Screw it." Okay, though, so, then what? You know, you can be a kid, saying, "Screw white people." Or you can look at this situation in a more realistic way where you have to earn a living in this world and you have your dreams, you know, that go beyond hanging out with your black friends rapping on white folks. So, for my situation, I realized I wanted to fulfill certain dreams of success, have certain things and a comfortable lifestyle to a certain extent and it was reality time for me. And you gotta go out there, you have to deal with people—I'm talking about white people, I mean—and for me, it was good: I knew the routine, I

knew how to handle those places and those situations because of (METCO). My mother knew what she was doing. [My job situations were] really like a natural extension of [my METCO suburban town] for me. And you realize you can deal with it fine.

You make that choice as a black person [growing up] in black communities whether to go out there or not. And I had that choice. But a lot of people don't. They are removed from that type of world because they have not been exposed to it. So, for me, it's a choice I had and made.

The type of practical reasoning that Jeremy and Carl represent leads many adults to a second justification. The post-METCO adults say it has been personally enriching to have sustained experiences in racially integrated settings. It is common for these adults to say they feel "expanded" or "broadened" from such experiences.

Bethany Cross, who graduated in the early 1980s, says her "personal values" were shaped in part by her early integration experiences as a black child in white suburbia.

I don't feel I'm better because of being around white people, for having white friends. But it's just the way my life is, and I like it. I have a lot of friends, black women, who have no white friends, they don't even really know a white person. They talk with white people. They have to deal with white people all the time. But they don't know any, not even on a casual basis. I'm not saying that this makes them less than me, just [as] I have friends who have traveled all over the world, and I haven't left the country. That doesn't make me less than them in any pure sense. It's just that I've had these experiences and I like that I have had white friends my whole life, that it's natural for me to have this circle of black and white and Asian, and that I learned this at a very young age. Speaking for myself as an individual, you don't have to be threatened or set up this little zone around you, where no whites are allowed. I used to be like that, like I felt closed off too much. And it's just my belief that you open up if you start off as a child being in different environments than where you come from.

Like Bethany, April Patterson is "proud" of her conviction that whites and blacks can "come together more than is happening now." April explains that her years in suburbia, while "difficult" and "trying" at times, played "at least some part in" shaping the values she lives by today:

> I am different from people who did not have this experience in terms of caring about race relations and feeling interested and curious about other cultures and wanting to know about those things. And I don't know if I'd be so believing that [whites and blacks] can work together, be allies, so to speak, on things. And [my METCO town] wasn't a great example of the races coming together, holding hands in coalitions. In a way it was sort of the opposite of that. But you see something, I think. You see people's side of things a little. And you start thinking more intelligently about your attitudes and you aren't going to just generalize about white-this, white-that. You see you can't make those kinds of comments and feel right inside so much anymore. I think I'm a little more thoughtful about these things now because of [my METCO experience], that it started something, some bells going off in my mind. And I'm proud of going past that fear and being able to learn from different kinds of people, accepting people, you know, not backing off because of skin color, being afraid to get too close because, well,

that person's white and we don't hang out with white people where I come from. However you want to see it, [METCO] expands the way you see things.

The third justification for returning to METCO is slightly less common than the first two. It is that programs such as METCO have the potential, however small, for improving race relations in the larger society. This might seem a surprising finding since, among these adults, racial integration, per se, was never a justification for going to METCO in the first place. But among adults reconsidering their experiences, the program's contribution to improved race relations as an important potential value.

It is important to emphasize here that most of the men and women who use this justification see improved race relations as a *potential* societal benefit of METCO and programs similar to it. While the adults might very well view METCO as a good opportunity to bring black and white closer together, it was also quite common for the former students to say that suburban educators and other adults in charge of the program failed to harness that potential to its fullest.

Margaret Redford dropped out of METCO and today does "wish I had finished. I just felt too sick of the bus ride. To tell the truth, I got sick on the bus. I missed my friends." But, Margaret explains, "My kids are going." She says METCO did help her "feel more comfortable, like more used to being in new places." And she hopes that giving her children exposure to schools "where going to college is what you do because it's what everyone's heading for" will improve their chances for economic security and "having choice for careers." But there's another, more idealistic reason why Margaret, like other post-METCO adults, wants her children in METCO.

"At least METCO's something," Margaret says. "It goes in that direction of bringing together instead of going apart, like the city and the other towns, bringing them together a little bit so we know where each other is coming from. I think it's better to live that way, blacks and whites more together, not so far apart. I'm a parent. And I am not into politics and things. But trying to bring people more together, I can say I believe in this. I can make this one choice for my kids that way."

Interestingly, few of the post-METCO adults focus exclusively on their negative perceptions of the Boston public schools in justifying their return to METCO. The adults often discussed such perceptions—including low academic standards, violence, environments not conducive to learning—and stressed that even if METCO did not exist, they themselves would not have attended a public city school nor would they enroll their children in one. They would instead investigate other options, including a religiously affiliated, independent, or charter school. The adults, however, are not choosing METCO just because they think Boston's schools are bad. In fact, they focus comparatively little on their negative perceptions of Boston and more on what they perceive their children would gain in suburbia.

Though the adults who say they'd return to METCO share similar justifications for returning, they have varying levels of enthusiasm and confidence in such decisions. The following three sections explore the considerable variation and complexities behind the adults' responses. In a later section, post-METCO adults who would not go back to the program offer explanations for their choice.

METCO's *Cheerleaders*

In her mind, Elaine Yardley sees a sequence of arrows representing orderly steps to opportunity in her life.

"I'll show you. You want me to show you?" Elaine asks, slipping a fresh piece of paper from the shelf above her desk.

"Okay," she begins, pulling the cap off a red magic marker. "Here's me, right?" Elaine sketches a little stick figure. Then an arrow. Above this arrow, Elaine writes the name of her old elementary school in an affluent suburban town. Then another arrow for her junior high. Then another for her high school. A fourth arrow leads to her summer job working with young children—a job a METCO counselor helped Elaine get. Then another arrow to junior college courses in early childhood education (a METCO teacher counseled Elaine about scholarships), another to a job in educational administration, another to a four-year college (about which a former teacher and host mother advised and helped Elaine to enter), another to a promotion, then to a savings account represented by dollar signs, and another to a condominium in a "safe, decent neighborhood" of "working people," and the last, to her children, represented by tiny stick figures carrying books. "These are my kids. They're going to school," Elaine explains. "Not a Boston school, either." Her children are going to school—and living, like Elaine—in a diverse suburban community near Boston.

"That's how it worked for me, anyway, okay? If it weren't for my mother putting me on that bus. Wait. She should be in here." Elaine revises her sketch. Giggles. Draws a second stick figure, a big one, one that overshadows the figure she drew of herself. She squeezes the mother stick figure in, right before the elementary school arrow. "But after that? It's METCO leading me from one thing to the other. I have to say that's how it works."

Elaine is typical of the small group—less than a dozen—of post-METCO adults who express no complaints about their experience in suburban schools. Predictably, they don't hesitate when asked whether they would return to METCO. Rhonda Johnson, for example, responds, "Of course."

Like Elaine, these adults see their time in white, suburban schools as having led directly to tangible benefits later in life. Their justifications for returning to METCO are similar to others' —this includes METCO's role in acquiring navigation skills, personal enrichment, and potential for helping to build a more tolerant society. But these respondents perceive a causal link from METCO to opportunity, which makes them more certain than most others of the wisdom of returning to METCO.

Not all of these men and women had wholly positive experiences while they were in their METCO schools. But in conversations, they simply do not focus on the negative aspects. They go so far as to evade discussion of any negative experience, often, explaining as Joseph Day does, that such past problems, "are irrelevant" now and "I'd like to ask not to discuss them, please." Joseph would rather stress, for example, that, prior to attending METCO in junior high school, he had not planned to attend college. (He later attended a four-year college part-time and is earning a law degree part-time.) Joseph says, "I can give myself credit for working hard, for getting [to college]. But until [METCO], [college] just wasn't something I was going for, something really on my mind. So, for me, I see METCO as the beginning of the time I set those goals and thought, 'All right. Cool. I can do this.'"

Even Elaine, with some prodding, acknowledges troubles fitting in at her affluent suburban schools. She did have some "personal problems" emerging from conflicts over "conforming to white people" that caused her to "mouth off a lot, to fight, even." But she adds hastily: "I wasn't there to make best friends. I didn't care about that stuff."

Yes, but ...

Far more of the post-METCO adults—just over thirty fit here—would place a child in METCO only on certain conditions (some do have children in the program). There are three principal conditions or concerns that the men and women expressed with regard to these decisions.

The most prevalent worry is that in white suburbia, their children would fail to maintain their cultural pride and would internalize white suburban standards of beauty, fashion, and lifestyles. Post-METCO adults with such fears think it important that their children remain connected to black institutions outside of schools—including church and community youth groups—and to form personal relationships with other blacks. These adults also want their children to learn extensively about blacks' contributions to American culture and history.

Several adults also lament the relatively low number of black teachers and administrators in the white, suburban schools. Failure to adequately teach black history and cultural contributions, these adults feel, is related to the small number of black authorities at most METCO schools. Barbara Michaels, for example, who graduated in the 1970s and is still connected to METCO through her work, says she would repeat the program herself and place a child in it. But her desire for more black teachers, administrators, and comprehensive teaching of black history is typical of adults who approach white suburbia with hesitation.

"What I would like to see is a black history course. A good one, something that everyone takes," Barbara says. "And these schools, it would be a very positive thing for these schools to really work harder at hiring some black teachers and administrators. There are a lot of people who are qualified, and you hear, 'Well [this town] isn't ready for a black principal,' and so forth. And that gets me angry."

A second complaint is that white teachers and administrators at the suburban schools don't seem to view METCO students as contributing to the school. Too often, complains Derrick Talbot, METCO students were viewed as "charity cases." Carla Lyon believes she was thought of as "a welfare case." Marie Lawlor always "got the feeling that they thought they were being great, generous folk for letting us in the door."

Rita Wood, who, with her husband placed their son on the METCO waiting list two weeks after his birth, feels that for all the program has to offer black children, members of the suburban communities may be benefiting even more merely by having black students in otherwise homogeneous schools. Rita's comments are typical of other post-METCO adults who, while seeing the benefit of suburbia, believe suburbia overlooks opportunity every day.

> As long as we live in this city—and we like living in this city—I'll want him in METCO. But it's true that the thing that they leave out all the time is what black students or the other minority students add to the school systems that they go to. They automatically assume that [only the minorities] are getting something out of it, that we are not adding something to it. I think that's unfair to say. I think that we add plenty because we teach the white kids who live out in the suburbs, "Hey, you know, life is not just about that little suburb that you live in. It's not the entire life in America at all. Not everybody looks like you." I mean, I think that black students add another perspective and I think that white teachers need to really begin recognizing that and seeing the benefits of it. I mean, we are forced to learn about other cultures because we live in a world where we are the minority, but you know, it's incredible, what we might be able to teach white students. There's got to be a change in attitude, I feel. That should be emphasized more and this is still something that I would be very concerned about.

It was difficult for the post-METCO adults to specify how evidence of such new attitudes might manifest themselves in the form of policies or educational practice. But several men and women do emphasize that as children, they grew tired of warnings not to mess up an important opportunity at their suburban schools.

It's quite clear that some of the current apprehensions about white suburbia—such as fears that children will not maintain community connections and will fail to learn about black history—are directly related to what adults feel they missed out on during their METCO years. The hesitation is also, however, a manifestation of adults' current-day ambivalence about some of the demands METCO placed upon them as children and teen-agers. Looking back at their own experiences, several of the adults are still unsure, for example, about how to advise their children about requirements to alter speech forms to conform to patterns and inflections prevalent in white-dominated settings.

Arlene Staples, for example, agrees that the acquisition of language patterns she picked up in suburbia is a "powerful tool" that she uses "every day of my life." But like other adults, she finds it difficult to reconcile this "reality of the world" with her opinion that encouraging a child to alter something so personal as verbal expression tells him "in effect that there is something wrong with his culture and his community." Arlene, whose di-lemma mirrors that expressed by many other METCO past partici-pants, explains that she does want METCO to model for young urban blacks the language of the "corporate America board-room," or the "surgical team" they might want to join one day. But Arlene does not want these children to be taught that their "cousins' and aunts' and uncles'" forms of expression are "in-correct" or that "the way whites talk in the downtown law firms" is "somehow better than." Arlene knows all about this conflict, because she felt it as a child. Like many other METCO graduates, Arlene is still trying to make sense of some of METCO's lessons twenty years later:

> These are words that come from somewhere, from a culture and a history and the rhythm of voices, of words. You hear it on the street, yes, you do. But what you're hearing is sometimes a lot like, or it grew from, in a lot of ways, literature and old narratives and a rich, rich tradi-tion. You hear it in the best African-American art forms —the same ones you white people like so much. So, it's

hard, you know, just to deny that to a child. You could say it's wrong, morally wrong, to tell a child, "You must speak this way, the way white people speak, not the way your beloved grandma talks."

On the other hand, I don't want my girl going for her job interviews speaking in slang, doing the rap thing, sounding uneducated and what have you. I am not in favor of that. She's got to practice talking in the white world. So, I don't know. I don't know what to do there.

Some of these adults feel, as Wanda Carter does, that, to the extent that METCO teaches or forces black students to "talk like whites," or, as Jeremy Shepard calls it, "to play the white words game," it should somehow help white students see and accept alternative language forms. Beyond the issue of language, these adults emphasize that METCO should not be singularly focused on what Wanda and others term "the white rules." It should also teach white students something about the rules of other cultures. For example, several post-METCO adults today struggle with the question of how to help their own children balance the need to display behaviors deemed appropriate by authority figures within the school with healthy self-expression and habits of socializing that are more common in the city.

Sean Thomas, for example, remembers feeling the need to "almost whisper" in the hallways of his suburban junior high and high schools. Merely greeting friends "naturally," he found, could bring stern looks and startled expressions from white teachers and friends. "So," Sean explains, "you learn to adapt to that" by "curtailing yourself, toning down your enthusiasm for seeing someone you like." Today, Sean explains, he is "thankful" that he "fits in so easily" in his management position at a racially diverse company. The atmosphere, he explains, is "casual but professional." Sean explains that "you need to know how to put people at ease, how to act in certain circles, with clients and over the phone. This tone you need to have."

Sean is ambivalent about the adaptations he has made and continues to make in white environments. About adaptations required of METCO, he explains: "I'm not sure how I feel about them, now. I got something out of them, right? Yes. But I look at my own kids and you have to ask: Am I telling them to be false people? Am I saying, white is right?"

Clearly, the hesitations about white suburbia that these adults express indicate that some of the issues about cultural belonging, assimilation, and acceptance that METCO evoked remain unresolved in their own minds. Seeing the benefits of METCO and even opting to repeat it, they surely do not accept all its lessons blindly. As adults, these men and women continue to think critically and deeply about the meaning of their past experiences as they try to settle remaining questions in their lives. This is especially true among the past participants who are raising or who have raised children. Child rearing, it seems, reignites some of the residual conflicts that first emerged in METCO and calls for the adults to resolve them.

There was a third common concern—a bit less common than the other two—related to academics. Men and women worried that their children might wrongly be deemed less academically able than white students and thus be enrolled in inappropriately lower-level courses. To guard against such discrimination, the post-METCO adults say they would be involved in their children's suburban schools, get to know their children's teachers, ask questions of teachers and administrators regularly, and attend school meetings and conferences.

Despite these three broadly defined concerns, the post-METCO adults justify the decisions by pointing, again, to the concrete benefits and personal gains they believe the program can offer its students. They are less likely than the first group to stress causal lines between their suburban schooling and specific opportunity in their lives. But members of this group do stress that, in spite of the potentially negative aspects of METCO, the potential benefits in the real world far outweigh their concerns.

Some members of this group reasoned that the problems and conflicts suburban schooling would present their children were no different from what they would confront in society.

Kevin Tyler, for example, says, "It's just more of the same thing, over and over. The same conflicts, between going and staying. Like, I want to have this opportunity in my life, so doesn't that mean I have to give up something of who I am? Do I? Is it right? Should I have to? Why? Why is it always the black guy who has to adapt?

I Guess I Have To

A relatively smaller group of post-METCO adults—just fourteen fall here—whose members, in saying they would repeat their experiences and place their children in white suburban schools, nevertheless see METCO as the best choice among inadequate options. They select the program with far more hesitation and uncertainty than do others. These adults commonly complain at length about what they perceive as the low quality of the public schools in Boston and the high cost of private schools in the Boston area. While they'd lean toward sending their child to METCO, a few said they would simultaneously "consider" other options, such as independent or charter schools.

Some of these adults wish for public schools in their own communities that are racially mixed and college preparatory. All these adults complained of there being too few spaces in Boston's elite college preparatory high schools, which require a high score on an exam and an admissions evaluation. Though these high schools, commonly termed "exam" schools, would be acceptable alternatives for members of this group, these respondents doubted that the city's elementary and middle schools would adequately prepare a student for a space at one of these rigorous public high schools. Several members of this group do express strong desires for racially integrated schools but would prefer it if such schools were located in their own urban neighborhoods. It is not so much METCO's physical inconvenience that causes these adults to hesitate—though this was certainly mentioned as a drawback—but more important was what Cherisse Clarkson, an early 1980s graduate, terms, "this feeling like you are an outsider all the time, that you are a visitor, like you are on a visa from the ghetto. It hurts that I'll be putting my kids through that." As is typical of other post-METCO adults, Cherisse would strongly favor a college preparatory city school that catered to a significant share of blacks as well as whites.

Absent a "solid" guarantee that "my kids could get into a school like that," Cherisse says, "I don't know what I'd do. I guess I'd put them in METCO. I guess that would be my only choice, really, except to move. But then, you get all the same issues that aren't that different just because you live in the suburbs. I'd like it if there was a school with a lot of black students, high-achievers, good kids who don't screw around or something like that, and some whites, a good, more mixed school that wasn't a token thing like METCO."

The concerns expressed by these men and women were often similar to those with more enthusiasm for the program. These fears related to discrimination and the potential for children to lose connections to black groups and culture. But unlike the enthusiastic group, members of this more hesitant group also expressed concerns about what they perceived as the relative lack of power that METCO parents have in suburban systems. These more hesitant adults, while not wanting their children to suffer because of their "visitor" status, often also have political concerns they believe might be solved in an independent school to which they pay tuition or in a public school in a community where they live.

No Going Back

It is rare for post-METCO adults to answer a plain "no" to the question of whether they would either repeat their experiences or send their child to METCO. But the justifications they provide are certainly revealing and worth considering in some detail. Just eight of the sixty-five people I talked with did not answer "yes" to the question of whether they would return to METCO in some fashion. Of these negative replies, four answered "no," to both the question about themselves and the question about their children. Three of these men and women said that the feelings of cultural isolation and identity confusion that stemmed from suburban schooling were too painful for them at the time and failed to diminish in later years. Thus, they speculated, METCO would be too painful for their own children. Three of the four say that if black children develop high self-esteem and personal power on their own, separate from whites, then society will be improved as these young blacks contribute to their communities. These adults, then, say that they would likely choose an all-black or nearly all-black learning environment for their children.

Paul Hammond, for example, believes that the "black condition" will improve only when blacks work together, outside the white "mainstream," to "build communities [and] teach each other our history."

"It is not that METCO was all bad for me. I didn't like it so much day to day, and there were kids on the bus with me who were into it a lot more," Paul explains. "But when you think about your children, they are the future. And I'd want to feel like my kids were part of the solution for black communities coming together. [In METCO] I was leaving a black community rather than staying in it and seeing the strength that exists inside of it. I would not want my child leaving that community, his community. First, I say, stay where you are, know where you come from, build it up. Don't run away. Then you see some improvement in our society."

A fourth past participant, Beth Davidson, acknowledges that METCO helped teach values of "appreciating others for what's inside," and "being understanding and appreciative of all different cultures, trying to see things from everyone's side." She nevertheless feels that it is important for her to pass those lessons of "acceptance" onto her sons herself rather than have an educational program "do it for me." Beth had generally positive experiences in METCO but never graduated from the program. After leaving, Beth earned a high school equivalency degree and is working as a manager in a state-run agency. While Beth's elementary and middle school years were "fine, no problem," in high school, she became pregnant and found little support from school administrators or METCO staff.

With one school-age child attending school in Boston and racially integrated camps in summer, Beth explains, "I got that [appreciation of other cultures] out of METCO, but I have it now and I'm giving that to my kids. I think it's important for me to do that for them. I don't need METCO to do that. And I'm watching over his school and he's going to be all right. I'm making sure of this. So, it's also a matter of wanting my kids close by, near home, near my work. That's important to me and I do think that what you get out of METCO can be important too. But I'll give that to them myself."

Two respondents were undecided, though stress that they lean strongly toward not sending their children to a METCO school. Each the parent of school-age children, the man lives out of state in a diverse, urban neighborhood and sends his children to independent schools, while the woman sends her children to public schools in Boston The woman, however, is exploring charter schools in the city as well, saying she'd consider METCO, but wants them closer to home even though she believes her children aren't offered enough "advanced" curriculum.

These parents were not concerned about cultural isolation, even though one said she experienced it "intensely" as a student. More specifically, these parents were concerned about the physical inconvenience of the program, including that the school's distance from their homes might make it difficult for them to take what they termed "active" or "influential" roles in their children's education.

Two other respondents would repeat the experience themselves, but, in considering the specific needs of their actual children, they say they would not send all their children to METCO. (Neither lives in the Boston city limits.) They concluded that their children might require small learning environments, possibly found in an independent school. Another worried that her daughters might require more structure and less freedom than she felt existed in some suburban high schools. These parents, however, were not opposed on principle to sending their children to predominantly white schools.

Therefore, there is a range of reasons post-METCO adults would not repeat their experience either themselves or through their children. It was common for the adults to cite a higher, societal purpose for their hypothetical decisions against METCO. Just as those in favor of repeating METCO often cited their belief that racial integration might lead to a better society, so did some of the nonrepeaters believe that *less* racial integration would improve blacks' self-worth and make them more likely to contribute in constructive ways to black communities.

Continuing the Cycle of Integration

Based on interviews with post-METCO adults, a striking number would opt to repeat their suburban schooling. And most would also send their children—actual or hypothetical—to suburban METCO schools. The decision isn't always easy, just as METCO wasn't always easy. For most people, METCO—and the policy and practice of racial integration it symbolizes—is a necessary, inescapable feature of American life. For many of these adults, who experienced racial integration in a most extreme form, it almost had to be "worth it" because it quite simply represents their way of life, their mode of existing in this society.

These adults did not board METCO buses thinking, as Elaine Yardley says, "that it was going to be an easy, good time." Most of them went because, as Rita Wood recalls, "my parents made me." Parents made them, it seems, because they thought the experience would pay off. And to varying degrees, for different reasons, most people believe their parents were probably right. And today, most of the now grown-up children—though not without hesitation—would make the same choice for their children.

Barbara Michaels, the first METCO student to graduate from her suburban school, spoke in the first chapter about the good and bad associated with being a black city child in a white, suburban school. She sums things up, again, now.

"You do see as a child what you're going to see later. Out there. In the real world. You see it in a METCO school, the good and the bad, right? Do you really have a choice about integrating and not integrating? I don't think so. So, fine. Let's try to make it work better for everyone."

7

City Life and Suburban Schools

What We Learn from
the Grown-up Children Who Crossed
Boston's Race Boundary

One fall Kevin Tyler, then just twelve or thirteen years old, looked around the suburban neighborhood near his new school. He felt "sick." Not disgusted, but "out of sorts, out of my element" with "everything feeling foreign, just weird." He was only ten or twelve miles from home, but through Kevin's Roxbury child's eyes, suburbia looked like "another world."

The differences assaulted his senses. There were so many shockingly white faces. The sidewalks here didn't seem made for walking. There weren't any people out. The streets hummed steadily with cars, but the neighborhood seemed "so silent." The quiet made him wince. Kevin startled easily. Suburbia smelled "cleaner, greener" than the city's "bus exhaust and smog." But the fresh new odors "felt weird to my nose, not pleasant."

Suburbia's space was cordoned off, privatized. This intimidated many young METCO students. In the city, they usually shared the greenery and the pools. In suburbia, people drove around by themselves or with their families in comfortable cars. In the city, they used the buses and the subway with many people they didn't know. People dressed differently out in the suburbs: to many black students it all looked more casual, despite the wealth. They talked differently "out there"—they "chatted" in what sounded to April Patterson, like "not a very expressive style." Despite its "weirdness," life in suburbia seemed, in April's words, to be "charmed, so easy for those kids, so easy." But years after they left suburbia, Kevin and April are glad they went, although life in the city—life around other black people—would always be more comfortable for them.

Thousands of METCO students like Kevin and April have experienced more personally and perhaps more profoundly than anyone the consequences of long-standing, deep racial and class divisions that characterize metropolitan Boston. Like most northern metropolitan areas, Boston and its suburbs are generally close in proximity and yet, as the cliché says aptly, they are worlds apart. The most important differences are not merely those sensory ones children might experience traveling back and forth between urban centers like Roxbury and suburban communities like Newton and Lexington. Differences in sight, sound, lifestyle, affluence, and skin color do indeed make the journeys across the boundary line more disconcerting, more difficult, and, in the long run, quite informative.

The principal mission of METCO was never solely to reveal and reconcile differences, though of that, it does its share. Its fundamental goal was to correct disparities. This highlights the distinction between "equal opportunity" and "diversity." On the one hand, METCO students and their parents were seeking to equalize their educational opportunities, not experience diversity, per se. But it's also important to see that just because a student is going to a program with one clear goal—equal education—it does not preclude that student from benefiting from the program's other mission, which is to create diversity. As we saw in the previous chapter, the former METCO students perceived that they derived many longer-term benefits from exposure to a different culture and slowly became more at ease in a predominantly white, opportunity-rich environment. While they might have initially gone to suburbia in order to get better prepared for college, they often found that preparing for college required learning how to navigate, negotiate, and build their own bridges to a nearly all-white environment. Today, Kevin and many other former METCO students place their own children on the program's long waiting list. These parents have learned to look critically at the long-standing divisions and inequality in Boston's metropolitan area. And they believe that because of these chasms and disparities, the educational opportunities in the urban and suburban communities aren't equal in what they offer to prepare students for post–high school life.

In this general asymmetrical structure of educational opportunity, most of the high-performing, well-regarded, well-connected public schools are located in suburban communities, while lower-performing, poorly perceived public schools are in the city. There are exceptions, of course. And public perception isn't always a fair and accurate reflection of reality. However, if parents were to compare school districts based on their evaluative test scores and other data—and some do—they would easily find evidence that confirms their perceptions.

According to the 1998 results of the Massachusetts Comprehensive Assessment System (MCAS) exam, for example, suburban schools generally performed far better than their urban counterparts. The percentages of students scoring either "proficient or advanced" on the test were lowest among the bulk of Boston's elementary schools. Elementary, middle, and high schools in Boston were clumped near the bottom of the widely published comparisons of regional test results. Meanwhile, as most would predict, the prosperous suburban schools—many of them METCO school districts—placed near the top of the list.

Newspapers and local magazines published the comparative results, not just of school districts, but also of individual schools within communities. (See, for example, Community Newspaper Company, 1998.) Of course the reasons for these outcomes are complicated and may be related to socioeconomic factors and resource disparities well beyond the control of individual schools. And there is a familiar exception: Tenth-graders at Boston's selective and prestigious Boston Latin School ranked the second-highest in the state when averaging "advanced" and "proficient" scores across the English, math, and science categories (Massachusetts Department of Education, 1998).

In the minds of the METCO past participants, many of whom are parents, the lopsided pattern of high achievement on one side and lagging achievement on the other points dramatically to some of the basic differences between Boston and its surrounding suburbs. The parents of METCO students understood these differences, and their children, who boarded buses out of their communities, sometimes reluctantly, have come to focus on the differences too.

There are other reasons METCO endures. A small program, METCO operates on terms that suburbanites can accept. It does not greatly alter the status quo of either suburbia's schools or their larger communities. Some post-METCO adults say that this is precisely the program's remaining flaw. Blacks adapt and accommodate. Whites need not adjust or empathize much. Thus, METCO is doing something few programs do in that it attempts to redress vast structural inequality by connecting urban and suburban communities. But while METCO lets urban blacks break in, it still lets suburban whites off the hook.

If the program can be stripped to an essential, it is this: METCO students break a long-standing, general pattern of inequality by jumping over the race boundary to what might seem to them at first to be foreign, distant worlds. And if the program is successful, young people come to learn that what seemed to be another world is, in fact, connected to their world. White suburbia and the white America it approximates become internalized parts of their expanding spheres, part of their familiar universe. A few years in suburbia usually showed METCO students what to expect—where they might find triumph and where they might find disappointment. Memories of race-based indignities rest alongside memories of challenges overcome, fears faced down.

The stories that these men and women tell require us to reexamine the terms of an important social policy debate. They have implications for educators, policy makers, and community leaders. The findings here also illuminate what is still not fully understood about this experience and what new questions researchers might try to answer.

Returning to the Questions

This study was guided by broad questions about black adults' memories and their perceptions of the long-range effects their years in white suburban schools had on their lives. The first set of questions is: What salient recollections do black adults have of their experiences of attending suburban schools while living in the city and what recollection do they say best characterizes such experiences? And as they look back on their school years, what do the prominent memories mean and symbolize to the adults today?

As black children or teenagers boarding a bus to suburbia, the METCO students quite commonly repeated a mantra in their minds. On bus rides that could last one, even two hours, students understood that they were in pursuit of "a better education." Parents placed a bet with METCO. They banked on those suburban schools to expand their children's options for the future. Parents and, later, their children valued the longer-term possibilities of suburban schooling, a practical logic that is in keeping with the earliest Supreme Court decisions on desegregation. These were decisions that upheld education's value, not just in its immediate effects, but in its potential to ameliorate inequality by equalizing access to opportunity over the course of one's life.

But day to day, METCO could try a young person's spirit. Occasionally, it seemed to some of the students that it would have been easier, and certainly more pleasant, just to stay in the city for school. But parents, confident of the bets they had made, thought otherwise. As the black adults encountered the new world of white suburbia, they couldn't help but notice differences between themselves and the students who lived in white communities. But it is not the mere existence of difference itself that endures in the memories of post-METCO adults. It was white students', teachers', and administrators' *reactions* to difference that shaped the METCO students' lasting impressions of suburbia and of their experiences there. Years later, the METCO adults haven't forgotten about incidents in which they were humiliated by ignorant questions and hurt by blatant racism. Meanwhile, memories of cross-cultural learning, few as they may be, co-exist as powerful forces with the negative recollections of stereotype and ignorance.

Students also were both awed and bothered by what seemed to them to be the white students' tendencies to take their own privileges for granted. But witnessing privileges inherent in white suburbia enabled the METCO students to comprehend fully the inequalities—related to power and to opportunity—between the places where they lived and the places where they went to school. They began to discern the forces that both created and exacerbated disparities in power, wealth, and prestige. Inequality, most of them began to understand, was the fault not merely of individuals, but of a complex system of barriers—barriers that many of the young students would later feel that METCO had helped them climb over.

The second set of questions driving this study considers

adults' perceptions of the longer-term effects of their early racial integration experiences. The questions are, simply, do black adults perceive longer-term effects of the METCO experience? And, if so, what are those perceived effects?

Most often, it was not until the adults began learning and living on college campuses and working in business firms and various social institutions that they began to more fully understand the reasons they were in suburban schools in the first place. If they attended predominantly white colleges—all but one of those who went to college did—the black students often found students who were similar to the suburbanites they had encountered during METCO. When hired into predominantly white settings—all but three of the post-METCO adults were—they found that their colleagues and supervisors and the very culture of those workplaces mirrored aspects of the suburban students and schools of their younger days. This, they perceive, could work to their advantage.

The former METCO students generally perceive that prior experience interacting in an environment that imitated college and the workforce made them more likely later to enter similar settings, feel more comfortable once they were there, and be more likely to succeed and less likely to be intimidated or scared off by initial awkwardness related to racial and cultural difference. Beyond this, the post-METCO adults say that the early years traveling between black and white worlds enables them now, as adults, to move fluidly in both worlds. Many were pleasantly surprised to find that such skills—often labeled as "intercultural communication" or "diversity training"—were in high demand in college and especially in racially diverse workplaces.

As they entered the "real world" armed with these personal skills, they had other tools to help them break down barriers to opportunity in society. Associating themselves with a powerful, well-regarded social institution, they perceive today, aided them in breaking the ice during interviews and forced others to see them as capable of success in an academically or professionally competitive environment. They began to see that certain forms of information they had received in their suburban schools—details and guidance about college, career paths, and connections—had been crucial for getting opportunity in their lives. Later, as adults, the former METCO students saw the utility of patching together a network of contacts and acquaintances—a network that included blacks and whites—to provide them with information about and connection to opportunity. Many perceive that METCO had helped them develop the political savvy to see this necessity and the interpersonal skills to actually create the contacts and connections.

Clearly, then, the post-METCO adults generally perceive that they gained a lot from their journeys to white suburbia. But they quite often paid a price. Bouncing between white and black worlds often made the young black students feel they didn't truly belong in either one. This confusion lingers for many of the adults, who remain sensitive to challenges about cultural integrity and sad about lost connections to community. Even adults who are sure they made the right choice, both about METCO and about attending predominantly white colleges, quite commonly have lingering questions about whether they might today be more secure in their racial identities had they attended all-black educational institutions. The vast majority of adults did manage to resolve such conflicts, through either reconnections to a black community or personal and professional commitments to organizations and causes concerned with blacks as a group or in predominantly black communities. But the confusion they experienced during METCO still gets re-ignited, forcing them to address questions about racial identity and assimilation.

The typical post-METCO adult thus carries two narratives in his or her mind. On the one hand, METCO yielded benefits. On the other hand, it had costs. And there are compelling stories associated with each narrative. Faced with this dual reality, how does one weigh the good against the bad? After considering the positive and negative stories, a reader might feel qualified to answer this question based merely on his or her own values. For example, one might believe that a relatively uncomplicated development of a healthy racial identity is more important than whatever increased opportunities METCO might plausibly provide. Or, one might conclude that if a program helps a child to succeed in college and the workplace, confusion over racial identity should be a secondary concern. But much more relevant, I believe, is the conclusion of people who actually lived through the experience.

This brings us to the third question driving this study. Balancing all the aspects of the experience and its perceived effects, how do post-METCO adults characterize and explain the value of the overall program based on their personal experience? From the perspective of post-METCO adults, the program's real world, practical worth generally outweighs its more negative aspects. And a striking number—fifty-seven of the sixty-five—say they would return to METCO if they were to go back in time and that they would make the same or a similar decision for their children. But there is much ambivalence within these answers. And for many, their particular reasons for their hesitation are reflections of what they feel was missing or lost as they crossed the boundary between black and white, city and suburb.

The following two sections move beyond general findings to place this work in the context of theory and existing knowledge about the longer-range effects of desegregated schooling for black Americans.

What's Known

A lot is already known about the longer-term effects of desegregated schools on the lives of blacks. The research findings, in fact, are far less ambiguous than the research on some other educational matters, including choice and magnet school options, which were comparatively more topical and more widely endorsed in the 1990s (Orfield & Eaton, 1996). But research on desegregation's longer-term impact has been widely ignored for decades, as policy makers and grant makers came to favor the more immediate results from shorter-term analyses on the effects of desegregation on the test scores of students still in school (Wells and Crain, 1997; Orfield and Eaton, 1996). The results from hundreds of these shorter-term studies have been inconclusive, conflicting, and problematic, as research usually failed to distinguish between types of desegregation plans, communities, and students (Schofield, 1989).

But the lesser-known, longer-term research generally shows that previously desegregated blacks are more likely than their otherwise similar but previously segregated counterparts to continue the trend of racial integration over the course of their lives (Wells and Crain, 1994; Braddock, McPartland and Trent, 1984; Crain & Weisman, 1972; Braddock & McPartland, 1983; Green, 1981; Crain, 1984). In their conclusions, the researchers who conducted the long-term studies often imply that more integration is desirable and segregation is not. This might seem an audacious assumption, since in the 1990s, the value of integration was regularly questioned by liberals and conservatives alike (Patterson, 1997; Eaton & Orfield, 1996). And as school segregation continues to increase, there seems to be little concern from policy makers (Orfield et. al., 1997).

But it is important to understand the context in which these researchers designed and conducted their studies. They do not examine integration and segregation as pure conditions of equal value. These scholars recognize that the structure of opportunity in America handicaps segregated blacks. The scholars suggest that segregation by race, whether imposed or chosen, physically excludes blacks from myriad forms of opportunity for social mobility that are simply more abundant in white settings. In plain terms, white, middle-class people, because of a history of advantage in the United States, perpetuate their privilege through friends, acquaintances, and their association with prestigious institutions. Segregated blacks, the theory goes, are left out of this powerful progenitor of success and prestige in American society.

Breaking the Cycle of Perpetual Segregation

University of Miami professor Jomills Henry Braddock (1980) first used the term "perpetuation theory" to describe the tendency of black Americans to perpetuate their segregated states over the course of their lives. Perpetuation theory posits that blacks who have not had sustained past experiences in racially mixed environments will probably perpetuate segregation by avoiding racially mixed settings in the future. Blacks do this, Braddock argues, because they overestimate the hostility they will find in such environments and believe themselves incapable of either coping with or succeeding in predominantly white workplaces, learning institutions, or social groups. Conversely, blacks who have had sustained experience in racially mixed settings, Braddock hypothesizes, will be more likely to choose to enter predominantly white settings when they perceive opportunity there.

Perpetuation theory, as Braddock articulated it, focuses on the motivations and actions of individuals. Principally, the theory addresses the question of how one's own behavior and state of mind might limit his or her chances for success. But Braddock, along with other scholars, also understood that removing personal or psychological barriers to racial integration would not be enough either to build a more integrated society or to improve black Americans' chances for social mobility. Braddock and other scholars saw that it was more than blacks' own fears holding them back. In Braddock's analysis, there are also structural barriers in the larger society that make it difficult for segregated blacks, whatever their levels of personal confidence, to gain entry to white settings where a disproportionate share of economic and higher educational opportunities are located. Such barriers include white prejudice and the fact that whites aren't familiar with predominantly black institutions and communities where blacks might have contacts and personal references. Also, whites generally have more access to information about jobs and they generally have more influential social networks. These advantages stem, in part, from the fact that whites have long been predominant in certain types of jobs.

Scholars who study such phenomena are sometimes referred to as "structural theorists" because they focus on the often-unseen barriers to opportunity that perpetuate inequality. Mark Granovetter (1986), for example, theorizes that school desegregation may enhance lifelong opportunity by bringing blacks into contact with affluent whites who are generally better-connected to job and economic opportunities. Several other scholars, referred to in the scholarly literature as "network analysts" (Montgomery, 1992; Lin, 1990), note that the economically and socially disadvantaged have less useful information about how to achieve economic success or win opportunity. And because such information is generally so common in white middle- and upper-middle-class settings, structural theorists suggest that tying blacks into those networks via integrated schools may level the playing field over the long term.

Previous research offers support for both the more behaviorally focused perpetuation theory as well as theories that speak to broader structural concerns. In their comprehensive review of the scholarly literature on the longer-term effects of school desegregation, Amy Stuart Wells and Robert Crain (1994) consider the policy's effect on students' choices of college, educational and occupational aspirations and planning, adult social networks, and occupational attainment. They conclude:

Beginning with the aspirations of high school students and ending with tangible results of black adults' social networks and participation in the work force, our analysis has attempted to trace the path of perpetual segregation and isolation, pointing out the various junctures at which the cycle can be broken by black students who have access to information about better education and occupational opportunities and who are less fearful of whites. We believe that this review supports the theory that interracial contact in elementary or secondary school can help blacks overcome perpetual segregation. (Wells and Crain, 1984, p. 552)

One study (Braddock, 1980), for example, found that black students who had attended predominantly white schools (at least seventy-five percent white) were more than twice as likely to chose a predominantly white college than were blacks who attended high schools that were more than seventy-five percent black. A later study (Braddock, 1987) found that the racial composition of a black student's high school has the greatest impact among many factors—including grades and even proximity to home—on whether a student will choose a predominantly white college. In a study that speaks to an experience that is similar to that of METCO students, researchers Julie Kaufman and James Rosenbaum (1992) compared college-going rates of two sets of black students from Chicago who participated in the Gautreaux program. Gautreaux relocated inner-city families to new homes and public schools. Drawn from a randomly selected pool of applicants, one set of students in the study had been moved to suburban neighborhoods while the other set was relocated to neighborhoods and schools within Chicago. The researchers found the suburban movers more likely to attend college than the urban students and also more likely than the urban students to attain a four-year rather than a two-year degree. (The researchers are not suggesting, of course, that white college campuses are somehow "better" than historically black ones. They use choice of college as merely one indicator of a respondent's willingness to enter a white setting when he or she believes opportunities exist there.)

Other studies have found that previously desegregated blacks were more likely than previously segregated blacks to have racially mixed social networks that may include contacts for jobs and other opportunities. Research has also found desegregated blacks more likely to be working in racially mixed settings. For example, Braddock and McPartland (1989) found that young black adults who attended majority black schools were less likely to have white work associates than their counterparts from predominantly white schools. In this study, the racial composition of a student's high school was the most powerful predictor of the degree of occupational desegregation later in life. Trent (1991) found that blacks, Latinos, and whites who attended racially homogeneous schools were far more likely than those from more integrated schools to perceive their racially mixed work environments as less friendly than workplaces dominated by members of their own race. Trent also found that blacks who graduated from racially mixed schools were more likely to work in settings with larger shares of whites. This was true even when he controlled for the racial composition of the county in which the workplace was located. Likewise, Dawkins (1991) found that for three age groups younger than forty, there were positive relationships between attendance at a desegregated school and degree of interracial contact as an adult.

Explaining the Findings

As Wells and Crain (1994) point out in their research review, the underlying reasons for these findings remain unclear. There are several plausible combinations of factors that may be at work. For example, it might be true that previously desegregated blacks do become comparably more comfortable in white settings. But it may also be that biased white employers are more comfortable with black applicants and employees who have acquired the ability to de-emphasize traits—such as speech patterns—that whites associate with blacks. Another explanation is that because white interviewers and employers are often unfamiliar with predominantly black institutions, they are more likely to favor a black person associated with the prestigious white institutions with which employers are familiar. A more hopeful explanation is that the employers perceive that the black applicant, because of his or her experience in desegregated settings, may be skilled at interracial communication and working in diverse groups. Finally, it's also possible that blacks in these studies did benefit from social networks that included more whites connected to opportunities and information.

Certainly, these are all plausible explanations. But there is some persuasive evidence that a black's association with an integrated school can counteract some biases, perceptions, and prejudices that whites might have. And it's been found that having a social network that includes some whites can be beneficial to blacks. This is because jobs often are acquired through "word of mouth" information among friends, acquaintances, and family members. Similarly, as Jankowski (1995) suggests, a school's status or prestige in society depends on the status and prestige of its students. Thus, Jankowski finds, schools that enroll students with higher status in society—in other words, those who are wealthy and white—will have better connections to prestigious colleges and good, high-status jobs.

Circumventing Discrimination

Braddock and McPartland (1987) found that minority applicants from segregated communities and schools may be discriminated against because their recommendations and references—major factors in getting hired—carry less weight than recommendations or references provided by white candidates. Braddock and McPartland argue: "Due to segregation of schools and communities, white employers may be less familiar with a black school, a black clergy, or a black firm that a minority individual may use for sponsorship of his or her job candidacy, or white employers may feel more suspect of information provided by minorities due to stigma or stereotypes attached to minority sources" (Braddock and McPartland, 1987, p. 19).

Another study related to the Braddock and McPartland research found that when asked under what circumstances they would hire minority high school graduates in their firms, employers had more confidence in minority graduates of suburban, rather than urban, schools (Braddock, Crain, McPartland, and Dawkins, 1986). Several studies have shown that unsolicited, walk-in applications and informal referrals from current employees are among the most important tools that employers use to create applicant pools. (See, for example, Braddock and McPartland, 1987; Becker, 1977; Baker et al., 1984; Granvovetter, 1974; Granovetter, 1982; Mangum, 1982.)

In their study of 4,078 employers, Braddock and McPartland (1987) found that for positions filled by workers with a college degree, the chances are significantly greater that an opening will be filled by whites when such "social networks" are used as a major recruiting method. The research further shows that black high school graduates who used racially integrated social networks to find their jobs were in higher-paying positions, while those who used segregated black social networks were, on average, in the lowest paying jobs in settings with comparatively low percentages of white co-workers.

These findings are compatible with more comprehensive research on poverty and disadvantage in American society. Perhaps the best known of such studies are those conducted by the sociologist William Julius Wilson. In two large-scale studies (Wilson, 1987, 1996), he found that the most significant barrier to success for segregated, poorer classes living in the inner city was their isolation from information networks, social interaction, and more formal association with connecting institutions that might tie them into the economic opportunity so prevalent in middle-class, predominantly white communities. Wilson's work does not relate directly to school desegregation, but his general findings support theories put forth by network analysts such as Mark Granovetter (1986), who hypothesize that even "weak" or "acquaintance" ties to networks rich in information and contacts from desegregated schools will increase opportunity for otherwise marginalized individuals.

Granovetter argues: "Because employers at all levels of work prefer to recruit by word-of-mouth, typically using recommendations of current employees, segregation of friendship and acquaintance means that workplaces that start out all white will remain so" (Granovetter, 1986, pp. 102–103).

Some research evidence supports the hypothesis that information and influence derived from racially integrated schools will enhance opportunity for blacks in American society. Gable, Thompson, and Iwanicki (1983) found that blacks who had attended desegregated schools were more likely than otherwise similar blacks from segregated schools to have received adequate information about careers and thus to pursue academic courses that best prepared them for the careers they wanted. Similarly, Wells and Crain (1997) found that black students who transferred from urban to suburban districts through a voluntary desegregation program benefited from college fairs and school personnel's clear connections to college—characteristics far more prevalent in suburbia than in the city of St. Louis. Kaufman and Rosenbaum (1992) found that black inner-city students who were relocated to suburban communities and schools benefited from teachers and counselors who provided information about college admissions and helped the students prepare adequately for college curriculums. In interviews conducted by Kaufman and Rosenbaum, black parents and students cited the benefits of attending a suburban school where information about college was provided constantly. Also important, the parents and students said, was that suburban classmates' older siblings who had gone to college provided up-to-date information and assistance with the college application process.

In their 1998 book, *The Shape of The River: Long Term Consequences of Considering Race in College and University Admissions,* Derek Bok and William G. Bowen consider affirmative action's longer-term effects on the lives of blacks who attended some of the most prestigious colleges. They find that even when their grades were relatively low in college, the students went on to succeed in graduate and professional schools and the workplace. Although this research involves higher education only, the findings are relevant to METCO research. The research is similar in that Bok and Bowen considered the policy over the long term and, like my research, considered not only effects upon achievement, but also black adults' involvement in civic life and their mature views about the benefits of diversity on campus.

Particularly relevant to this study is Bok and Bowen's conclusion about the social benefits of diversity. The benefits cited by black students in their study are similar to the long-term gains cited by METCO's past participants. Based on survey data, Bok and Bowen conclude: "Both the growing diversity of American society and the increasing interaction with other cultures worldwide make it evident that going to school only with 'the likes of oneself' will be increasingly anachronistic. The advantages of being able to understand how others think and function, to cope across racial divides, and to lead groups composed of diverse individuals are certain to increase" (Bok and Bowen, p. 279).

Researchers Richard Zweigenhaft and G. William Domhoff (1991), meanwhile, have examined the interplay of social structure and social psychology among black students from poor, inner-city neighborhoods who attended some of the nation's most elite boarding schools through the program called A Better Chance (ABC). (A Better Chance recruits racial minority students from inner cities and offers them scholarships to the schools.) In their book *Blacks in the White Establishment* (1991) they provide a rare, dual consideration of both identity and social structure in the experience of American blacks. Through interviews with 38 ABC graduates, the researchers found that the black students acquired two skills with tangible rewards for social mobility following graduation. The graduates acquired the skill to "talk with anyone about anything." In other words, the graduates perceive that they grew to feel comfortable interacting in many types of settings, including upper-class social events and predominantly white, affluent workplaces. Second, the ABC graduates learned the importance of networking and were able to use contacts with influential people met through the ABC program to accomplish their goals. These skills, the researchers say, are powerful forms of social capital that contribute to social mobility.

But even after winning success equal to that earned by elite whites from boarding schools, the ABC graduates discovered that race would continue to be an important factor in their lives. On the job, for example, the graduates continued to face subtle forms of racism, which they found deeply discouraging. In considering the intersection of identity and social structure, Zweigenhaft and Domhoff also analyzed their findings within a framework of racial identity development as identified by anthropologists John Ogbu and Signithia Fordham.

Racial Identity Development

Fordham and Ogbu (1986) found that, as black teenagers become more aware of whites' historical exclusion of blacks in the United States, they develop an "oppositional identity" to the dominant white culture. Such an identity is characterized by behaviors, speech, taste, even gesturing and moving defined as not only "truly black" but, quite significantly, the polar opposite of what black peers have defined as being "white." This identity in opposition to whites, Ogbu and Fordham contend, protects young blacks psychologically from racism in part by distancing themselves from whites.

Particularly significant, Fordham and Ogbu found, is that, in the minds of these adolescents, academic achievement is commonly associated with "white" behavior, and this often is negatively sanctioned in black peer groups. This is because, the researchers explain, whites have neither expected nor valued black intellectual achievement. Thus, black students perceive academic success to be a characteristic exclusively of whites. Black students who do achieve are then labeled as "acting white" by their peers. And when the black students are high achievers, according to Fordham (1988), they often succeed at the expense of adopting painful "raceless" identities characterized by a lack of concern for or connection to black culture or black peer groups.

Ogbu and Fordham carried out their research primarily in predominantly black high schools. But it seems likely that such phenomena may be even more common or more pronounced in heavily white settings of the sort Zweigenhaft and Domhoff studied, where black adolescents have intense immersions in a white dominant culture. Indeed, Banks (1984), in an exploratory survey of ninety-eight black suburban children and their families, found that the white suburban communities in which the children were socialized did not prevent them from developing positive attitudes toward themselves, their communities, and their schools. The children had positive attitudes toward both blacks and whites in general. However, the study also found that as assimilation increased, the black children felt increasingly positive toward their schools and neighborhoods and about whites in general, but less positive about blacks.

Interestingly, Zweigenhaft and Domhoff (1991) found that the ABC students did not develop oppositional identities hostile to academic achievement or even associate academic achievement with whites only. The researchers offer two explanations for their findings. They theorize that the students, who lived on campus and were immersed in a prep school culture, incorporated the school's strong emphasis on academic achievement into their identities. It was the twenty-four-hour immersion in prep school culture, the researchers theorize, that may have caused this difference. Indeed, the prep school students don't have to contend with the challenge of moving daily between white schools and predominantly black neighborhoods. Zweigenhaft and Domhoff also suggest that rather than adopting an anti-achievement identity, the black students viewed themselves as achieving in order to advance the cause of all blacks. In his earlier work, Ogbu (1978, 1981) had identified such a trend among academically successful blacks who emphasized that if they were to succeed, this would result in advancement for other blacks. In this strategy, a young person sees his intellectual achievement not as a betrayal but as a contribution to blacks as a group. Zweigenhaft and Domhoff say that this personal strategy may "offer the most promising approach," as it allows for educational achievement and still "openly challenges white racism and maintains close ties with the black community."

What We Learn from METCO's Adults

The stories and recollections of post-METCO adults offer new insight into some of the questions that previous research on school integration had left unanswered. Much of the previous research that looks specifically at the longer-term effects of school desegregation has been statistical. This means that the research, by its nature, is not intended to capture the nuances of a complex human experience or to explain events and outcomes from the perspectives of participants themselves.

For example, research on METCO adults sheds light on the statistical findings that previously desegregated blacks are more likely than previously segregated blacks to enter and remain in desegregated settings later in life. In doing so, this research tests the validity of theories about social structure, educational opportunity, and the interplay of racial identity and integration. The research suggests that the perpetuation of racial integration is probably the result of a complicated interplay of several factors. This includes increased personal self-confidence and diminishing racial self-consciousness, the acquisition of behaviors and associations that counteract white prejudice, and an enhanced structure of opportunity that includes connections to information and influence.

In the eyes of program participants, METCO did reduce their personal fears of predominantly white—and in some cases, predominantly affluent—settings. There is much support found here, then, for Braddock's perpetuation theory that early experience with integration might prevent a potentially self-limiting behavior, namely self-segregation. The meaning of feeling comfortable in a white setting, however, is complex. For many of these black adults, comfort comes not just from knowing and applying unwritten rules of the so-called white world, but from finding a way to express themselves specifically as blacks within white settings.

These former METCO students did learn what so many still refer to today as "the white rules" in their suburban schools. And they are able to play by these rules when they want to. Just as it did in suburbia, playing by the rules might require altered speech patterns, toning down their expression of enthusiasm, and simply de-emphasizing traits they suspect might make whites feel uncomfortable. Each person finds his or her own way to respond to these rules. Some choose to follow. Others choose to rebel against them. Still others operate by white rules for a period of time and then, once they feel more comfortable, tend to express their identities as blacks according to their own personal definitions. It would be simplistic to say that black identity is lost in the process of decoding and using the so-called white rules. On the contrary, these adults generally perceive that because of METCO, they had to think intensely about what it means to them to be black and had to work arduously to form connections to their culture and identity. That process continues for adults who find themselves, years after METCO, learning and working in environments that mirror aspects of the suburban schools they attended.

Previous theory and research suggested that black students might also benefit from suburbia's pervasive flow of information about higher education and other opportunities. Similarly, it's long been theorized that networks of personal contacts, links to other opportunities in society, and diffusion of influence in white suburban schools might very well enhance possibilities for black students who would be excluded from these opportunities were they to remain segregated.

Past METCO participants offer much support for these ideas, as they recount the many paths by which crucial information about colleges, financial aid, internships, and jobs reached them. Valuable information about college and its requirements reached METCO students via official and informal channels at their suburban schools, including college fairs, numerous advertisements and written information, and counseling sessions about college and financial aid. But information also came from other METCO families and from contacts families made through the METCO program specifically, rather than the suburban school. This includes siblings of friends who had attended METCO, parents of other METCO students, METCO counselors and directors at the suburban schools, and even administrators in METCO's central office, located in Roxbury and thus accessible to many METCO students' homes. And when it came to personal contacts who could exert influence to help students get opportunity, the former METCO students were far more likely to have received help from these black sources than from white parents, students, counselors, or others in their suburban schools.

The fact that other blacks, rather than whites, appear to have been more likely to provide direct links to opportunity does not mean that network analysis, as articulated by Granovetter and others, is not accurate. More likely, the stories of METCO participants teach that organized and institutionalized programs may complement the powerful suburban connections and flow of information, and that these programs are important enhancers of opportunity. This predominantly black network was also a helpful counterweight to the influence of white guidance counselors who seemed to lack confidence in the intellectual abilities of black METCO students.

As research by Braddock and others has demonstrated, segregated blacks are often disadvantaged at the job hiring stage, in part because white employers are unfamiliar with blacks' learning institutions and also because blacks do not have personal contacts among employees or associates who can exert influence on who gets a job. Many former METCO students say such disadvantages are real and that these barriers may go unnoticed by whites, who have benefited greatly from having the insider track over the years.

These same METCO students often say that METCO did help them get past these barriers. For example, the METCO students perceive that they benefited from the status and prestige of their suburban schools and that the program provided the practice they needed to later form and maintain connections and links to opportunity.

After high school, however, many of the former METCO students continued to struggle with painful, confusing questions about where they fit in relationship to other blacks, to whites, to their home communities, to friends, and to relatives. Because METCO students had such early and, sometimes, harsh encounters with white stereotypes and prejudice about blacks, it's certainly plausible that they might develop protective identities that stand in opposition to whites or, in trying to adapt to their suburban schools, they might adopt "raceless" identities.

Chapter 3 discussed how the young METCO students would often consciously adopt behaviors, tastes, and manners of speech and then flaunt them as authentically black. In doing so, they reacted to the dominant white culture in suburban schools—a culture that often seemed to ignore or devalue black, urban culture. Talking to the adults today, we find that such oppositional identities were usually transient, though some adults still struggle with imposed definitions of what it means to be black. And interestingly, oppositional identity for these students did not manifest itself in academic failure. It is true that many of the adults I talked with struggled academically when they were in suburban schools. But the reasons for their problems, according to their accounts, were complicated and varied. The problems, according to them, were not a function of their thinking that academic achievement was somehow "too white." Certainly, racism in the school environment could have had some negative effect on academic achievement, as some students speculate that it did.

But the reason that low academic achievement didn't grow from a desire to develop an oppositional identity may be because METCO parents, as the former students commonly recall, provided strong messages about the need to succeed in school and offered examples of other academically successful blacks. Thus, these students might associate academic success with blackness. It is also plausible that, as METCO participants, the students developed specific identities that included academic striving and, in some cases, stood in opposition to some of their neighborhood acquaintances who did not seem to value academic achievement.

Both possibilities were common themes in the interviews, but the range of academic performance represented in my sample precludes my data from definitively answering questions about the role of racial identity in academic performance.

Other scholars have noted the importance of educators and parents offering black students definitions of blackness that include examples of academically successful blacks. Beverly Daniel Tatum (1997), for example, suggests that such definitions might lead students to associate success with being black and thus the students might not develop an oppositional identity that expresses itself in academic failure. Tatum reminds us that the black adolescents who see success in school as being "too white" are, of course, basing their definition of what it means to be black mostly on cultural stereotypes.

The METCO students, even the most academically successful ones, generally did not adopt so-called raceless identities over the long term. In fact, most of these former students consciously sought out and maintained professional, volunteer, and personal connections to black culture and history, predominantly black communities or causes, and organizations operating in the interest of helping blacks as a group. Even when black former students sometimes tried to camouflage behaviors they associated with or believed others associated with being black, the strategy was temporary and did not represent a total disassociation from black culture and relationships with other blacks. The strategy was abandoned, as it proved too psychologically painful in later years. It was then revised, and at times drastically altered, as the adults found comfortable ways to express themselves as blacks in white settings. The adults do generally perceive that their process of racial identity development was more intense, more painful, and perhaps more deliberate than it might have been if they had remained in a predominantly black urban setting for schooling. Despite this perception, the pattern of racial identity development described by the former students does not differ dramatically from the typical patterns of racial identity development as outlined by scholars whose studies focused mostly on blacks who did not have such early and intense experiences living within black and white worlds.

Recall that, quite similarly, Zweigenhaft's and Domhoff's prep-school graduates did not develop oppositional identities. Neither did the students develop "raceless" identities. The prep school graduates did not seem to face confusion about fitting in black and white communities as intensely or as commonly as the former METCO students report. This may be because the prep school students live on their campuses and thus are not bouncing back and forth daily between the "two worlds" the METCO adults so often described.

Also, the successful prep-school graduates often incorporated into their identities the idea that they were emissaries for the black community and that whatever personal success they had would benefit blacks as a group. The METCO graduates were less likely to view themselves this way. But, in later years, the METCO graduates were likely to see themselves as "giving back" to their communities. They did this, in part, as a payback for the opportunities they were given through METCO. But more significantly, they did this as a way to remain connected to a community from which they were once separated.

Expanding a Narrow Public Debate

The ongoing debate between advocates of integration and segregation is often a fight between those who see possibility and those who see disappointment. In recent years, there has been much public questioning, from blacks and whites alike, about whether racial integration in schools is a productive course either for improving the social condition of blacks or for improving race relations.

Despite well-publicized disappointments with the policy, no

one has yet articulated a serious, systematic policy alternative to racial integration. There are frequent calls for all-black Afrocentric schools designed to enhance self-esteem and efforts, such as the Million Man March, that preach self-help and individual responsibility. But these compelling calls don't address the questions of how segregated blacks, disproportionate numbers of whom are poor and near poor, can achieve economic success within a society where whites control most of the wealth and political power.

On the other hand, integrationists have had few answers for blacks who have been personally disappointed, even humiliated and hurt by their own experiences with integration. In 1997, the leading integrationist group, the NAACP, even considered abandoning its long-held policy in favor of racially integrated schools. The group finally chose not to vote on a proposal to abandon its supportive stance on integration. Leaders acknowledged the conflicts and difficulties of integration but offered no plan for addressing the problems (Williams, 1997; Maxwell, 1998). Even blacks who admit that they have benefited from policies designed to create racial integration nevertheless complain frequently of personal indignities, of glass ceilings that limit success, and of subtle forms of bigotry that linger in the hearts and minds of white colleagues (Cose, 1993; Cose, 1997; Collins, 1989; Patterson, 1997).

Therefore, scholars and advocates of integration, focusing on the progress and potential of integration, seem to be begging for patience. They do point to integration's successes thus far. But focusing only on longer-term benefits fails to acknowledge that blacks, who have historically been oppressed and discriminated against as a group, are also searching for personal meaning and psychological well-being in what's still a very race-conscious society.

Members on each side of the debate, then, are not so much arguing with each other as they are ignoring each other's basic interests and concerns. Integrationists focus on external success in higher education, jobs, and race relations. Both those who question integration and those who reject it outright are increasingly concerned with questions of racial identity and black community and cultural cohesion. There is, of course, still the occasional wrangling over the true extent of integration's successes. And the question still arises over whether integration is inherently impossible to achieve or whether federal and state governments have simply failed to pursue it (Wicker, 1996). But these important questions have become tangential in the more popular debate where pro and con participants circle each other, pitting economic reality against identity, and social mobility against self-actualization. (See, for example, Fineman, 1996; Kozol, 1994; Shaper Walters, 1996; Shlinkman, 1997; Patterson, 1997; Maxwell, 1997.)

If the stories and lives of post-METCO adults contribute anything to this debate, it is that the concepts of racial identity and connection to culture should not be separated from discussions about social mobility and economic opportunity in American society. Using the experiences of these adults as a guide, we learn that the two concepts—social mobility and identity—are intertwined. Most researchers have treated these ideas as separate and discrete. But for people experiencing integration programs such as METCO, it is difficult and illogical to separate the two.

Thus, the stories and perspectives of post-METCO adults suggest that advocates of integration should neither minimize nor dismiss the very real problems that are by-products of integrated schools. White resistance to integration has inspired understandable urges on the part of many post-METCO adults to flee integrated settings for the comfort and well-being they associate with predominantly black environments. But from the perspective of past METCO participants, remaining forever in segregated black communities and learning institutions is not a realistic option. Segregated schools, they perceive, neither approximate nor prepare them for the larger society where employment and higher education opportunities exist. Advocates of integration, then, would do better to acknowledge the conflicts that arise and focus on ways to reduce the problems.

Meanwhile, most past METCO adults would say that black leaders who urge segregation by choice, or an as-yet unarticulated policy of self-help, are offering a self-defeating option. This brings us to the first of the three most prevalent public conflicts that have shaped the debate over METCO-like programs that promote racial integration across urban and suburban lines.

The first such conflict relates to resources and the question of who should get them—inner-city, predominantly black communities, or the urban blacks who choose suburban schools. There are two types of resources—good students and money. The objections to such programs go like this: *Programs that encourage transfer between city and suburb steal the most motivated students and parents, whose presence might enhance public inner-city schools. Whatever money is spent transferring these students across municipal boundary lines would be better spent in the black community's urban system.*

This is a compelling and important argument. But the justifications that post-METCO adults give for having attended suburban schools, and for choosing to send their children there, may make the first part of the objection irrelevant. Segregated schooling is not an option they would seriously consider. This is because, in their minds, the urban system replicates a segregated community that fails to offer a full range of opportunity. The suburban school, the adults believe, offers something most city schools—no matter how objectively good they might be—usually cannot. It offers prestige, connections, exposure, and clear links to opportunity in the larger society. The one exception, they agree, is Boston Latin High School, where places are limited.

Based on their own testimony, families who are motivated to transfer to predominantly white suburban schools in the first place are simply not good candidates for being fenced in to limited educational options. It is likely that if they had the money, such families would pursue an independent or religious school. As for those without tuition money, one has to consider: Is it right to force lower-income families to attend school in what are generally poor-performing urban systems when they would rather be elsewhere? This is a question that research can't answer, but that enlightened public discourse might. (This argument is similar to that forwarded by advocates of market-based voucher programs, but METCO differs from such schemes in important ways, as I discuss later.)

As for monetary resources, METCO and programs like it usually are funded by the state and, to some extent, by the suburban communities that participate. Theoretically, the money spent on this program could indeed be funneled to the city schools instead. But the state money spent on METCO-like programs goes to address not an urban problem specifically, but a problem within a metropolitan area that thus requires metropolitan solutions. In other words, reducing the plausibly negative effects of racial isolation—lack of connection to opportunity; lack of association with prestigious, influential schools that are connected to higher education opportunity; lack of connection to social networks that relay vital information about jobs—requires the participation of not merely the city, but also the suburbs.

The broad mission of increasing opportunity is reflected in the stories of past METCO participants. After some former students entered the real world, they began to comprehend quite clearly the importance of bridging the divide between urban and suburban communities. And many of them came to see the problems that continued in their lives—subtle racism and stereotyping and race-related misunderstandings—as manifestations of the vast divisions between blacks and whites in America.

Black community leaders and politicians commonly raise a second objection to metropolitan-wide solutions that center on schools, arguing that they threaten efforts to strengthen black communities. The argument is that *such programs disconnect blacks from their neighborhoods. As a result, the black child/future adult will think poorly of himself and internalize racism. Moreover, as young people become disconnected from the community, they fail to assist in strengthening their neighborhoods, aspiring instead to white, suburban lifestyles.*

The stories and recollections from METCO graduates offer some support for this contention. There is, indeed, a pattern of lasting conflict as children confront racism and stereotypes and are influenced by dominant white standards in lifestyle, clothing, dress, and personal style. Many of the former students do, in fact, recall thinking poorly of their communities and feeling bad about where they lived and who they are. And many do believe that it was their immersion in white suburbia that provoked these negative feelings. But these early reactions weren't permanent. Childhood attitudes did not predict future attachments or opinions about their culture and their home communities.

As noted repeatedly, the vast majority of these adults remain deliberately connected to black communities. Even the relatively small share who left black neighborhoods to live in suburbia found ways to stay connected to black social groups, culture, and communities, through either worship, friends, or volunteer service, or by passing down cultural traditions and pride to their children.

The third objection is that *confrontations with racism and white ignorance will hurt young black children in suburban schools.* The logic is that integration does not work because the racism in schools negatively affects the experiences of black children. Therefore, it's better to have segregated learning environments. The METCO adults certainly recall varied forms of racism and stereotyping in the suburban schools they attended. As one would expect, confrontations with this reality were quite unpleasant and evoked a range of reactions: anger, disgust, rage, scorn, mocking humor, and cynicism. Sometimes this aspect of the suburban experience was, in itself, enough to make students want to transfer. Some did.

But the former METCO students began to see, later in life, that what they experienced in suburbia was a reflection of what existed in the larger society. The adults continued to face racism and deal with race-based misunderstanding. Many perceive they may be better prepared to traverse that terrain because of their early schooling experiences. Moreover, when adults look back on their suburban experience, they rarely focus exclusively on negative aspects of black and white relationships. They find important meaning and hope in the positive examples of healthy relationships between blacks and whites. The majority of adults do acknowledge that suburbia could indeed become more welcoming to and appreciative of METCO students. But remarkably, many say that they'd choose METCO for their own children. They nearly always look at their choice critically, viewing racial integration as difficult but unavoidable.

Implications for Schools, Policy Makers, and Community Leaders

This research can inform educators who have METCO-like programs in their schools in addition to policy makers and educational leaders considering the adoption of such programs, as well as teachers and administrators in increasingly diverse suburban schools. The research doesn't lead to clear prescriptions; nor are the stories and recollections necessarily indicative of what goes on in all schools. Yet, the longer-term perspective of these former students illuminates problems, challenges, and positive potential that might otherwise go unseen.

As the nation becomes more diverse, some educational leaders are growing critical of schools that do not reflect that diversity. They ask: How will we prepare students to work and live with people from backgrounds different from their own? If students, no matter their ethnicity, don't learn such skills in school, where in society will they learn them? According to surveys, most parents still believe that, in an ideal world, schools would be racially integrated. Just how to make those schools integrated, however, is where matters become contentious. The METCO program is a potentially appealing route toward such diversity, if only because it does not alter the established nature of school organization. Granted, for many suburban districts, space limitations may hinder implementation of METCO-like programs, which would require currently crowded suburban districts to enroll even more students. In light of this impediment, it might be more practical for individual communities to begin with smaller-scale programs that begin to bridge boundary lines between communities with the intent of moving toward larger-scale efforts similar to METCO when spaces became available. Such programs might include shared academic projects, such as newspapers, student magazines, or theater programs that include urban and suburban students and educators. These programs would likely not be comprehensive enough or of long enough duration to make marked differences in students' lives, but they could be important steps toward efforts that allow students to cross city boundary lines to attend school.

But educational leaders should look at METCO in a broad way—as an example of the potential for cross-district educational efforts. In the current discussions about school reform, while there is often polite mention of the benefits of diversity, the interdistrict efforts that would actually create that diversity are rarely explored. As one model of such an approach, METCO often is criticized because of its one-way nature that does not allow for white suburban students to transfer to more diverse urban environments. In looking to suburban-urban options, then, educators might consider the potential, also, of interdistrict magnet schools that enroll a mix of students from various municipalities.

Such efforts would likely need the support of state government, of course, to provide funding. Though we sometimes forget this, it is still the states, not local communities, that has the ultimate authority over public education. It is the state that has substantial, though usually untapped, power to create and sustain such cross-district efforts. As space tightens in overwhelmingly white segregated suburban districts and superintendents dutifully make requests for costly new school construction, state officials would do well to instead encourage construction of schools that would include students from more than a single, small district. Such seemingly mundane efforts would be powerful steps that leave a legacy of working toward a true democratic society. The other option, suburban school construction and expansion, serves to further cement divisions among children based on where their parents can afford to live. Because our local communities, especially in the northern metropolitan areas, are still heavily segregated by race and income level, dividing school districts along municipal lines is, for all practical purposes, segregation by race and class.

Once a cross-district program is created, educators should expect to face challenges that come from efforts to address major social problems. Just getting students into different schools to learn together is only a first step. It was common for the respondents in this study to recall that educators and students in their suburban schools seemed to think that racial integration, via METCO, held benefits only for black students. There was little indication, as these adults remember anyway, that the white educators, students, or administrators believed that they were benefiting from having a more racially diverse school. Though these complaints were common, it was particularly difficult for the former METCO students to say, specifically, how the school environment should change to reflect the view that black students enrich the school environment.

There is, of course, no prescription for change in this case, and thus it may be most useful for educators to examine their own attitudes about the purpose of such transfer programs and of racially diverse learning environments in general. Educators might then reexamine classroom discussion, counseling, and various school policies. Simply asking racial minority students for their insights and reflections about the school environment might very well inform educators about problems or prevalent attitudes unseen by white administrators, teachers, and counselors.

The black adults also remember being stereotyped. For example, black students from middle-class families recall that teachers and other students routinely assumed that they were poor. Likewise, classroom discussions and questions revealed the assumption that all the black students from the city lived amidst violence and despair. This suggests that educators might benefit from further education about the diversity that exists within racial minority groups in terms of income, education level, and other factors. It may be useful for teachers and counselors to become familiar with the qualities of the neighborhoods and communities from which their students come, rather than relying on reputation or widespread images not based upon actual experience with the communities. This might be accomplished simply through discussions with METCO staff members. Also, districts could conduct more formal workshops in which suburban educators learn from city residents about the history and characteristics of the various urban neighborhoods, including information about what distinguishes the neighborhoods from each other. Similar to the suburban host families, some METCO families might open their homes and become formal hosts to teachers and other educators from the suburban schools. This might encourage the type of two-way learning that so many former METCO students perceived to be missing from their suburban schools.

A third possibility focuses on the former METCO students' frustration that race and race-related matters were taboo subjects in their schools. They remember the awkwardness around these subjects, and they responded in a variety of ways, including anger, withdrawal, and resentment. Not all students wanted to address such topics. But some do remember trying to bring up discussions of race-related issues, or offering perspectives that emerged specifically from their experiences as blacks. They found themselves humiliated and frustrated because their efforts elicited few constructive responses from white educators or students. On the other hand, students recall occasions when they encountered teachers who openly discussed racial issues, which made diversity enriching rather than scary. These remain hopeful examples of the potential for improved race relations. Certainly, educators and administrators need to decide for themselves how to approach the complicated and potentially contentious topic of race. But the stories and recollections of post-METCO adults suggest that remaining silent about a difficult subject carries its own message.

The program's former students can offer important information to policy makers and community leaders who are trying to improve, sustain, or establish similar programs. The former METCO students can point specifically to the program qualities from which they feel they benefited. Their long-term perspectives suggest that such benefits might not be derived from more traditional forms of desegregation that are limited to a single city. This is because the METCO programs' benefits are related not just to objective quality, but to the reality that the suburban schools are seen in such a positive light by the larger society. In addition, skills earned from navigating in a predominantly white, often affluent terrain were precisely those with long-term tangible pay-offs. In the eyes of post-METCO adults, merely transferring students from one similar school to another within the same community, while it might achieve a racial balance within what is overall an isolated urban system, would likely not carry the same benefits they feel they received in their suburban schools. For this reason, then, metropolitan, cross-district desegregation programs should not be presented either in public discussion or in policy debates as similar to traditional forms of northern-style school desegregation limited to one city. The public certainly attaches stereotype and fear to traditional forms of "busing," and thus, enlightened public discourse about voluntary, cross-district programs may get overshadowed by misdirected controversy if distinctions between the policies aren't made clear.

Similarly, while METCO is a school choice program in the sense that it is voluntary, there are particular aspects of METCO that were important for students—aspects that are not typically part of free-market choice schemes that are gaining in popularity. Under a free-market choice plan, for example, students might be given the option of transferring to a community outside of the one where they live, such as to a suburban school. The merits of such choice plans aside, the programs may very well get more racial minority students to suburban schools. But the black students may not find the special, institutionalized entity like METCO within the school district. Students in METCO rely on METCO staff, not just for bureaucratic matters, but often for emotional support as well. The METCO central office in Boston, too, was often an important place for students and their families who had questions and concerns. Through these institutionalized groups, METCO students had a specific place to turn for guidance and fellowship and identifiable adults to help them during an often difficult experience. Further, the informal network of METCO parents and students appears to have been a powerful one for many students in that members shared information, influence, and connections to opportunity. Letting black city children transfer to white suburbia under a free-market choice plan will likely not offer the same supports or encourage similar powerful networks, unless those supports are deliberately built into such a scheme. Again, it is important to distinguish between two very different types of policies.

It is important to stress again that because METCO, in practice, gives preferences to racial minority students, it may be vulnerable to court challenges. So far, recent circuit court decisions suggest the wisest course might be for suburban school and METCO administrators to document clearly the justifications and benefits of METCO-type programs for *all* students, so that the programs are concretely tied to educational missions and pedagogical goals and narrowly tailored to meet them.

For example, educators should be able to answer the following types of questions, in concrete, empirical terms: "What benefits has this program demonstrated with regard to students' learning, including such things as critical thinking, exploration of different points of view, debate, and empathy?" Also, "What larger goals of the school system is this program helping to achieve, and how?" Thinking these questions over would be useful not only in preparation for a possible court challenge, but also to help educators reflect upon and understand the importance of such programs to the system as a whole.

Finally, to judge METCO and similar programs fairly, it is necessary to take the long view; that is, policy makers and others who evaluate such programs should not gauge success solely against short-term improvements on test scores. Surely, better school achievement is a principal objective of any academic program. But, as the former METCO students testify, the program has other, longer-term academic and social benefits that should not be ignored. Moving beyond this, we should take seriously the suggestions METCO students have long been giving teachers and administrators in their white schools: evaluators should consider the effects programs such as METCO have on white students, especially in schools where there would be little racial diversity if not for this desegregation program.

In the end, it may be that METCO's best test is whether teachers and administrators, students, and parents can tap what its past participants see as the program's potential to prepare all students—both black and white—to be good, productive citizens in an increasingly diverse democracy. By design, METCO escapes some of the contention and resentment that accompanies—and that often dismantles—traditional busing and affirmative action policies. If potential legal vulnerabilities can be addressed, programs such as METCO may be especially well positioned over the long term to benefit not only black students who travel miles to white suburbia, but also the white people they meet at the schoolhouse door.

Next Steps for New Research

My research on post-METCO adults points to additional questions and concerns that other scholars might examine. First, however, it is important that readers understand that I am not systematically comparing the long-term outcomes of METCO participants with those of their peers in urban settings. Although the participants often speculate about such differences, these speculations are presented only as elements of narratives about the men's and women's experiences in METCO. They should not be mistaken for research conclusions.

Nor am I assessing the objective "success" of METCO or of programs similar to it. Because it is a voluntary program, METCO is difficult, though not impossible, to study in this manner. Such self-selected programs create big problems for researchers conducting comparative studies because the mere fact that participants get to choose a program indicates that their desire to be in the program could be a key factor in what makes a program successful. Similarly, the fact that students choose the program may be indicative of other characteristics (such as motivation, parental involvement, and ambition) that might contribute to their ability to do well in school or in life regardless of the educational institutions they attend. Thus, I focus here on the experiences of the men and women in the program, in their own words, evaluated in their own way.

That said, there is much more work to be done. For example, I did not focus on the experiences of students who drop out of the program and either return to the Boston public schools, transfer to other schools, or leave school altogether. It would be useful to determine the reasons students leave, why they are unsuccessful in the program, and what happens to them after they are no longer enrolled in METCO.

Second, my research strongly suggests that parents play a crucial role in the METCO program, both in encouraging students to stay in the program and in stressing the importance not only of educational success, but of success within the suburban environment. The strong role of parents is hardly surprising, of course, but it's still unclear exactly how various parental attitudes about suburbia or the importance of connections to black culture affect a child's development of racial identity, academic achievement, and adjustment to schooling in predominantly white suburbia.

Third, because this study is qualitative in nature, it is not intended to reach broad conclusions about whether participation in METCO, specifically, is associated with external measures of success later in life. A statistical study comparing METCO graduates with non-METCO graduates might answer such a question although the general positive relationship between similar programs and later success has been well established. Since METCO is a self-selecting program, randomly chosen inner-city Boston students are not an adequate control group. It might be possible, however, to use as controls either non-METCO siblings of METCO students or students who were on the waiting list for the METCO program but who did not get in.

The adults talk frequently about what they perceive as relatively easy adjustments in white-dominated colleges and workplaces. They often compare their experiences with the seemingly more difficult adjustments for other blacks who did not have prior experiences in racially integrated schools. A focused qualitative study that more systematically compares such experiences between previously segregated and previously desegregated blacks might offer more insight into these matters.

Previous research has suggested that, in general, blacks fare better on historically black college campuses than they do on predominantly white college campuses (Allen, 1991; Allen et al., 1992). But the experience of METCO graduates, some of whom transferred from historically black campuses to predominantly white ones, suggests the possibility that previous exposure to racially integrated schools may increase the likelihood that a black student will feel comfortable and succeed on a white college campus. A study that focuses on these questions would be a useful contribution.

Finally, the research literature on racial integration in schools reflects the prevailing assumption that racial integration carries benefits only for black students. Surely, there is a continuing desire for racial diversity in learning environments for its own sake. Witness, for example, the concerted efforts and public comments of college-level educators who want to maintain diversity on their campuses in the wake of anti–affirmative action policies that reduce the share of black and Latino students (Bok and Bowen, 1998; also see Rosen, 1998). These educators and advocates have long held that exposure to racial diversity prepares white students for participation in an increasingly multicultural society. But next to nothing is known about the actual lives of whites who have had racially integrated school experiences. A wide-scale study on the effects of a sustained racially integrated schooling experience on the longer-term attitudes, decisions, and racial attitudes of whites would be a tremendously useful contribution.

Methodology

This study's findings are drawn from 65 interviews that I conducted with men and women between 1995 and 1998.

White Studying Black

That I am a white person studying and writing about aspects of the black experience has escaped me scarcely for a minute. Of course race has tremendous social significance in American society, and race-consciousness, whatever its broad effects in society, is likely to trickle down into personal relationships. This includes even the typically transient and brief personal encounters between an interviewer and her interviewee.

There have been studies and commentary on the question of the effects a white researcher might have upon black respondents. Generally, blacks have been found to be more forthcoming with black interviewers (e.g. Pettigrew, 1964; Feagin, 1989a, Feagin, 1989b). These studies and commentary suggest that the answers from blacks differ not in type, but in depth. There might be more details offered, and anecdotes told with more frequency than they would have been with white interviewers. But the general characterizations and reported patterns of an experience do not seem to differ. In my particular case, however, I believe racial difference created challenges and had drawbacks and benefits.

Because I am white, I believe I did need to probe more deeply into respondents' answers and explanations, both so I might receive adequate material for my study and so I might personally understand the meaning of the participants' words and the character of their experiences and feelings. It was quite common, for example, for a participant to ask, off-handedly, "You know what I mean?" These were awkward moments at first, as I responded, "No." In one example, a participant said, "You know. The usual problems for a black woman." And I would, of course, have to say, as I did in that case: "No. I don't know."

On the one hand, this situation could be viewed positively, as the lack of common experiences required more in-depth discussions. Participants necessarily offered what seemed to me to be precise and detailed responses. I also believe my candor led to an open and honest discussion that might not have occurred otherwise as respondents seemed to me to accept that I was trying to understand their experiences from their perspectives and that I did not presume, from my vantage point as a student of race relations, to understand what they thought and felt. Following the interviews, some of the participants did say in varying ways that they appreciated my efforts to listen and my ability to admit when I did not fully comprehend what was on their minds.

But I suspect this frustrated some respondents, who may have been less forthcoming as a result. I did worry that because I am white, the black men and women I talked with might be holding back the more negative aspects of their experiences with white people or were being less than honest about their opinions of white people in general. To mitigate such problems, I often explained that I had much previous experience interviewing people of many races. I told many respondents that they should not hold back their opinions or negative feelings for fear that I would be offended. Sometimes I opened the interview with this discussion, but other times I offered this information in the course of discussions, usually if a participant was not being specific or was talking negatively only in implicit ways. This seemed to me to be effective in establishing rapport and encouraging interviewees to "let down their guards," so to speak.

I did ask just about less than one quarter of the respondents (mostly the later interviews) what effect they felt my race had upon their responses to my questions. Their answers were quite revealing and point to the potential drawbacks and benefits of cross-racial interviewing. Generally, the participants said that if I had been black, they might have opened up more quickly and, many said, talked in a different style, with different inflection, which one respondent described as "more casual," or as another said, "more real . . . the way I talk around other blacks." A few said they might, indeed, have spent more time complaining about past interactions with white teachers. This is a drawback because of course I would prefer discussions that reflect what is on one's mind and "real" styles of communication of the type the respondents might have with friends.

Conversely, several said that, had I been black, they might have been less forthcoming about their conflicts over assimilation and adaptation to white environments since they were unsure how some blacks might react to those concerns. Several added that had I been black, they might have been less likely to recall or discuss the development of positive relationships with whites and their own changing racial attitudes.

This study is about black men and women who have spent much of their lives crossing the race line. White people, generally speaking, are required to cross that line much less frequently. Despite the potential challenges inherent in such a study, I wanted to cross the race line myself to some extent. Truly listening to and learning to empathize with people whose experiences differ from mine are the values at the core of my scholarship.

The Sample

I created this sample through the "chain-referral," or "snowball sampling," method, used widely and effectively in studies of diffuse populations not accounted for as an official group (Biernaki and Waldorf, 1981). I began with a list of 27 past METCO participants provided to me by METCO directors in several communities. I contacted and interviewed 13 people on this list. (The others had incorrect phone numbers or never returned phone messages I left on answering machines.) Four of these initial interviewees referred me to METCO past participants, including siblings, friends, and colleagues. I interviewed two of these references, who, in turn, provided me other names. I continued getting referrals from the past participants I interviewed. Simultaneously, I sought names of METCO graduates through other means, including personal contacts within the African-American community in Boston and other organizations. In a few cases, personal friends provided me with names and phone numbers of acquaintances and colleagues who were METCO graduates. I conducted a pilot study of 24 past participants, which helped me test the effectiveness of my interview methods and, most important, determine whether I had included the most important themes in the protocol.

Through this chain-referral process, I ended up with a list of 189 potential interviewees. I then selected interviewees so that I would have a sample with particular dimensions. I sought to balance the sample by gender because past research on METCO finds gender-linked differences in the students' experiences. I also assured variation and balance in the age of respondents in order to have respondents close in time to life experiences that typically fall within given age ranges. Variation also increases the possibility that a wide range of life experiences is represented. I created three age bands: (23–29; 30–36; 37 and older). The adults vary in age, with 18 who graduated high school or who were of graduation age (18) between the years 1971 and 1977; 24 who graduated or who were of graduation age between the years 1978 and 1983; and 23 who graduated or who were of graduation age between the years 1984 and 1991.

I also ensured variation in the socioeconomic status of METCO communities represented. Some of the METCO communities have among the highest degrees of concentrated wealth in the state, but others are more economically mixed. I based these judgments on median salary and assessed home value obtained from municipal offices in METCO communities. I assumed that variety might allow me to see if differences emerge in respondents' perceptions based on the socioeconomic status of different METCO communities. Thus, I was able to consider whether differences in perception and experience exist on this dimension and then, whether such differences should be examined more closely not only in my analysis, but in future research.

So that my sample would match the study needs, I kept a running record, in the form of a chart, displaying the changing dimensions of my sample. For example, if I had interviewed 10 people and was making arrangements for my eleventh interview, I examined the chart to see what characteristics I might need in order to keep the sample balanced on the dimensions I outlined. If a review of the chart revealed that I had more middle-aged than young respondents, I searched my master list for younger potential respondents and contacted them. Once contacted, only three people declined to participate in the study, though seven people failed to show up for interviews. I estimate that about 15 to 17 potential respondents did not return messages I left on their answering machines, though I did not keep records of this.

Chain-referral sampling has limitations, as it may produce only respondents connected to social networks (Waldorf & Biernaki, 1981). I was also concerned that relying on my own contacts might produce a skewed sample of people similar to me with regard to education and economic status. Thus, I sought referrals outside my social circle and stressed that I was looking not just for "success" stories, but people with varied opinions and experiences. Likewise, in requesting names from METCO directors, I also stressed that I did not want only those former students who had succeeded or who would say only positive things about the METCO program. Based on the diversity of experience and opinion present in those early interviews, I believe the METCO directors did provide me the type of respondents I requested.

In the end, the chain-referral method produced a sample somewhat diverse in education level, occupation, and life experience. Ideally, I would have begun this study with a master list of METCO past participants that indicated such dimensions as income level, education level, etc., and then created a sample that represents those important dimensions. However, as is usual in long-running K–12 programs such as METCO, no such alumni record exists. The second-best choice, then, was to consider some of the dimensions of current graduates and try to represent that larger group. Based on previous surveys (Batson & Hayden, 1987; Orfield, 1997), my sample does appear to be representative of current and past METCO students on several key dimensions, including parents' education levels at the time of METCO enrollment, childhood neighborhood of residence, and higher education plans after high school.

The sample includes 30 men and 35 women. Because of the plausible impact of classmates' socioeconomic status on a school environment, the sample also includes a mix of affluent, middle-class/affluent and economically mixed school districts, though it is not perfectly balanced on that dimension. Just 16 of the 32 METCO districts are represented in this sample. My goal is not to make comparisons between districts, and I therefore decided that mentioning the districts by name would serve no purpose. It is important to understand that my goal is to look for common patterns in the general experience. While I am not making systematic comparisons based on adults' current socioeconomic status, this sample does contain diversity (though not balance) on that dimension. About 42 of the adults would be classified as middle class and college educated; 17 could be classified as working class with a college degree, some college education, or a high school diploma, and the remaining 6 could be classified either as working poor or poor with no college education. Forty-nine of the 65 adults were graduated from a four-year college or, at the time I met with them, finishing work toward degrees. Twenty of the 65 had completed some graduate work (a law,

master's, or other professional degree). Several more had immediate plans to pursue graduate studies.

It was difficult to classify the socioeconomic standing of
adults at the time of their growing up since such matters are
highly subjective. For example, a few students who grew up in
public housing and whose parents had low-wage, nonunion jobs
characterized their families as middle class. Suffice it to say there
is a range of childhood backgrounds represented here—from
children who grew up in public housing and whose parents
were, at least for some period of time, receiving public aid, to
those from double-income households who traveled occasionally
and who owned homes. None of the parents of the past participants had high-wage jobs that put them in the upper middle
classes, and only six, in fact, had parents who had graduated
from four-year colleges, though several of the adults' parents did
earn bachelor's degrees later on.

Of the 65 adults in this sample, 59 graduated from a METCO
high school. Six either dropped out of the program in high
school or graduated from another school or earned a graduation
equivalency diploma (GED).

A Caveat

It is crucial that readers understand that I am not comparing the
long-term outcomes of METCO participants with those of their
peers in urban settings. Neither am I assessing the objective
"success" of METCO or programs similar to it. Because it is a
voluntary program, METCO is difficult, though not impossible, to
study in this manner. Such "self-selected" programs create big
problems for researchers conducting comparative studies because the mere fact that participants get to choose a program
indicates that their motivation and desire to be in the program
could be key factors in why they are successful in it. Similarly, the
fact that students and their families choose a given program may

be indicative of other characteristics that would cause them to do well in school or in life, no matter what educational institution they attended.

I make no comparative judgments between the experience of suburban educated blacks and urban educated blacks. Through this study, I'm seeking to understand the personal effects of a particular educational experience from the participants' perspectives only, not in comparison to a more seemingly typical black experience.

Data Collection

I chose intensive interviewing because I wanted to articulate complicated, varied perspectives and meanings people make of an educational experience (Seidman, 1991). Intensive interviewing is the most appropriate method, as respondents tell their stories from *their* perspectives—stories framed in large part by their values and specific experiences. I assigned pseudonyms to all the participants. Several of the study participants (all still connected to the METCO program in some form) were concerned that they would be identifiable even with pseudonyms. Thus, to be consistent, I did not name workplaces, unusual occupations, or the colleges that the participants attended. I did characterize these places when details were relevant, however.

In all, I conducted seventy-three interviews. I conducted all but seven of these interviews in person. I conducted the other seven by telephone. I eliminated five of the pilot interviews, as, early in the process, I failed to touch on the very themes and issues that ended up being crucial to the final study. I also eliminated three more later interviews because the participants were biracial and said during the course of the interview that they did not identify themselves as black.

I tape-recorded all but three of the interviews. Twice, I forgot recording equipment and once I met a METCO graduate by coincidence who was visiting from out of state and I did not have a tape recorder. I did take notes on a laptop computer during these interviews. The interviews lasted between one-half hour and three hours. They were conducted at locations chosen by respondents—usually homes and workplaces.

I conducted about a dozen follow-up phone interviews early in the data collection process, as I discovered questions I had forgotten to ask and material on which I wanted more elaboration. A semistructured interview guide is included in Appendix III. The guide's topics emerged first from my theoretical framework, and then were refined during pilot interviews. However, I did not follow strict questioning but moved interviews forward chronologically by building upon what respondents said (Seidman, 1991). I remained flexible in this way, because through their explanations, respondents, especially early in the process, established issues or categories I had not considered. An integral part of understanding the perceived enduring effects of METCO is understanding METCO's perceived place or position within the larger context of respondents' lives. Thus, I provided ample room for respondents to discuss the impact of other events, institutions, and relationships on key aspects of their lives, and then room to characterize the place and position of their urban-suburban educational experience.

Thus, this work is biographical insofar as it seeks a full picture of each respondent's life. Then, within the context of this larger narrative, I focused on the role and force of an educational experience with respondents providing their links (if any) to METCO. Certainly, there are issues and life characteristics that research literature and my pilot interviews suggest are relevant to theory and that have implications for research. If a discussion of these issues did not emerge spontaneously, I asked specifically about them. In later interviews, I focused most intently upon aspects of the experience that I did not yet understand. For example, early in the process, I felt I understood, through extensive elaboration from participants, the details of a family's initial contact with METCO and their justifications for it. I understood less well the perceived longer-term effects upon racial identity and the participants' meanings of comfort. Thus, in later interviews, I focused more on those issues.

I did ask each respondent in his or her own words to characterize his or her "social class" or economic situation while growing up. (I also inquired about parent occupation, home ownership, parent education level[s].) I paid attention to these issues in my analysis and looked for differences that might help forge hypotheses for further research. But this is not a comparative study, as I did not find differences based on a social class dimension in preliminary data and because categories such as "middle class" do not, for my purposes, work either as neat or telling descriptors of the lives of respondents.

Analysis

I did not divide my study strictly into "collection" and "analysis" phases but conducted analyses concurrently with data collection by coding and displaying data and writing "rough draft" expositions of tentative theories and findings (Miles and Huberman, 1994). My pilot study and literature review led to a preliminary coding list, construction of visual displays, and development of routines for refining coding, checking for bias, and verifying conclusions (Miles and Huberman, 1994).

I began with several copies of a transcribed interview, making marginal notes on one copy about potential coding categories. Later, I coded another, then compared the two for consistencies and inconsistencies (Strauss and Corbin, 1990). Soon after interviews, I wrote field notes and memos on forms that provided space for spontaneous writing about an interview or idea, but also had consistently labeled sections under which I recorded specific types of information for each interview (Miles and Huberman,

1994). The field notes form, for example, contains sections labeled "interview's important elements," "follow-up questions," "improving future interviews," "personal reaction/bias to respondent." Memos are related more to the implications of an interview. The "memo" form contains such labeled sections as "implications for coding," "relevance to theory," and "interview's fit with current ideas/tentative findings."

In a separate section, I articulated "mini-theories" (Weiss, 1994). These are "rough draft" expositions of ideas and possible findings. Here, I concentrated primarily on key themes emerging from my theoretical framework and the interviews. I organized "mini-theories" into one section to keep a trackable running record. I examined these drafts while conducting my analysis. Then, I constructed a matrix (Miles and Huberman, 1994) displaying summary answers to the research questions from each interview. I did this *not* to have a kind of quantitative "count" of responses, but to display data in an extremely condensed form, thereby aiding analysis and helping me verify/negate tentative conclusions or findings (Miles & Huberman, 1994). When I thought I fully understood something, I returned to the data and examined it again to help verify findings/conclusions. As said, I also focused parts of subsequent interviews on testing ideas as they emerged (Miles and Huberman, 1991; Weiss, 1994).

When writing field notes and memos or developing mini-theories and potential codes, I linked my thinking and analysis as starting points, to the theories and research outlined in the literature review. For example, I considered whether data is relevant to perpetuation theory or network analysis or whether, for example, participants offered evidence or stories of challenges to their cultural integrity, as identified by most research. In linking my research to past research and theories, I considered whether my findings negated, complicated, further explained, or confirmed past work.

Limitations

Retrospective interviewing has weaknesses because of the potential for memory loss. Cross-sectional analysis, which, in this case, means one interview with each person, also has some risks associated with memory loss, as the respondent may not, at the time of the interview, be undergoing the experience significant to the interviewer.

However, this study is not primarily a reconstruction but more an examination of how participants perceive the effects of a past experience. Given infinite time and resources, I would have preferred to conduct a longitudinal study. In a longitudinal design, the same respondents would have been interviewed repeatedly over time. This design diminishes memory loss, as the researcher can talk with the respondent while s/he is undergoing a particular experience. However, because of the limited funds and time-bounded nature of this project, cross-sectional analysis was more feasible. And because I conducted just one interview with each respondent, I did not have attrition over time.

I do not believe this excludes the study from being useful, especially if considered among other sources. Certainly, it could establish questions and themes for a longitudinal study. Overall, this study will further understanding of a public education experience whose perceived effects have never been examined from either a long-term perspective or by asking questions that emerge from more than one academic discipline.

Interview Guide

Section I—Background

1.1 Name

1.2 District attended during METCO

1.3 Year of graduation

1.4 Neighborhood/Street resided in during METCO
a. Ask respondent to characterize neighborhood

1.5 Parents/Family
a. Job and education level at time of METCO
b. Siblings (any in METCO)
c. Extended family (cousins, etc.)
d. Characterize economic situation of family
e. Why did you go to METCO? Understanding of why you were going? Family role in this.

1.6 Educational/Life trajectory since METCO. What have you been doing since you left high school? (education/work/family/travel/relationships/etc.)
a. College, process of making decision about college, GED, etc.
b. Involvement in organizations at college/African-American focused organizations?
c. Friends in college
d. College major and interests

1.7 Occupational history since METCO
a. Jobs, decisions about work
b. Favorite job

c. Describe ideal job/career goal
d. How was job obtained?

1.8 Religious affiliation
a. Characterize church involvement over time

1.9 Current address
a. Characterize neighborhood
b. Decisions about where to live
c. Community/neighborhood involvement

Section 2—METCO History/METCO Effect in Life

2.1 Process of involvement in METCO

2.2 Besides METCO, characterize past experience with suburbia and predominantly white settings

2.3 Any impressions of "white people" prior to METCO?

2.4 What was understanding at the time regarding why you were in METCO?
a. How did you explain this to friends in your neighborhood?

2.5 Earliest memory of METCO?

2.6 First impression of the resident students?

2.7 Tell about your experience in METCO years.
a. Courses taken?
b. Who helped you?
c. Academic life
d. Social life
e. Dating
f. Racism

g. Perceived impact of gender upon experience

h. Perceived impact of class upon experience

2.8 Socioeconomic class of resident students

a. When did you become aware of the concentrated wealth (if relevant)?

b. Any impact upon your experience?

c. Interaction between your social class background and that of students

d. Long-term effect? Any practical uses?

2.9 Friends/family outside of METCO

a. How did neighborhood friends/family react to METCO?

b. Effects of METCO upon these relationships

2.10 Racial identity

a. Thinking about being black

b. Conflict

c. Did you feel like you had to act somehow "less black" in METCO? If yes, did you act differently around your neighborhood? Explain this to me.

d. Awareness of difference?

2.11 Did you change as a result of METCO?

2.12 Current understanding of why you went to METCO

2.13 Did you get anything useful out of METCO, in the sense that you used it in life?

a. How did you apply these things?

b. Examples

c. Anything useful from exposure to whites?

d. Anything useful from exposure to affluence/upper middle class?

e. College/higher ed.

f. The workplace

2.14 Did anything negative come out of METCO?

a. Anything negative that stays with you today?

b. Friendships/relationships

c. Identity

d. Adaptation strategies

* Position of METCO—other factors influencing? family, friends, community, church

2.15 Did you use any contacts in high school to help you get a job or get into college?

a. Networking skills

b. Current "network" (Affected by METCO?)

2.16 Decisions you made influenced by the METCO experience?

a. Regarding friendships

b. Community involvement

c. Jobs

d. College

* Position of METCO—other factors influencing?

2.17 Current involvement in specifically "African-American" organizations or work?

a. Degree of interest/involvement affected by METCO?

b. Church, etc.

2.18 Relationship with family today?

a. Mother/father/siblings/extended

2.19 Old neighborhood friends/current friends

a. Any contact?

b. How did their lives turn out?

c. Describe closest friends

d. Who are the people you feel most comfortable with?

2.20 Racial identity

a. Relationship to African-American culture and history?

b. Would this be different if not for METCO? If yes, how?

2.21 How did you choose current address/neighborhood?

a. Do you see yourself in a particular type of community in the future?

b. Would you ever choose to live in a community similar to the METCO community where you went to school? Why? Why not?

2.22 Overall, considering all the aspects of the program, do you consider the program was "worth it?" Why? Why not?

2.23 Would you want your child or one close to you to have the experience? Why? Why not?

a. If yes, would you want that child's experience to be different from yours in any way? Would you want it to be the same in any particular way? If yes, how?

b. If it were your child, would you play a particular role in that experience? Can you explain this?

2.24 If you could go back in time, would you repeat the METCO experience? Why? Why not?

Bibliography

Allen, W. R. (1992). The color of success: African-American college students outcomes at predominantly white and historically black public colleges and universities. *Harvard Educational Review* 62, no.1, 26–44.

Allen, W. R., Epp, E. G., and Haniff, N. Z. (Eds.) (1991). *College in black and white: African American students in predominantly white and in historically black public universities*. Albany: State University of New York Press.

Armor, D. (1972). The evidence on busing. *The Public Interest* 28:90.

Baker, P., Carpenter S., Crowley, J. E., D'Amico, R., Kim, C., Morgan, W., and Weilgosz, J. (1984). *Pathways to the future: A longitudinal study of young Americans*. Vol. 4. Columbus, Ohio: Center for Human Research, Ohio State University.

Banks, James A. (1984). Black youths in predominantly white suburbs: An exploratory study of their attitudes and self-concepts. *Journal of Negro Education* Vol. 53. No. 1.

Batson, R. and Hayden, R. C. (1987). *A history of METCO: The metropolitan council for educational opportunity*. Boston: Select Publications.

Becker, H. J. (1977). *How young people find career entry jobs: A review of the literature*. Report No. 241. Baltimore, Md.: The Johns Hopkins University Center for Social Organization of Schools.

Bok, D. and Bowen, W. G. (1998). *The shape of the river: Long-term consequences of considering race in college and university admissions*. Princeton: Princeton University Press.

Braddock, J. H. and McPartland, J. M. (1989). Social-psychological processes that perpetuate racial segregation: The relationship between school and employment desegregation. *Journal of Black Studies* 19, 267–289.

Braddock, J. H., Crain, R. L., McPartland, J. M., and Dawkins, R. L. (1986). Applicant race and job placement decisions: A national survey experiment. *International Journal of Sociology and Social Policy* 6 (1), 3–24.

Braddock, J. H. and McPartland, J. M. (1983). *More evidence on the social psychological processes that perpetuate minority segregation: The relationship of school desegregation and employment segregation.* Report No. 33. Baltimore: Center for Social Organization of Schools. The Johns Hopkins University.

Braddock, J. H. (1980). The perpetuation of segregation across levels of education: A behavioral assessment of the contact-hypothesis. *Sociology of Education* 53: 178–186.

Braddock, J. H. (1987, June). *Segregated high school experiences and black student's college and major field choices.* Paper presented at the National Conference on School Desegregation. Chicago, Ill.

Braddock, J. H. and McPartland, J. M. (1997). How minorities continue to be excluded from equal employment opportunities: Research on labor market and institutional barriers. *Journal of Social Issues* Vol. 43. No. 1, 5–39.

Braddock, J. H., McPartland, J. M., and Trent, W. (1984). *Desegregated schools and desegregated work environments,* paper presented at the annual meeting of the American Educational Research Association, New Orleans.

Brewer v. The West Irondequoit Central School District, 212 f.3d 738; 2000 U.S. App. LEXIS 9866 (2000).

Brown v. Board of Education, 347 .S. 438 (1954).

Collins, S. (1989). The marginalization of black executives. *Social Problems* Vol. 36. No. 4.

Community Newspaper Company (1998, December). MCAS '98: By the numbers. A guide to the Massachusetts Comprehensive Assessment System exam.

Cose, E. (1993). *The rage of a privileged class: Why are middle class blacks angry? Why should America care?* Harper Collins: New York.

Cose, E. (1997). *Color blind: Seeing beyond race in a race-obsessed world.* New York: Harper Collins.

Crain, R. L. and Weisman, C. (1974). *Discrimination, personality and achievement.* New York: Seminar Press.

Crain, R. L. and Strauss, J. (1985). *School desegregation and black occupa-*

tional attainments: Results from a long-term experiment. (Rep. No. 359) Baltimore: Center for the Social Organization of Schools. The Johns Hopkins University.

Crain, R. L. (1984). *The quality of American high school graduates: What personnel officers say and do about it.* Report No. 354 Baltimore: Center for Social Organization of Schools. The Johns Hopkins University.

Crain, R. L. (1984). *Desegregated schools and the non-academic side of college survival.* Paper presented at the annual meeting of the American Educational Research Association, New Orleans.

Cross, W. E. (1991). *Shades of black: Diversity in African-American identity.* Philadelphia: Temple University Press.

Cross, W. E. (1995). The psychology of nigrescence: Revising the Cross model. In J. G. Ponterotto, J. M. Casas, L. A. Suzuki and C. M. Alexander (Eds.). *Handbook of multicultural counseling.* Thousand Oaks, Calif.: Sage.

Dawkins, M. P. (1991). Long-term effects of school desegregation on African Americans: Evidence from the national survey of black Americans. Unpublished paper.

Duchesne, P. D. and Hotakainen, R. (1996, July 11). Activists hail desegregation ruling: Connecticut case called 'road map' for suit against Minnesota. *The Star Tribune.* p. 1B.

Eaton, S. E. (1999, March 9). The legacy of METCO. *The Boston Globe.* p. 11.

Eaton S. E. and Orfield, G. (1994). Brown v. Board of Education and the continuing struggle for racially integrated schools. In K. Lomoftey (Ed.), *Readings in equal education (5).* Baton Rouge: Louisiana State University Press.

Eisenberg v. Montgomery County Public Schools, 197 f.3d 123 (1999).

Fineman, H. (1996, April 29). Redrawing the color line. *Newsweek* p. 34.

Fordham, S. and Ogbu, J. U. (1986). Black students' school success: Coping with the burden of "acting white." *The Urban Review* 18(3) 176–206.

Fordham, S. (1982, December). *Cultural inversion and black children's school performance.* Paper presented at the annual meeting, American Anthropological Association, Washington, D.C.

Fordham, S. (1988). Racelessness as a factor in black students' school success: Pragmatic strategy or pyrrhic victory? *Harvard Educational Review* 58(1), 54–84.

Gable, R. K., Thompson, D. L., and Iwanicki, E. F. (1983). The effects of voluntary desegregation on occupational outcomes. *The Vocational Guidance Quarterly* 31, 230–239.

Granovetter, M. (1973). The strength of weak ties. *American Journal of Sociology* 78, 1360–1380.

Granovetter, M. (1974). *Getting a job: A study of contacts and careers.* Cambridge, Mass.: Harvard University Press.

Granovetter, M. (1982). The strength of weak ties: A network theory revisited. In P. V. Marden and N. Lin (Eds.), *Social structure and network analysis.* pp. 105–130. Beverly Hills, Calif.: Sage.

Granovetter, M. (1986). The micro-structure of school desegregation. In J. Prager, D. Longshore, and M. Seeman (Eds.), *School desegregation research. New directions in situational analysis.* pp. 81–110. New York: Plenum Press.

Green, Kenneth. (1981). *Integration and attainment: Preliminary results from a national longitudinal study of the impact of school desegregation.* Paper presented at the annual meeting of the American Education Research Association. Los Angeles, Calif.

Hart, J. (1997, Sept. 25). Metco's popularity confirmed in survey; most parents prefer suburban schools. *The Boston Globe.* p. B1.

Hopwood v. Texas, 78 f.3d 932 (5th Cir. 1996).

Jankowski, M. S. (1995). The rising significance of status in U.S. race relations, in M. P. Smith and J. R. Feagin, eds. *The bubbling cauldron.* Minneapolis: University of Minnesota Press.

Judson, G. (1996, August 15). Civil rights lawyers hope to use Hartford schools case as a model. *The New York Times.* p. 1B.

Kaufman, J. E. and Rosenbaum, J. (1992). The education and employment of low income black youth in white suburbs. *Education Evaluation and Policy Analysis* 14, 229–240.

Kluger, R. (1975). *Simple justice: The history of Brown v. Board of Education and black America's struggle for justice.* New York: Vintage.

Kozol, J. (1994, May 23). Giant steps backward: The romance of the ghetto school. *The Nation.*

Lin, N. (1990). Social resources and instrumental action. In R. Breiger (Ed.), *Social mobility and social structure.* Cambridge: Cambridge University Press.

MacQuarrie, B. (1997, May 5). Amid pain, a call for action: Old colony's new crisis. Second of two parts. *The Boston Globe.* P. A1.

Mangum, S. I. (1970). *Job search: A review of the literature.* Report submitted to the U.S. Department of Labor, Employment and Training Administration. Office of Research and Development. Washington, D.C.

Massachusetts Department of Education (1998). Results: Massachusetts Comprehensive Assessment System Examination. Boston, Mass.

Maxwell, B. (1998, July 12). Reassessing the value of desegregation. *St. Petersburg Times.* p. D1.

McLaurin v. Oklahoma State Regents for Higher Education, 339 U.S. 637 (1950).

Milliken v. Bradley, 418 U.S. 717 (1974).

Montgomery, J. D. (1992). Job search and network composition: Implications for the strength-of-weak-ties hypothesis. *American Sociological Review* 57:586–596.

O'Connor, A. (Aug. 15. 1997). Mediation in schools suit? State, NAACP hire firm, ponder out of court talks. *The Star Tribune.* p. 1B.

Ogbu, J. (1981). Education, clientage and social mobility: Caste and social change in the United States and Nigeria. In *Social inequality: Comparative and developmental approaches,* G. D. Berreman (Ed.), pp. 277–306. New York: Academic Press.

Ogbu, J. (1978). *Minority education and caste: The American system in cross-cultural perspective.* New York: Academic Press.

Orfield, G. and Eaton, S. E. (1996). *Dismantling desegregation: The quiet reversal of Brown v. Board of Education.* New York: The New Press.

Orfield, G. (1994). Public opinion and school desegregation. In E. C. Lagemann and L. P. Miller (Eds.), *Brown v. board of education: The challenge for today's schools,* 59–70. New York: Teachers College Press.

Orfield, G. (1997). *City-suburban desegregation: Parent and student perspectives in metropolitan Boston.* Cambridge, Mass.: The Harvard Civil Rights Project.

Orfield, G., Bachmeier, M. D., James, D. R., and Eitle, T. (1997, April). *Deepening segregation in American public schools.* Paper prepared at the Conference on Civil Rights and Equal Opportunity in Public Schools. Atlanta, Ga.

Patterson, O. (1997). *The ordeal of integration: Progress and resentment in America's "racial" crisis.* Washington, D.C.: Publishers Group West.

Plessy v. Ferguson 163 U.S. 537 (1896).

Regents of the University of California v. Bakke, 438 U.S. 265, 270 (1978).

Rosen, Jeffrey (1998, February 23 and March 2). Damage control. *New Yorker.* 58–68.

Schlinkman, M. (1997, February 9). Bosley calls for an end to busing: Says desegregation disconnects children from neighborhoods. *The St. Louis Post Dispatch.* p. 6D.

Schofield, J. W. (1989). Review of research on school desegregation's impact on elementary and secondary school students. Paper commissioned by the Connecticut State Department of Education.

Seidman, I. (1998). *Interviewing as qualitative research: A guide for researchers in education and the social sciences.* New York: Teachers College Press.

Shaper Walters, L. (1996, March 4). School busing at end of line in Missouri? *The Christian Science Monitor.* p. 1.

Sheff v. O'Neill 238 Conn. 1, 678 A.2d. 1267 (CT Sup.Ct., 1996).

Smith, M. (1997, August 6). Multicultural model: The inaugural year of a voluntary integration school in Maplewood is coming to a close amid praise from educators and parents who say the project has enriched children's lives and education. *The Star Tribune.* p 1A.

Strauss, A. L. and Corbin, J. (1990). *Basics of qualitative research: Grounded theory, procedures and techniques.* Newbury Park, Calif: Sage Publications.

Sweatt v. Painter, 339 U.S. 629 (1950).

Tatum, B. D. (1992). African American identity, academic achievement and missing history. *Social Education* 56 No. 6. 331-344.

Tatum, B. D. (1996). Out there stranded? Black youth in white communities. In H. McAdoo (Ed.), *Black families.* 3rd. ed. Thousand Oaks, Calif.: Sage.

Tatum, B. D. (1997). *Why are all the black kids sitting together in the cafeteria and other conversations about race.* New York: Basic Books.

Trent, W. (1991). *Desegregation Analysis Report.* New York: The Legal Defense and Educational Fund.

U.S. Commission of Civil Rights (1967). Racial isolation in the public schools. Vols. I and II. Washington, D.C.: U.S. Government Printing Office.

U.S. Census Bureau (1990). Race and Hispanic Origin in 1990: Massachusetts Cities, Towns, and Counties Ranked by Per Cent Minority. 1990 Census of Population and Housing, Summary Tape File 1A, Table 10.

Weiss, R. (1994). *Learning from strangers: The art and method of qualitative research.* New York: Free Press.

Wells, A. S. and Crain, R. L. (Winter 1994). Perpetuation theory and the long term effects of school desegregation. *Review of Educational Research* 64(4):531-555.

Wells, A. S. and Crain, R. L. (1997). *Stepping over the color line: African-American students in white suburban schools.* New Haven: Yale University Press.

Wessman v. Gittens, 160 f.3d 790 (1st Cir. 1998).

Wicker, T. (1996). *Tragic failure: Racial integration in America.* New York: William Morrow.

Williams, A. (1997, July 17). Forced integration loses appeal among blacks. *The Columbus Dispatch.* p. A13.

Wilson, W. J. (1987). *The truly disadvantaged: The inner city, the underclass and public policy.* Chicago: University of Chicago Press.

Wilson, W. J. (1996). *When work disappears: The world of the new urban poor.* New York: Vintage.

Yemma, J. (1997, September 15). The new segregation: Black community reexamining school busing; rethinking integration. *The Boston Globe*. Second of four parts, pp. A1, A15.

Zweigenhaft, R. L. and Domhoff, G. W. (1991). *Blacks in the white establishment: A study of race and class in America*. New Haven: Yale University Press.

Index

ABC (A Better Chance) program, 236, 238, 244

academic achievement: and criticism of METCO, 6–7; and METCO parental involvement, 242; and racial stereotypes, 92–95, 237, 243

academic grouping, in suburban schools, 34–35, 71–72, 211

"acting white," 19, 69–70, 94–95, 237

administrators, suburban, and METCO students, 96. *See also* guidance counselors; teachers

Afro-American studies, and racial identity development, 173–74

Afro-centric schools, 245

alienation: and class mobility, 165–67; and racial identity development, 168, 170–83; and suburban school experience, 158–64

assimilation behavior: and METCO experience, 79, 184–87; and verbal self-expression, 209–10

athletic involvement, and social integration, 2, 29, 87, 102

behavior, social: misinterpretations of, 76–79; and "white rules," 239

"better education" mantra, 30–31, 38, 222

black colleges: and METCO participants, 174, 225; and racial identity, 187–90

black culture: commitments to, by post-METCO participants, 180–82; family attitudes toward, 186–87; and racial identity development, 172–83; stereotypes of, 50–57

black educational institutions, employers' perceptions of, 232, 233

black history: importance of, to METCO participants, 168–69; and racial identity development, 172–183; teaching of, in suburban schools, 2–3, 49–50, 206–7

black identity. *See also* racial identity development: expressions of, and coping strategies, 124–29; and racial integration, 245

blackness, symbols of, and racial identity development, 175

black organizations, on college campuses, 134, 174

boarding schools, and ABC program, 235–36, 238, 244

Bok, Derek, and William G. Bowen, *The Shape of The River: Long Term Consequences of Considering Race in College and University Admissions,* 37, 235

book bag, as symbol, 33

Boston: metropolitan areas of, 218–22; racial and economic separation in, 7–8; and school busing order, 23–24

Boston Latin School, 8, 11, 40, 221, 247